# BEING GURU RINPOCHE

May the sweet dew
Of Guru Rinpoche's blessing
Soften the hard skin
Of ignorance everywhere

\* \* \*

Sponsor's dedication

With gratitude to the Teachers of the Lineage
I dedicate
The merit of sponsoring this book
To my late parents
Mary and Stan Thompson
And to all who study and practise the Buddhadharma

Pamela Carr

# BEING GURU RINPOCHE

A COMMENTARY ON THE
VIDYADHARA GURU
SADHANA

BY
JAMES LOW

Khordong Commentary Series III

The commentary text is from seminars held in the Black Forest, Germany, 2000, 2001

Transcription by Mani

Edited by Gordon Ellis

Typesetting and Design by Andreas Ruft

Tibetan unicode font: XenoType Tibetan New.ttf

© Copyright 2006 James Low.
All rights reserved. No part of this publication may be reproduced, stored in a retrieval system, or transmitted, in any form or by any means, electronic, mechanical, photocopying, recording, or otherwise, without the written prior permission of the author.

Note for Librarians: A cataloguing record for this book is available from Library and Archives Canada at
www.collectionscanada.ca/amicus/index-e.html
ISBN 1-4120-8407-5

# TRAFFORD
PUBLISHING

*Offices in Canada, USA, Ireland and UK*

**Book sales for North America and international:**
Trafford Publishing, 6E–2333 Government St.,
Victoria, BC V8T 4P4 CANADA
phone 250 383 6864 (toll-free 1 888 232 4444)
fax 250 383 6804; email to orders@trafford.com
**Book sales in Europe:**
Trafford Publishing (UK) Limited, 9 Park End Street, 2nd Floor
Oxford, UK OX1 1HH UNITED KINGDOM
phone 44 (0)1865 722 113 (local rate 0845 230 9601)
facsimile 44 (0)1865 722 868; info.uk@trafford.com
**Order online at:**
trafford.com/06-0162

10    9    8    7    6    5    4    3    2    1

# Table of Content

| | |
|---|---|
| **Preface** | 7 |
| **Introduction: Some Aspects of Tantra** | 11 |
| **Commentary on the Vidyadhara Guru Sadhana** | 31 |
|   **A. First Prayers** | 31 |
|   **B. Preparatory Practice** | 41 |
|     a. The Four Reflections | 42 |
|     b. Refuge and Developing an Enlightened Attitude | 47 |
|     c. Seven Branch Practice | 48 |
|     d. Dorje Sempa Meditation | 50 |
|     e. Guru Yoga | 62 |
|   **C. SADHANA: Introductory Part** | 69 |
|     a. Seven Line Prayer | 71 |
|     b. General Prayers for the Lineage | 78 |
|   **D. SADHANA: Preparatory Practices** | 91 |
|     a. The Visualisation | 92 |
|     b. Refuge and Bodhicitta | 92 |
|     c. Cutting the Boundary | 102 |
|     d. Confession | 107 |
|     e. Invitation | 113 |
|     f. Purifying and Blessing the Offerings | 116 |
|   **E. SADHANA: Main Part** | 129 |
|     a. Visualisation of the Mandala and the Deity | 129 |
|     b. Padmasambhava and his Manifestations | 133 |
|     c. The Invocation | 144 |
|     d. Offerings | 154 |
|     e. Praise of the Three Kayas | 160 |
|     f. Mantra Recitation | 168 |

|   |   |
|---|---|
| g. Offerings and Praise | 174 |
| h. Encouragement on Impermanence | 192 |
| i. Praying for What We Want | 207 |
| j. Short Phowa Practice | 214 |
| k. Receiving the Four Initiations | 215 |
| l. Dissolving into the Guru and Maintaining the View | 219 |

## F. Dharma Protector Practice — 231

## G. Offerings — 243

|   |   |
|---|---|
| a. Blessing the Offerings and Inviting the High Guests | 243 |
| b. Making Confession | 249 |
| c. Sacrifice | 252 |
| d. Offerings we Share | 257 |
| e. Remains | 260 |

## H. Concluding Section — 265

|   |   |
|---|---|
| a. Stabilising the Result | 266 |
| b. Prayers of Aspiration | 278 |
| c. Auspicious Verses | 283 |

# Appendices — 293

|   |   |
|---|---|
| Authorisation to Practice | 293 |
| Contact Details and Further Reading | 293 |
| Table of Pictures | 294 |
| Available Titles of Khordong Commentaries | 294 |

# Preface

THIS BOOK CONTAINS THE TEXT of the tantric ritual practice called *The Vidyadhara Guru Sadhana* and my brief commentary on it. The commentary is the edited transcript of two talks and in no way claims to be a complete account of the text. Rather, it is offered as a way for western people to approach the engagement with tantric practice. The text itself is from the nyingmapa tradition of Tibetan buddhism and is a treasure text of Nuden Dorje. I first translated it with C R Lama (Chhimed Rigdzin Rinpoche) over twenty-five years ago and it has become the most frequently practised larger text amongst his students.

This ritual text is a very important one because of the depth of its content and the shortness of its lineage, in other words, its closeness to Padmasambhava, the root of all the nyingma lineages. C R Lama gave the following account of the text:

> When Padmasambhava was at the great cave of Samye Chimpu in Tibet he gave very important initiations to Yeshe Tsogyal, Nanam Dorje Dudjom, Khyeuchung Lotsawa, Achar Sale, and so forth, the twenty-five great disciples known as the Je Bang Nyer Nga. This present treasure dharma is part of the doctrines he taught then. In this sadhana Padmasambhava himself is seen as the emanation of all the buddhas and the encompasser of all herukas and dakinis. When the teachings were allotted this practice was part of Khyeuchung Lotsawa's share. Khyeuchung Lotsawa had seven important incarnations, the seven Nuden Dorjes, namely Terchen Dundul Dorje and so on. Nuden Dorje Drophan Lingpa Drolo Tsal was the seventh of the Nuden Dorjes and it was he who revealed this treasure dharma. After he had taken it out he kept it secret for twenty-five years during which time he did much practice and recited thirteen million of the benza guru mantra with this practice and also with Rigdzin Godem's Rigdzin Dung Drub. This

was his first treasure (gTer) and subsequent to it, he revealed and wrote down a further sixteen volumes.

According to the text Nuden Dorje Drophan Lingpa gave this practice first to the wife of Lhachen, the King of A-Kyong, Tamdrin Wangmo. When she did this practice light rays issued from her body, and when she died she resembled an eight-year-old girl. At her funeral many rainbows appeared. This happened at A-Kyong near Lake Ko Ko Nor. Then secondly, Drophan Lingpa's own son, Gyalsae Padma Don Sal received the teachings from that queen. The third person to receive it was Gonpo Wangyal, the nephew of Nuden Dorje Drophan Lingpa. He received it from Gyalsae Padma Don Sal. The fourth person was Tulku Tsorlo (Tsultrim Zangpo) who gained it from his father and root guru, Gonpo Wangyal, who was the incarnation of Achar Sale, one of the twenty-five great disciples. The fifth person is myself, and I received it from Tulku Tsorlo, the incarnation of Vimalamitra and Vairocana who received Padmasambhava's mind blessing.

From Nuden Dorje until now this lineage has only five members. The first four of these five lineage holders gained great results and recited many or at least one hundred thousand benza guru mantras for each syllable of the mantra.

I myself have less opportunity, and for this practice and Byangter Rigdzin Dungdrub I have recited just two million six hundred thousand benza guru mantras. But anyway when I die, I will not be afraid, and am competent to go to some other place not in the six realms of beings. It may not be a very high place, but I am sure that it will not be a low place.

At this time and in accordance with some of my dreams and the predictions of some former terchens (according to Drophan Lingpa's prediction) I have decided to give this teaching to those who will practise it.

Perhaps this is right. Perhaps it is wrong. We do not know. But it is certain that whoever has faith and belief free from doubt in Padmasambhava and this terton (treasure-revealer) system, and the nyingma kama and terma lineages, and who does practice, will get result. The lineage for this practice is not long. From Padmasambhava to my guru there are only five in the lineage. There is also another short lineage for when I did practice in Tsonae Nang in Kham, East Tibet. I also got some direct lineage from Drophan

> Lingpa, Khyeuchung Lotsawa and Padmasambhava, all not different in form. This occurred on the tsechu (tenth day of the waxing moon) when I received this initiation. Now I think that whoever does this practice and reads the seven-line prayer (*Tsig Dun Sol Deb*) one hundred thousand times, and the benza guru mantra one million three hundred thousand times, is sure to get some result.

C R Lama[1] was a very powerful yogi, a master of energy, and the root text was translated and printed in a wrathful mandala of terrifying anger and intensity. Hesitation was burnt up on the spot, and the flow of transmission was a ceaseless river of molten lava from beginning to end. Rinpoche said that the translation and the first initiation, which would open out the lineage to a wider group of disciples, was at the time mainly for the benefit of Barbara Terris and Robbie Terris. One of Rinpoche's favourite expressions was 'full faith', and our work in Shantiniketan from 1974 to 1982 was based on this principle.

Since the Tibetan diaspora there has been an opening up of the ways in which such practices are approached. Many people engaging in tantric practice lack a thorough grounding in the philosophical views embedded in them. They also often lack the ripeness that comes with diligent attention to the preliminary practices. However these are difficult times, and if anyone has a sincere interest in the practice they should, I feel, be welcomed and eased into this approach to existence, to the transformation of daily life into the mandala of the enlightened ones. Hopefully this commentary will show how the various parts of the practice function, for the text is method from beginning to end. Reading the text alone can in no way substitute for receiving the three-fold aspects of initiation, transmission and instruction from an authorised teacher.

Karma is a strange theory. On the one hand it seems very orderly: actions have consequences. In early translations into English of buddhist texts it was often presented as the Law, something inescapable, inexorable and therefore a fearful call to awakening. Yet in our own lives it reveals itself as luck, as chance, as our share, our slice of life which, as it lands on our plate, looks rather different from what other beings are getting. The complexity of why things happen as they do will inevitably always evade us. More important perhaps is how we can work best with our share, a share which is not fixed but revealed though a dynamic co-provocation of the potential of any situation, and our capacity to attend to it from a state of openness.

---

[1] For details of some aspects of Rinpoche's life see the Khordong website at http://www.khordong.net

This text arises from a sequence of events in which I am implicated, and feel assisted by, and yet which seemed to just happen. The interweaving of active and passive moments in which others lead with their intention and I follow, and moments where I have an intention (find myself intending, tending towards) and others come aboard, is unceasing. When what takes one's fancy also captivates others, releasing inspiration and energy, it is marvellous, for it reveals the synergy of the mandala, the collaborative effortless effort of getting on with it by being fully in it, up for it, longing for it, living for it, filled and emptied by it, all at the same time. Dharma is the great 'it', the ungraspable revelation that returns us to ourselves, subverting ordinary identity by dropping us back into the groundless ground which is always emerging as this or that.

The initial wish that I say something about the Rigdzin practice came from Ruth Kürman who also organised the two small retreats in which this took place. The warm wind of good fortune blew in Robert Jaroslawski as the translator for German. His easy presence meant the pauses were harmonious and pleasing, creating an atmosphere of flow running through the continuity and disruption of two languages. For some reason the thought of transcribing the tapes appealed to Mani and she applied herself with diligence although, as she said clearly, the topic was not really her path. Then, for a while, the transcripts languished, accumulating dust among my myriad papers. Suddenly there was a new breeze in town, a sweet gust of enthusiasm swept Gordon Ellis into the major task of ordering and editing the material of the two retreats. This he did with patience, skill, and love and the fruits of that work are what you see before you. Final preparation was done by Ruth Rickard and Barbara Terris.

The Tibetan text in this volume was collated from several versions and revised by Anne Gäbler. Timely sponsorship from Pamela Carr speeded the final work and ensured publication. Andreas Ruft did the final layout with the care and diligence which he has brought to previous Khordong publications and Elisabeth Poller-Frischengruber provided help with the cover design.

# Introduction: Some Aspects of Tantra

IN THIS BRIEF COMMENTARY we will look firstly at the structure of tantra, and secondly at how the *Vidyadhara Guru Sadhana*, or *Big Rigdzin* as it is known, relates to the main themes of tantra.

What I will try to do is to bring together two streams of explanation. One is the traditional explanation and the other is a more socio-political, historical, psychological interpretation. I think both of these can be very useful because as westerners we have grown up with a particular way of analysing situations. If dharma is to become fully integrated into the western way of life it is important that it doesn't just get bracketed off as some strange, foreign — and thus alien — set of beliefs. Rather, there needs to be some way in which it can be processed and so incorporated. Also, I think both of these two streams of explanation are contained within dharma itself.

The first stream of explanation relates to buddhist principles of cause and effect and why things come into existence. The second stream is to do with ideas of validity, that things have a truth because of their source. In general, it is said that in this treasure tradition, the *terma* tradition, if we believe that a terma is authentic then we can believe it is reliable because it has originated with Padmasambhava, so the proof of its validity lies in its origin. As Padmasambhava integrates the three *kayas*, so we believe this teaching is a display, a manifestation of the natural condition of existence. In this way all the terma teachings, including the one that we shall go on to study, the *Big Rigdzin*, arise from a dimension of space and time which is beyond our ordinary space and time. They arise from the *dharmadhatu* as a manifestation of the nature of awareness.

On the other hand, at a relative level, we have the idea of dependent co-origination. The basic principle involved here is that everything manifests on the basis of other factors which have already manifested. One of the clearest expositions of this is in the *Arya Salistamba Sutra* in which it is set forth very clearly in these terms: on the basis of *this, that* arises.

Without causes and conditions nothing manifests. We see that in the birth story of Padmasambhava. If you remember, in the land of Uddiyana there was a king, Indrabhuti, and this king was old and blind and without any children, and in that country, due to causes and conditions, there were many, many problems; there was famine and drought and illness. Although the royal priests and the other holy people in the country did many pujas and practices, there was no benefit from these actions, but then, due to other causes and conditions, the idea of praying to Amitabha arose and because of these prayers there manifested, out of the heart of Amitabha, a lotus surrounded by five-coloured lights upon which sat a letter *Hri*. It is from this letter *Hri* on the lotus in the Dhanakosha lake that Padmasambhava then manifested. That is to say, he didn't just flow out for no reason; there was a stimulus, there was a hook in some way, and in response to this hook compassion took on a particular form, namely that of Padmasambhava.

In a similar way we can see, if we take a western historical view of the development of buddhism, that after Prince Siddhartha had gained enlightenment under the bodhi tree in Bodhgaya and started, with some doubts and hesitancy, to teach the dharma, this too developed according to causes and conditions.

The Buddha, who was Prince Siddhartha in his new state, thought that there was no point in teaching any of what he had discovered because nobody would understand it, but then all the gods, led by Brahma, came and prayed to him and said, "Please, what you have understood is very important, please teach it to us". And he said, "Okay!" That's how it happened, because of causes and conditions.

Also, if you look at the structure of the monastic system that was established at the time of the Buddha, you will find in the commentaries on the *vinaya* that there were very precise situations in which the various specific rules for monks' behaviour came into being. For example, somebody at that time came up to the Buddha and said, "Buddha, do you know that some of your monks are going to houses and asking for meat?" Buddha said, "Oh, this is terrible, from now on, my monks will hold out their bowl and take whatever is put into it". The same message was reinforced when, at another time, someone came and said, "Your monks are throwing out the meat that I put in the bowl," and then the Buddha said, "No, you should eat whatever is there. No matter what somebody puts in your bowl, you should eat that". As more and more people came to the Buddha, to tell him all the bad things his monks were doing, he gave more and more instructions. Then there is the famous story that when the Buddha died, all the monks were crying and crying except one monk who was laughing, and they said to him, "Why are you laughing?" He said, "The Buddha is dead. No more rules!" That is causes and conditions.

The development of buddhism, as is the case with most organisations, moves between, is constructed out of, develops from a tension between two positions. There is both a centripetal force and a centrifugal one. That's really what a mandala is, it holds the tension between these two forces. Just as in a laboratory we use a centrifuge to separate things out so, in the history of the dharma, points of difference between different monks, different philosophers, led to the rising of different schools and sometimes these tensions led to killings, to the destruction of monasteries and so forth. On the other hand, we have a direction of devotion to the Buddha, a belief in certain basic principles such as impermanence and so forth, and these factors keep bringing the whole movement of dharma together, so that it is also possible for buddhists from all parts of the world to come together and find a common ground. So these two strands of explanation are important.

Generally speaking, tantra is concerned with continuity, with linking. This concept itself is especially important in relation to what Tibetans call the hinayana position. This is because the basic view, according to the hinayana, is one of renunciation and renunciation means separation. For example, according to the hinayana view, if you find things that disturb you then you should try to avoid them. You can look therefore at the normal cues or the normal supports for emotional disturbance, and then try to get rid of them. Thus, for example, if you decide to become a monk or a nun you should avoid close contact with people of the opposite sex (and people of your own sex as well), and you should carry out the analysis of the body that reveals its raw and crude components. When you get used to this way of looking, instead of being hooked by the perception of someone you find attractive you can rapidly turn them into something disgusting. In this way, by reducing the whole world to shit, you will feel free from attachment. That view doesn't appeal to everyone because one of the things about living in shit is, even if you try to separate from it, the smell goes up your nose. Simply trying to create a schizoid world of avoidance of difficulties will be ineffective because, by our very nature, we are dependent on other people.

It is possible for us to take this idea of dependent origination, that everything arises in relation to something else, and experience it as a very persecutory negative idea. One can feel like somebody with a big octopus hanging onto them who is constantly trying to pull off all these connections. This arises from not recognising that we ourselves, everything about us, arises interdependently, without any stable essence standing apart from the process. But even when we see that, we may feel that we need to shut the whole system down, loosen connection, extinguish the lamp.

Alternatively, as we experience the shift from the hinayana to the mahayana view we can come to see that dependent co-origination and the interdependence of all things takes on a much more positive connotation: because I am connected with all sentient beings, my liberation is dependent on their liberation; there can be no finite solution; the only way out is through, with, and as, infinity.

From a basic mahayana point of view I can say, "It is because I recognise I am connected with you that I need to make a gesture of compassion towards you." This is further supported by the idea that I have been born many, many times, that in all my lives I have had a mother, and therefore it is obvious that at one time or another you have been my mother. I can, therefore, arrive at the conclusion that, as my mother, you have done good things for me and so I have a debt of obligation to you.

From a British position that is a little bit like the idea of the European Union, in which people tell all kinds of sweet stories about their deep connections but actually, underneath, there are many historical conflicts which are still very much present. That is to say, you have to keep reminding yourself, "Oh, this person has been my mother, they did this to me, therefore..." There's a huge adjustment to make because the habitual impulse is something else altogether.

As the understanding of dependent co-origination started to be woven into the understanding of emptiness, particularly after the work of Nagarjuna and then the *yogacara* work of Asanga Maitreya, what we see is that connectedness is taken as a given. It's not that I have a choice whether I am connected but that connectedness is given by the very nature of reality, and one of the functions of ignorance is to not be aware of this basic connectedness.

Someone can make a decision that they don't wish to belong in their family any longer, yet nevertheless family-ness, blood-relatedness is a given. It is an insanity for someone to claim that they are not connected with their family. For many young people there is a strong psychological feeling that arises that they have to separate out from their parents in order to work out who they are. Yet the inescapable biological basis of someone's existence is their parents. Feeding, being clothed, being taught to speak language, being supported in going to school, all the complex formative experiences of life, of personal development, are generated inside the family. However, it is clearly the case for many young people that, by holding strongly to the idea that they don't want anything to do with their family, they cover over what is actually a manifest, undeniable reality. From the mahayana buddhist point of view this is the same with all sentient beings. We're all part of the same family, and to deny our connection with other people is part of what is meant by ignorance — it's just part of our madness.

One of the notable things about buddhism is that it is very intentional: it has a teleological orientation. Buddhism's intention is towards the enlightenment of all beings. This has an important implication because if I, through studying the dharma get some idea of what enlightenment is, then I will want to bring this enlightenment to other people and I will want to help them to get enlightened. This gives me a sense that I should do things to help other people get enlightened. In which case I might pray, "Oh, may all beings go to Zangdopalri". But not all sentient beings might want to go to Zangdopalri; some might want to go to Sukhavati. So, due to the power of my prayer, some people may find themselves in Zangdopalri and they're thinking, "I don't want to be here! Here in Zangdopalri there are all these very big, angry, powerful people but in Sukhavati you sit nicely inside your lotus and there is very sweet music; it is much more peaceful".

This raises a very important question. If we like people, if we love people, we want to do something for them but what will help them? Usually what we want to do for them is an extension of *our* desire, we want to take them into *our* world. Is it possible to know what is good for another? If we ask them, can they tell us? Do they know?

Many positions within buddhism are dogmatic in that they are connected with having an idea in advance of what applies with respect to a particular situation. It is much easier to apply a dogmatic solution rather than to actually investigate or inquire. In terms of the centripetal-centrifugal tension within buddhism much of the difficulty is located in the tension between the discourse of faith, of dogma, on the one hand and the discourse of practice on the other. For instance, in the practice of meditation we develop attention, a phenomenological attention, which is an attention to what is actually there, but when we learn dharma, when we have the dogma, the discourse of dharma, we don't need to attend to what is there any more because we know in advance what it will be. It seems that all the major religions have this kind of tension. On one hand you have scholars and dogmatists and on the other you have the people who do a practice of some kind; between them there is a major tension which, if it is not held creatively, results in avoidance, non-resolution and schism rather than synthesis.

Now, in tantra, part of the continuity is a continuity between dogmatic positioning and open, free attention. According to tradition, the tantras arose as a set of skilful means taught by Buddha Shakyamuni as part of the third turning of the wheel of dharma. That is to say, Buddha Shakyamuni manifested in the form of Vajrapani on Mount Malaya in South India. Some think this mountain is similar to Adam's Peak in Sri Lanka. Arising out of the wisdom of the Buddha there was a movement, a gesture of his compassion, in which he manifested in the form of Vajrapani and began to teach the methods of tantra. Each of the tantras has its own story of origin, and in Tibet there are many, many tantras, some originating in India, some developed in Tibet. If a tantric initiation is given in its complete form, the first thing a teacher will do is read a history of that particular tantra and how it came into existence. These stories are very important for they point to the moment when the infinite becomes finite, the timeless enters time; they indicate the non-duality of the ever-open ground and the unique specificity of lived contingents and contextual existence. Some of these stories have now been translated, for instance the story of the *Guhyasamajatantra* has been translated by Alex Wayman[2].

The important thing in these stories is that at a certain point some event happens which provokes or stimulates the Buddha, often in the form of Dorje Sempa (Vajrasattva), to manifest in a particular form. Although possessing the three key qualities of infinite wisdom or understanding, infinite compassion and infinite power, a buddha only manifests in the world if there is a cause from that direction. This is a very, very important principle in buddhism. It is exactly the same principle that we find in the story about Buddha Shakyamuni in Bodhgaya when he decided, "No, I won't teach, it won't be helpful." Then somebody requested him, and then many people came and asked him to teach, and as a result he taught.

It is a general principle that buddhist teachers should teach only if somebody invites them. Likewise there is a strong tradition in Tibet that if you want an initiation from a master you should ask many times. They'll often say, "No, no, no," for a long, long time. A good example of that is with Milarepa who for many, many, many years asked Marpa for instruction and Marpa always told him to fuck off. Marpa was very rough to Milarepa — it's not sweet. That very roughness is seen as important because it shows, developing in Milarepa, the power of a kind of hook. Marpa always had the ring

---

[2] Alex Wayman: *Yoga of the Guhyasamajatantra. The Arcane Lore of Forty Verses. A Buddhist Tantra Commentary* (Motilal Banarsidass, 1991)

but at first Milarepa didn't have a good hook so if Marpa had given the teaching to Milarepa it would have just slipped away. However, due to this longing being built-up, being cooked-up again and again to a total desperation, Milarepa developed a very strong hook and then, when he eventually got the teaching, he locked on very solidly, and stayed fully locked on until he died.

This is very, very important I think, because we can easily fantasize and project onto the Buddha or Padmasambhava the idea that they are some kind of good papa figure and that somehow all good things will just come to us from them. This is okay if it serves as a support for devotional practice. However, if it develops as a formalistic position in which one does the puja as a ritual function and imagines that Padmasambhava will come by just doing this, it is probably not very helpful. The reason for this is the notion of dependent co-origination: all things arise from causes. This is fundamental for everything. Obscurations and limiting patterns run very deep in us: great effort invested in the great method of tantra is necessary if liberation is to be achieved.

Generally speaking, although there are different buddhist philosophical views, only three things are said to have no cause and to be unconditioned: the first is the blue sky, which is always just there; the second is enlightenment, which is the manifestation of the buddha nature, which is always there; and the third is the moment of enlightenment itself. If this were not the case then buddhahood, or enlightenment, would be a construct.

You do your practice and, on the basis of your practice, you approach enlightenment or enlightenment becomes a possibility for you, but the actual moment of enlightenment itself is not dependent on any of the causes and conditions that have been operating to bring it about, it is an entirely separate occurrence. Everything else arises due to dependent co-origination and is therefore contingent and unstable. Thus, even the Buddha's compassion manifests in response to people's practice, and the opportunities to experience it are both rare and fleeting, although it is ever-present as potential.

Following from this, it is said that if you see your teacher as a buddha you get a buddha's blessing, but if you see him as a human being you only get a human being's blessing. This is because even if the teacher is a buddha he cannot give a buddha's blessing to somebody who is not in a state to receive a buddha's blessing. The relationship between teacher and student is a collaborative relationship. The teacher needs the student otherwise he can't teach, and the student needs the teacher otherwise he can't learn.

Chhimed Rigdzin Rinpoche used to tell the following story. When he was a small boy and he had to be involved in giving initiations, he'd be sitting on his tall throne and at the end people would come forward to make an offering and give a white scarf or *katag*. However, there were many of these small boy tulkus in a row and the people who were coming forward didn't give a katag to everyone; so he had to sit there, and if somebody went to give him a katag he had to bend forward and put it back over their neck. But it wasn't necessarily the case that if somebody came towards him holding a katag that they were going to offer it to him. If he leaned forward to receive it and the person didn't offer the katag then his teacher would get very, very angry with him. This was because the required position was to *respond* rather than to manifest any desire for himself. This is very important to maintain, otherwise, instead of paying attention to what is there, we work on the basis of assumptions.

In general we may say, in accordance with the tradition, that the flow of tantric teachings arises from many situations far, far in the distant past, just on the very edge of time. On a more ordinary level, the level which is being increasingly revealed through the studies of many western scholars, tantra arose as a socio-cultural phenomena. It arose in hinduism, jainism, and buddhism at pretty much the same time. Tantra was a reaction to religious traditions which had become increasing concerned with the avoidance of worldly affairs and which had a negative view of the world.

Tantra, as it manifests in buddhism, is a very interesting link between, on the one hand, the understanding of madhyamika philosophy, involving a profound intellectual grasp of emptiness and on the other, an aesthetically oriented manifestation which is linked with devotional practice and a path of enjoyment and ecstasy.

We know that there was a very profound connection between ancient Greece and the India of early buddhism. There was a huge cultural and economic exchange between these areas. Some of this involved movement along the ancient silk route, some of it involved movement further south and some involved movement along by the coast. We know for instance that Alexander the Great moved as far as the Indus river, while there are still people in Afghanistan and Pakistan who claim their blood origin from him. These people still talk of him, 'Sikander' as he is called, and he is still very much a cultural presence for them.

Indian buddhist art was just beginning at this time and initially depictions of the Buddha were in terms of abstract symbols, like the bodhi tree (for enlightenment), the stupa (for his death) and the lotus steps (for him taking his first steps), etc. This was because it was decided that the Buddha was too splendid to be represented directly and so only aspects of his life should be represented. . It was only after some time, perhaps in response to hindu depictions of Siva, that there arose the first actual representations of the Buddha as a human being and shortly after that there was the development of Gandharvan art in what is now Pakistan and east Afghanistan, where buddhas and bodhisattvas were depicted in a strikingly Greek manner. It might be suggested that it wasn't just Greek notions of art that were introduced, but also Greek aspects of thought.

One of the great tensions in ancient Greek culture was that between the apollonian and the dionysian, or between the gods Apollo and Dionysus. Apollo was the son of Zeus. He was a sky god, a bit like Mercury, but his principal function was to do with clarity. It was his role to give order, direction and also to give perfect form. He represented the clarity that arises through getting things into perspective in the same way that distance gives us clarity by enabling us to have an overview. By contrast, there is Dionysus. The cult of Dionysus was probably a transformation of earlier, mother-worshipping cults which became directed through this male form when the power of matriarchy started to collapse. Practices associated with Dionysus were absolutely through the body, using the body as a means of linking into both nature and ecstasy. They involved nakedness, dancing, (particularly at night, in dark places in the forest), sex, sacrifice, meat-eating and a lot of alcohol, so you can see there is a contrast and a tension here between the apollonian and the dionysian. Very similar tensions existed in Indian culture, even before buddhism.

The Aryan people who moved down into India, anywhere between 6000 to 2000 b.c., came from near the Caucasus. These Aryans shared a common linguistic identity with the people of western Europe, specifically the proto-Indo-European language from which arose both ancient Greek and Sanskrit. The Aryans were cattle herders so, not surprisingly, the cow and the bull were very, very sacred to them, as they still are in modern India.

Now, if you have cows you don't like the forest, because cows get lost in the forest and there are wolves there and many other kind of dangerous animals: you want to clear the forest. You want to have a place where there is grass, with easy things to eat and not too many snakes. As the Aryans developed, a lot of their religion became orientated around the sky, around space, around openness. They were quite afraid of darkness and enclosure. This resulted in a very strong polarization of 'light is good and dark is bad'. A parallel dualism is found in Manichaeism, which emerged in what is now

Iran probably around 260 a.d. For them, Ahura Mazda was a light god in the sky, with his great over-arching blue dome, while underneath were the forces of darkness and water.

When the life of the mind and the life of the body were set up in opposition, the mind of abstract thoughts free of emotions became linked with purity, while the body, with its needs and waste products, became linked with defilements. Childbirth leads to impurity; menstruation leads to impurity. There was an enormous fear around that kind of embodied existence. No culture can hold the split between the apollian and the dionysian for very long. What you start to see, in the development of the cult of Krishna in India for example, is an integration.

Krishna is blue in colour; blue is pretty close to black. He is connected with cows because he liked to eat yoghurt when he was small. He liked to have sex with the cowgirls when he got older, enjoying freedom and indulgence of the senses in the forest. He had many women, was not a married man and he played his music, so he was really the outsider. There is a very interesting cultural transformation, in which a position which has been denied and rejected can be integrated by moving it up. This means that the anxious brahmins, with all their rules and regulations about eating and bathing and ritual purity, could also have a relationship with this much freer figure, this archetypal figure, who is concerned with embodied existence, sexuality, pleasure and so forth.

A very similar thing happened in buddhism, where in early tantra you have people who were outsiders — washer women, prostitutes, for instance, people involved in very low-caste activities — establishing powerful and liberating connections with people who have high-caste status. One famous example of this is found in the story of Saraha.

Saraha was a brahmin from a very good family. He became a great scholar but he made no real progress in his spiritual work until one day he encountered a woman who made arrows. This arrow-maker woman is clearly connected with tribal culture because arrows are for hunting, something brahmins don't do. She asked him some questions which he couldn't answer, questions related to experience. The effect was to wake him up from his apollonian discourse, from his scholarly discourse connected with ideas from the sky, with his concern with clarity, with books. Suddenly somebody says, "What is life? Who are you?" and he doesn't know what to say. So she opens to him the secret mandala hidden in her underwear and he gains awakening through the shift from concepts to non-conceptual experience.

It is very interesting, because here you have a structure in which this outsider-woman, who perhaps previously would have been simply a kind of secret pleasure and an indulgence for the powerful male, is integrated rather than excluded, and so becomes somebody who flips him into a wholly different realm of experience.

There is a similar story about Naropa. One day when he was teaching, an old woman came to see Naropa and similarly asked him questions he couldn't understand. As he couldn't answer her, she said, "Oh, you need to see my brother." So Naropa went to see this man, who was called Tilopa, and who was living a very wild life, the life of an untouchable, sitting on the bank of a river eating discarded fish intestines and heads. Tilopa sets Naropa a series of tests which bring him in contact with the more primitive aspects of himself that he has avoided, his anger, fear, doubt and so on. It is through his intuitive trust in Tilopa that Naropa manages to break through the seemingly protective yet profoundly limiting cocoon of his habitual concepts. There are many stories like this from the early days of tantra.

The teaching site of many of the tantras was a cemetery. A cemetery was a place where nobody wanted to go; it was a place of fear; it was a place where there was the possibility of indulging in the darkest fantasies. You could eat human flesh there, you could bring dead people back to life and you could probably have sex with them too, if you wanted.

What you have here is a breaking of boundaries, where things which had been kept separate are now brought together. Normally, when you bring together things which were separate this results in anxiety. However, where there is anxiety there is the possibility of transforming it into excitement. We know this from riding motorbikes or going mountain climbing and so forth. It is also the key principle for understanding sexual perversion. This process is made use of in tantra by taking all the things that would normally frighten, disgust and dismay you, then by engaging with this anxiety, there arises a kind of existential angst, one that really stirs the bottom of your existence, and this is transformed into excitement. In this way you can mobilise the heart energy which can be used for liberation. People who are able to manage this transformation of anxiety into excitement become known as 'heroes' or 'heroines'. This is a general principle, I think, in world culture and it is absolutely true in buddhism.

In the case of Padmasambhava, whatever else he is, whatever else we believe, he is certainly a mythic hero. His power arises from his fearlessness. He is not overcome by anxiety, he doesn't turn away from situations, he goes right into them. He is the real yogi because a yogi is somebody who can take the events and feelings, the behaviours which would normally tie people in knots and bind them to samsara, and use these very things as a means for liberation.

So, if we think, what are the two greatest fears in life, they are sex and death. And what is tantra but a very long discussion of sex and death? Tantra works with the images of killing and copulating, destroying the manifestation to which we are attached, and attachment itself, in order to copulate and fuse with emptiness. This reverses the ordinary pattern of samsara where we copulate with manifestation while destroying awareness of emptiness.

Tantra at its root is about ecstasy, and what is ecstasy but *ek-stasis*, a stepping out of yourself, a being-taken-out-of-yourself? By stepping outside yourself you recognise yourself, because the self that you think you are is a self that is constructed from assumptions, from karma, from habitual tendencies. That is one of the reasons why in tantra we visualize ourselves as gods and goddesses, so that we can move out of our ordinary sense of self and leave all our assumptions and fears behind and then, in this imagined identity, we feel free to act in a different way.

Some of you may be familiar with the writings of Herbert Marcuse. Although some of his ideas are not very wise, one interesting thing he wrote particularly, I think in *One-dimensional Man*[3], is that if a revolution is to occur, if radical change is to occur, it can only be brought about by people who have no place in the system; only outsiders make revolutions. Grand gestures, however, don't last very long. For example, you may have been around in 1968 and maybe enjoyed a little bit of excitement. Those days are long gone. This is because revolutionary movements always provoke a counter-attack by the forces of conservatism.

In the dialogue between Trotsky and Stalin you have a theme which is very general in left-wing politics, about whether to take a sudden approach or a gradualist approach. In other words, whether you go for success in the revolution in one country, build on that, and then move on to the next stage, or whether you go for universal disturbance.

This is a very important theme also in Tibetan buddhism. One of the founding moments of Tibetan buddhism is what is called the Council of Lhasa, which was convened after the departure of Padmasambhava from Tibet. This involved an Indian monk called Kamalashila, a principal student of Shantarakshita, who engaged in a debate with Hwa Shang Mahayana, a proponent of an alternative Chinese view. Kamalashila was a great scholar

---

[3] Herbert Marcuse: *One-dimensional Man: Studies in the Ideology of Advanced Industrial Society* (Routledge, 1964)

and meditator. He wrote the *Bhavanakrama*[4], an important meditation guide. In this debate Kamalashila set out the gradualist position whereby moving through the stages and progressions of buddhist practice one would gradually remove one's defilements and impediments, and in the other direction build up wisdom and compassion, and so gradually come to a state of enlightenment. Hwa Shang Mahayana, on the other hand, spoke about instant enlightenment. He took the position that since the mind has been enlightened from the very beginning and all obscuration is simply contingent or adventitious — in other words, something which arises but which is not innate — so it can be instantly removed.

In this debate, which was convened by the king, Kamalashila won. We can give many, many readings as to why this was, such as better trade relations with India and so forth, but it is also very unlikely that any king, anywhere, is going to say that something spontaneous is a good idea. To be a king is to be concerned with control. The king is a manifest aspect of patriarchy, and patriarchy tends to be gradualist. The history of democracy in Europe shows this again and again: that people, when they stand up for their rights, are suppressed; that the forces of conservatism, of established wealth and power, don't give up easily.

Nowadays we learn more and more about the history of what is called the Wild West in America. According to the Hollywood narrative, which is very seductive, the border was opened up by a peculiar combination of good, gentle folk and crazy madmen. I have watched many, many cowboy movies and it seems to me that there are basically two kinds of cowboy film. One is where you get a wagon-train of settlers going out, protected by good men and attacked by bad Indians. The other is where you get a bunch of bad boys causing a lot of trouble. Usually the bad boys go first and kill all the Indians. Then they kill a lot of each other, after which the good sheriff arrives, puts them under control, and finally the wagon-train rolls up and civilisation progresses.

If we think about it in these terms, Padmasambhava, aka Guru Rinpoche, is a mixture of the very, very bad boy and the good sheriff. He is clearly a little bit nuts. When he arrives in Tibet, according to the story, he is naked. You can imagine, if you're a Tibetan, that when you go down to India you might want to take your clothes off, but if you are an Indian going up to Tibet, you'll want to put something on! He is mad — he doesn't care. The local people say, "Don't go there. These local gods are very powerful". He says,

---

[4] Kamalashila: *Stages of Meditation* (Dalai Lama, et al : Snow Lion Publications, 2001)

"Whatever, I'm going there!" He carries a pair of colt mantra specials that he can fire with both hands, and he always gets victory. This is very important, because without his wildness, the Tibetan belief is that buddhism would never have been established. Remember Shantarakshita: his name means 'peaceful protection'; this was not enough to do the business; they had to bring in a hired killer, this man with Dorje Phurba, who says, "I'll stab you! Phat!" This is a wild man who comes in and says, "I don't take any enemies. You are my slave, otherwise you're dead!" Bang! Dharmadhatu! That is the story of Padmasambhava. Due to his activity the country becomes peaceful, the local gods are controlled. Subsequently other peaceful sheriffs simply have to repeat what Padmasambhava did and everything is under control.

A victory has been achieved. A psycho-spiritual, social, ecological system of symbolic control over the forces of disorder and confusion has been established by Padmasambhava. This brought with it a centralized metaphor of power because here we have one person who can control everything. We can see in this the structure of a mandala: the principal god is in the middle and power moves out through the doors into the world.

Before Padmasambhava's intervention there were many local gods each with their own local cult which was often woven into the structure of power and autonomy of the Tibetan tribal chiefs. However, with the establishment of Samye monastery, brought about by the power of Padmasambhava, there arose a centralised site for the control of all these psycho-spiritual forces in Tibet.

It was often the case that when buddhism arrived in a new country it was through the conversion of the king who then authorized its spread. That was exactly the pattern in Tibet. By the time Padmasambhava arrived the royal commitment to dharma had been there for several generations. The then current king, Trisong Deutsen, became more and more involved in buddhism, becoming a close personal disciple of Guru Rinpoche The buddhism of gradualism, of order, of prediction, exactly fitted in with a centralised authority functioning through a bureaucracy. It conforms to the confucian idea of the role of the king as a mediator between the gods and the people. It also fits in well with the structure of monasteries in India where the notion of a hierarchical religious structure was well established. However, where there is a movement towards centralised power, as we know very well from European history, resistance arises from the provinces, the local barons, and landowners. This is what we hear happened in Tibet, after Trisong Deutsen and his sons, who succeeded him. Then Ralpachen became king of Tibet who is especially remembered because of his very long hair. Supposedly, when he sat he let his hair out and monks came and sat on it, which was symbolically to sit on the top of his head. His successor was Langdarma who had much more sympathy with the traditional bon religion, and was much more in communication with local leaders. He began to slow down the expansion of buddhism. We have to remember, of course, that Kamalashila had already been murdered: a butcher came and squeezed his kidneys till he died. Langdarma, in turn, was murdered. He was murdered by a monk who had been expelled from the monastery as it was being closed and who returned wearing a two-coloured cape, and a big black hat. He killed Langdarma using a bow and arrow. That led, pretty much, to a collapse of centralised rule in Tibet for two hundred years, and with it a big decline in buddhism, which moved out to the peripheries, to the Far East, to Kham and Amdo, and to the west, to Guge and that area. The monk who killed Langdarma, while wearing his black hat, became symbolically the basis for black hat dancing, which is seen as the ritual act of destroying the forces that usurped the proper power of established buddhism.

Much later we have what is called the *new translation* period, when many kinds of teachers come to Tibet from India. Some of these new teachers gave rise to the three other main schools: the kagyupa, the sakya and the gelugpa. These were little, little strands which gradually, much later, came to be seen as having an identity. At first it is just that some teacher came from India and had a few students.

By the time of this second dissemination of dharma in Tibet there had been big changes in Indian culture. There had been, for example, the first muslim attacks on India and the destruction of the Somnath temple in Gujarat; consequently a lot of fear was spread. This new muslim force was very scary.

There was also a regeneration of hinduism. Modern hinduism was just beginning to appear. This was around the eleventh century, christian time. This resulted in some of the more easy exchanges between hinduism and buddhism starting to break down. People had to make decisions about which side they belonged to.

The buddhist monasteries by that time were very, very big and required a huge number of donors to give land and food, as well as servants, to maintain them. A monastery was like a small city. It was within this milieu that tantra, as a practice of ecstatic liberation, of the free interplay between male and female forces constituting a radical alternative, started to enter a dialogue with other, monastic, structures. Through a dialectical tension a new synthesis arose in which the practice of tantra became less physical, more symbolic, and more integratable within existing rigid monastic structures. So tantra went from being something very wild and free on the outside to being something woven into the structure of power.

One of the big concerns that emerged during this new period of dharma dissemination in Tibet was with respect to possible contamination. A lot of questions started to be asked. Are these teachers coming from India really hindus, or are they *proper* people? This resulted in a lot of vetting of people, and kings, local kings, started to control who was allowed to teach. It became necessary to get a certificate of permission to teach dharma, and dharma itself became more and more institutionalised. The result was a culture where, if somebody started to teach something, somebody would say, "Stop! Who are you? Who is your teacher? What is the origin of your teaching?" So, rather than trying to work out whether the teaching made sense, people wanted to know whether it was true or not, according to its origins, and to the established status of the teacher.

You find that, if you travel around Tibetan groups in India, they always ask, "Oh, so who is your teacher? Oh, yes, he's very good, oh, oh, oh". They will locate you inside that. We are familiar with this kind of snobbishness in Europe when people ask, "Are these Gucci shoes you're wearing?" or "Did you go to Oxford?" We find this everywhere. There is a discourse of lineage, which means if the lineage is pure then everyone in the lineage is pure. In logic this is called *solipsism*, which means that the argument chases its own ass. Yet underneath there is a phenomenological reality that people know only too well. It is difficult to trust our capacity to make considered adult evaluations. It is much quicker and easier to trust titles, logos, sanctioned ascriptions of value. The simple fact is that thinking, reflective discriminatory thinking, is hard work, especially in relation to power hierarchies that hide a lot of the necessary information. You have to be in the system before you can access the knowledge that lets you know whether you want to be in the system! That someone has a title doesn't necessarily answer the question of whether they have any special qualities. This is a problem with any kind of bureaucratic structure. The name does not necessarily describe the goods. There is a very real issue here because, if you have to honour the lineage because the lineage is pure, and the only proof is the reiteration of the statements, then often some sub-standard goods are being covered over.

In Tibet there were a few lamas who were very interested in ecstasy. C R Lama, when he was young, was very, very vibrant, energetically. When we did a puja in his house in Shantiniketan there were, maybe, six people there, and we had a very, very big drum made from a huge old wine barrel that he got from Calcutta. Very often, while doing a puja, he would stop and say to his wife, "Oh, bring some alcohol!", then we all had to drink quite a lot of whisky or brandy, or whatever. This was designed to loosen us up, so that we wouldn't be too serious. The mood in the puja would be very, very wild and intense. We'd make a lot of noise and the body would be really shaking. Rinpoche would always take big handfuls of rice and throw them at us, peppering us with blessing. As a result you would get completely lost. You wouldn't know *where* you were. You wouldn't know *who* you were: without the usual reference points the mind could experience itself directly. This style is not so common in the world. Rather, if you go into many Tibetan monasteries it's more like watching a corps de ballet. The Dorje Lopon is operating like some grand old dame of the Kirov, the St. Petersburg ballet company, who is shouting to keep everyone in line, all the drums together, and stopping them from shaking their bells at the wrong time. This takes us back to the tension between Apollo and Dionysos. From the apollonian point of view, a puja has to be done in the right way, with the right tune, and the right mudra, and so forth. From the point of view of Dionysus, on the other hand, the only reason to do these long pujas is to 'get' something. The purpose is to get something, not karma, (good karma is accumulated through counting mantras), but to get something direct, something, as a result of which you can go out of your usual state and experience something radically different. There is an inherent tension here between these two, between the apollonian and the dionysian. They're not the same. That's one of the reasons why I myself don't like to do these tantric rituals with anyone else, because I like to do them in a way that makes sense for me. This means, if I do a part of the practice, and I don't like how I've done it, I do it again, and I can do it again until it becomes real for me.

It will very often say, in the instruction about reciting mantras, "Recite this mantra until you see a sign in your dreams, or until you have done a hundred thousand mantras for each syllable, or until you really see Padmasambhava". This is important. It gives you two choices. The first is to recite it in a formal way, keeping count, no matter what happens, with the attitude of: anyway, it's good for you! The second is try to get something that is an experience. So, of course, if you go to do some practice with a lama like Chhimed Rigdzin, it is very important to fit in with the system, because there are many, many people there. Everybody has to stay in rhythm, otherwise it is just a cacophony. However, we also have to see that that is an aspect, a dimension of a mass of people. You have to stay in rhythm, otherwise it gets crazy. If you are doing this, you are aligning yourself with a normative rhythm; the rhythm is such that everybody can join in. This is something it is important to be able to do, it's part of being in a sangha and practicing together, but if you are going to use the dharma directly for your own transformation, it is very important to examine your own situation, to see what is your own rhythm is, and that will change from day to day. When you do this, you can then bring the practice into a direct relationship with your own experience.

An important aspect here is to attend to your body. Just as when someone learns t'ai chi, there are systems of the long form and the short form, but there is also spontaneous t'ai chi, and you have that in almost all the martial arts. There are the standard forms, and there is also the free, spontaneous responsiveness. That's what we need to have, I think, for the dharma, we need to have both of these. This is because sometimes the body wants to do funny things in the puja and, if you are on your own, you can let your body do that. Maybe you feel as if you want to rock, you might want to howl, you might find yourself doing many, many different things.

You are probably already familiar with the stories of the eighty-four mahasiddhas. These mahasiddhas are very important in the development of tantra, and of mahamudra in particular. Most commonly they are depicted as very crazy people. There is one, for example, Kukuripa, who was a great friend of dogs. He lived on an island, in the middle of a cemetery, with hundreds of dogs. If you go to Berlin, you can see some of his reincarnations there, wandering the streets looking completely 'not-there', but with many, many dogs! In the lineage we say that Kukuripa was great, but what the neighbours thought, we don't know. When C R Lama was in Shantiniketan in Bengal where I lived with him, many local people thought he was a black magician. They thought he was a very dangerous person, and they didn't like him at all.

That's part of the reality, you cannot please everyone. You take up a position in life, you do something, you try to stay close to your own experience yet other people will not necessarily find any value in it. So this again is a tension I think we all have to live with. On the one hand we have normative dharma, following the rules and regulations, being very polite to other people, and being very thoughtful about other people. Clearly that is useful, and it also gives people who are not buddhists the idea that, "Wow, buddhists are very good people". The danger is that by looking just towards the tradition, and towards what other people think, we can avoid ever really looking at ourselves, and so we end up making ourselves a kind of dharma clone. On the other hand we can move mainly in the direction of experience, and stay true to our experience, which can be very real and very important but we can then become very self-indulgent, not caring about other people and, worst of all, inventing our own kind of dharma as a justification for the psychological position we want to take up. In buddhism, when we talk of the middle way, it is a middle way between these kind of things. But the middle way itself is not a thing, it's a dynamic movement of managing the tension between the constraints of existence.

We will now look at the first verse of the *Vidyadhara Guru Sadhana* or *Big Rigdzin*.

Padmasambhava

※

# A. First Prayers

### Invocation of the Guru

ཨོག་མིན་ཆོས་ཀྱི་དབྱིངས་ཀྱི་ཕོ་བྲང་ན།
དུས་གསུམ་སངས་རྒྱས་ཀུན་གྱི་ངོ་བོ་ཉིད།
རང་སེམས་ཆོས་སྐུར་མངོན་སུམ་སྟོན་མཛད་པའི།
རྩ་བའི་བླ་མའི་ཞབས་ལ་གསོལ་བ་འདེབས།

**OG MIN CHOE KYI YING KYI PHO DRANG NA
DUE SUM SANG GYE KUN GYI NGO WO NYID
RANG SEM CHOE KUR NGON SUM TON DZAD PAI
TSA WAI LA MAI ZHAB LA SOL WA DEB**

*In the palace of Akanishta dharmadhatu are you
who have the nature of all buddhas of the three times,
the one who directly shows me my mind as dharmakaya.
I pray to you my root guru.*

HERE WE SEE THE USUAL STRUCTURE. Firstly, you always have a description of the place, then of the person. That is the normal way of describing it, and you'll see it again later, in the description of the development of the mandala, where the description of the place also comes before that of the person. That's how it is in life: the world is here before we arrive. We don't come first and then the world comes, although it appears like that to us. What is important here is the idea that according to the particular place, we become a particular kind of person. Again, what we see here is like the idea of interdependent co-origination: how we manifest in the world depends on our setting. This *og min choe ying*, or Akanishta dharmadhatu, is the closest we can get to talking about where the dharmakaya can be said to be. If you are not used to this kind of language, it sounds, at first, just like a string of funny names. However, these are really technical terms for describing a function. It is as if you don't know anything about car engines, and someone says," Oh, this is a carburettor". You know what a carburettor is, then gradually you see the function, and so the word becomes more meaningful. In this realm being referred to, the highest realm of existence is that of the one who is the essence of all the buddhas. And 'all buddhas of the three times' means the buddhas of the past, the present and the future. Who are the buddhas of the future? Some people not so very far away from us.

This is very important because we are included in this. It is very important in this kind of practice. On the one hand we put something up and we say this is very, very special and we speak the language of hierarchy, while at the same time we identify into this structure and find a place in the structure which brings it down to a very democratic or horizontal level. And who is this person who is referred to? It is our own root guru who shows us the dharmakaya nature of our own mind.

An important question that always arises is why is there such a stress on *gurus* in tantric buddhism? Essentially, it is because the task ahead of us is not a task which can be achieved by the rational function of our mind, by logical deduction, or by very intelligent inquiry. Who we are is not a problem to be solved, but a state of experience to enter into. If it is, like it says here, the one who directly shows you the nature of your mind, then maybe all we have to do is to invite some special research neurologist who could come in here, inside the brain and say, "This is the nature of your mind." No doubt he could then tell you all about it, and you could accumulate a lot of information but this wouldn't necessarily transform anything, it would simply be a further accumulation of knowledge.

Now, in a peculiar way, our own usual sense of identity is composed of knowledge. When we come to an event, like this gathering, to hear teachings on the *Big Rigdzin*, we meet people we haven't met before, and we say "Hello" and "Where are you from?" and "What do you do?" We ask them questions about themselves, and they give us some answer. In this way we get to know something about the person. That, however, is not the same as knowing the person. Even if you met someone at an event like this and decided to live with them, and you're together for twenty years, in that time you wouldn't necessarily know them. The guru is not a psychotherapist, he doesn't earn a lot of money by asking you questions about your life. Indeed, someone can be your guru and not know anything about your life at all.

This is because what we are talking about here is a level of experience which is different from that which is constructed out of stories, historical events, feelings, sensations, and so forth. One of the reasons that good gurus are often very rude is because they are not confirming the assumptions that you have about yourself. We all have some strong notions about who we are. If we remain within this field of assumptive knowledge that we have about who we are, maybe we don't see anything new, we simply add on a new kind of story. So the task of the guru is to try to open up something new, a new kind of experience, and because every person is a bit different, the same guru figure will behave in different ways to different people. If you've been around C R Lama you will have seen that very often. Sometimes he was very horrible to someone and the next minute he was smiling at someone else. He could be nice to someone one day, and the next day be very horrible to them. C R Lama himself was a very unreliable person. Not in a profound sense, but in an ordinary sense he was very unreliable. He changed his mind about things, "I want to do this…and that…and that."

One of the qualities of a guru, certainly in our lineage within the Tibetan tradition, is that he is integrated with the shamanic idea of the trickster figure such as you find in many North American Indian cultures, as well as in those of Central Asia. The trickster is someone who will do things that other people find difficult, a bit like Drukpa Kunleg or Mulla Nasruddin, about whom there are many, many well-known stories. He is a bit like the king's fool in the old royal court system, the person who can say what shouldn't be said. I remember somebody, who is now a student of C R Lama, saying that the first time she met him, he had been invited to give a talk in Paris at some big university institute, at a conference. The conference speakers were presenting papers and all discussing together. When C R Lama's turn came he just started saying any odd thing. He talked about the weather and the journey, and the more he went on and on, the more people started to leave, thinking, "What is this?" Eventually, there were only about twenty people left and then he started to say something about dharma. That was not at all polite to the conference organisers, so, in these kind of situations, one has to be careful. If you're on the inside of a story like this, it can be nice. If you're on the outside, it's a pain in the ass, which is the story of tricksters everywhere.

Within the tradition they would say the important thing is that people should be ripe. If people are not ripe, there is nothing to be done with them. It's just a waste of time if somebody is not ready. It's just the same in a hospital. When somebody comes for psychotherapy and they are not able to participate, or they don't want to participate, we just send them home saying come back when you want to do some work. Some people might say that the resistance is itself the work, and that one should just stay with it but fusion with states, or moods, creates a very dense, sticky surface, and it is very difficult to maintain clarity when close to it. Ripeness reveals itself through gestures of affinity.

Unlike in Western culture, where we have much more of a tradition of giving explanations, in Tibetan culture, particularly this guru kind of culture, this isn't the case. It's not about explanation, it's about experience. Additionally, however, in a Tibetan monastery, you would also have had a scholar. Young people coming into the monastery, wanting to learn something, would have had a lot of explanation from the scholar, the *khenpo*, the *geshe*. They would then have had some more direct instruction from the guru. So it's very important for Western people, I think, if you are around somebody who is operating primarily in a guru role, also to read some books, to give yourself some background knowledge. Otherwise this strong wind is blowing, and if the roots of your dharma tree are not very deep, then you can be blown over.

More generally speaking, what is dharma? There are many different explanations, but we can identify two main aspects to dharma. One is, dharma can mean reality, the true nature of how things are. The second means the teaching, in other words, what Buddha Shakyamuni and people following after him in the same family, have taught. Of course, dharma is a sanskrit word, and hindus also talk about dharma. Jains, too, talk about dharma. It's not just buddhists who have dharma.

In the dharma taught by Buddha Shakyamuni, the main thing he tries to do is to explain why we get into difficulties in life, and then to teach us some paths, some methods, for getting out of those difficulties. This is the basic structure of all the teachings. On the side of wisdom, we try to understand how things are. On the side of method, which is another way of saying compassion, because we can have compassion towards ourselves and towards others, we try to employ methods which help us to turn away from confusion and towards clarity. Method here includes both skills and tools. If you are going to saw some wood, you need to have a saw, but you also need to know how to use a saw. Similarly, with respect to a practice, which is how we approach a text like this one, we need a method as a tool, and then we need to have the skill to use it.

This text, the *Big Rigdzin*, generally people speak of as a *puja*. Puja means worship. This kind of puja text has been taken from hinduism. Historically speaking, this kind of text was present in hinduism before buddhism. Whereas the tradition which developed in buddhism involved monks practicing renunciation and meditation, the tradition for brahmins, in hinduism, was to do puja. During the development of buddhism in India, many hindus became buddhists, and they brought with them many of their hindu ideas. Thus the structure of a buddhist puja practice is quite similar to that of a hindu puja, but the view underlying the practice is different. What is very important, with any method, is to realise the view involved in why you use it. For instance, if you are a soldier, it's very important that your bayonet is sharp, because you want to cut into someone. If you are a surgeon, it's very important that your scalpel is sharp, because you want to cut into someone. The method is the same. Aspects of the technique might even be the same, a little bit of physical effort. Hopefully, the view is slightly different!

Now we're just going to start to go into the *Preliminary Practices* which set out the orientation of the view, and which then shows us how to make use of the method. Before that, however, we have first of all, praise of the root guru who directly shows me the nature of my mind, as discussed above; this is then followed by a verse giving an overview.

## Praise to the Guru

ལྟ་བ་ཀློང་ཆེན་ཡངས་པའི་དོན་རྟོགས་ཤིང་།
སྒོམ་པ་སྤྲིན་བྲལ་ཉི་མ་ལྟ་བུར་གསལ།
སྤྱོད་པ་མཐར་ཕྱིན་གྲུབ་པའི་རྟགས་ཐོན་ཅིང་།
འབྲས་བུ་ཀུན་བཟང་གོ་འཕང་མངོན་དུ་གྱུར།
དྲིན་ཅན་བླ་མའི་ཞབས་ལ་གསོལ་བ་འདེབས།

**TA WA LONG CHEN YANG PAI DON TOG SHING**
**GOM PA TRIN DRAL NYI MA TA BUR SAL**
**CHOD PA TAR CHIN DRUB PAI TAG THON CHING**
**DRAE BU KUN ZANG GO PHANG NGON DU GYUR**
**DRIN CHEN LA MAI ZHAB LA SOL WA DEB**

*You realize the vast meaning of the infinite view, and have meditation that is clear like the sun free of clouds. You gained the signs of the siddhis of the fulfilment of your deeds, and gained the result of the stage of Kuntu Zangpo. We pray to the most kind guru.*

This is a very, very nice verse, because it sets out the four aspects of practice: the view, the meditation, the activity, and the result.

The view is to understand the meaning of the experience of this infinite expansive awareness, that's to say, dharmadhatu. This is the view that we should have, and it is suggesting that this is also the view we should take into this practice, that what we are here attempting to realise is this infinite emptiness. This means that we are willing to put our whole trust, our whole belief, and the whole of our existence, through this connection with something which is open and empty like the sky.

This *long chen yang pai don*, very deep, vast meaning, what is this? It is ourselves. We are this dimension, and because we are this, we should understand what it is. At first the view is just something you try to see, it's a bit like a map. But we are trying to maintain this view, that is to say, to hold this attitude. So what is being said here is, 'Your own nature, from the very beginning, is infinite emptiness without any limitation.' It is not a compound. It is not dependent upon anything at all. This is the view. That is very, very important to understand, because the view is how you are trying to see the world.

I went to see my optician last year, and he checked my eyes. Then he looked in his records and he said, "Oh, you have some spectacles from me but you don't wear them." He said, "You know, when the spectacles are sitting in their little box, they don't see anything at all." This is the reality. The view is like the spectacles. You can have the view in a book, put in on a shelf, or you can have it in front of you and read the puja very quickly, but the only way for the view to become real is to put it on and view the world through it. That's why it's called a view. *Tawa* means 'to see', it means 'this is how to experience.' In order to help us to really look through these spectacles of the view, we have to practise doing it. When you put on spectacles for the first time your eyes start to hurt. You have to get used to this new kind of experience, to both maintain it and relax into it.

That is the meaning of meditation, *gompa*. Meditation is the opportunity to try to shift your view. It says here that the meditation should be 'clear like the sun free of clouds.' The 'clouds' are the assumptions that we have, the karmic habits that we have, the impulses we have, our own personal history out of which we create some notion as to who we are. Now, clearly, what happens when we try to meditate is that there are more clouds than sun. We get distracted very easily. Our understanding is not very clear. We drift off, get caught up in stuff, and so forth. These are the clouds. Through the practice of the meditation, however, we try to let the clouds lift off so that clarity is there, and then the view manifests through us. The advantage of meditation is that not too much is going on while you're doing it. You are usually just sitting, and the most you have to do is to hold things in your hand and shake them about. Given the complexity of our usual behaviour that's really quite simple. It's not the same as just quietly watching your breath, it's much more complicated than that. Tantric meditation is complicated. It's complicated because it tries to replicate the events of ordinary life, but in a simplified form, so that you can understand the structure of how you get lost.

Then, the third line is about the *chod pa*. *Chod pa* means behaviour or conduct. It means, essentially, everything you do when you're not meditating. And it says that this activity should show the sign of the highest achievement, which raises, of course, the question, how should a buddha behave?

In traditional buddhism there are many books on the etiquette of a buddha. Generally speaking, a buddha should sit very quietly and not cause too much trouble. He should wear clean clothes, and have many rainbows coming out from him. As far as we know, although much food and drink is offered to him, he doesn't eat or drink it, and he certainly doesn't shit or piss. In that way, people have many, many ideas of what a buddha looks like. There is a traditional listing of the thirty-two major and sixty-four minor marks of a buddha's body. For example, he has an *ushnisha*, a physical growth, on top of his head, and he has a little bump, the *urna*, between his eyes. He has images on the palms of his hands, of conch shells, and he has webbing between his fingers, and a retracted penis like a horse. This is what the tradition tells us.

In England they believed, in the old days, that royal people had blue blood. It was a belief that special people had a different physiological reality. They also believed that the touch of the king or the queen could cure leprosy. Of course, in the birth stories of Buddha Shakyamuni, there was a wise man who was consulted by the king, Siddhartha's father, who said, "Oh, this baby that will be born will either be a great king, ruler of all the world, or he will be a great yogi." In the buddhist tradition there are many examples of the powers and attributes of the king being added to descriptions of the Buddha, so there is one very important question that we need to ask here: how would you ever know if you met a buddha? Who knows? Most of the qualities of a buddha are invisible. Very often people think they're meeting a buddha because somebody else has told them it's a buddha. Somebody says, "Oh, Papa Rinpoche is coming to town. Are you going to see Papa Rinpoche? He's very wonderful!." You go into a hall, and there's Papa Rinpoche. First of all you can see there is the throne and the seat and some nice flowers, and you sit there waiting, and then suddenly everybody stands up. So you stand up. In comes Papa Rinpoche, and Papa Rinpoche sits down. Then you get to sit down. This is what you did in primary school when the teacher came into the classroom. These are the marks of hierarchy, power, differentiation and so forth, socialisation into the acceptance of authority structures. This is something we shall return to again. What is the conduct of a buddha? How should they behave?

Finally, the result, *drae bu*, that you gain is the stage of Kuntu Zangpo. Kuntu Zangpo is the original buddha, meaning a symbol of perfect enlightenment, so you become fully established in the realisation of your own true nature. Now who has got all of this? "Oh, it's my, my....Oh! My precious guru, he has got all these nice things!" That's a surprise! So, if you want to know how a buddha behaves, look at what your guru does. This is very important.

There are two possible views here. One is, you can identify rules and regulations which will let you establish whether something is good or not. There are certain criteria, certain categories, such that if something fits into these categories, then you know you are safe. The second view, which is the view established here, is: everything comes out of dharmadhatu. The nature of everything which manifests, whatever it looks like on the surface, is pure from the very beginning. If you understand that, that is enlightenment. Buddhahood is to recognise the nature of your own ground, your own basis, and in that all faults and limitations are self-liberated. This is very important. That's why in the text by Chetsangpa[5] it says very clearly some gurus are businessmen, lying and cheating to make a profit, some gurus are very rough and angry, some gurus have many women, some gurus get drunk a lot, some gurus are monks. However, the form the person shows is not important. What is important is that they realise the ground of their own nature. This is very important. One basic view follows from this: because we don't know what other people's realisation is, we should treat everyone as if they are a buddha; we should treat everyone with infinite respect; we should treat everyone with validation and belief in their potential and their possibility.

---

[5] See Chapter 1 of *Simply Being* (James Low: Vajra Press, 1998)

# B. Preparatory Practice

MANY OF US HAVE TO LIVE in very ugly cities and we see how sad and depressed people can become, just through the daily exposure to noise and dirt and the lack of concern from other people. It is worth remembering in these circumstances that beauty is very important in tantra. In the introduction to this sadhana, in the foreword, C R Lama has set out the lineage of the transmission of the main part of the text. Then we have the first *ngondro* part, which is not from that collection directly, it is more of a general ngondro that is used in connection with many of the *termas* of Nuden Dorje Drophan Lingpa. In the preamble, before the ngondro, he says simply, "We bow to this *rangrig gyalpo*," which means the enlightened nature of our own mind. He then goes on to say that in future times life will be very difficult for beings. They will easily succumb to the power of distraction. At that time, although dharma will not have changed, although the nature of reality will not have changed, people will have no time to do any practice. Therefore, for the sake of these stupid people who don't have much intelligence, I am teaching this very simple practice. The text reads:

*Salutation to my own natural awareness.*
*In the future sentient beings will have the five poisons (stupidity, anger, desire, pride, jealousy) very roughly and strongly and will go under the power of wavering laziness and many social affairs. Although all dharmas are free of relative positions and are vast as pervading space, who will do sadhana meditation practice to realize this truth? This is written for dull and stupid people who want to do practice, for laymen and beings of weak intelligence, so that they can get the refuge vows and can practice the dharma unceasingly in the six periods of each day,*
*I (Padmasambhava) have taught this.*

## a. The Four Reflections

ཀྱེ་མ་རིན་ཆེན་ལུས་འདི་ཨུ་དུམ་ཝཱ་ར་ལྟར༔
རྙེད་དཀའ་ཕྱིས་ནས་མི་ཐོབ་ཚེ་འདིར་རྙེད༔
དལ་འབྱོར་སྟོང་ལོག་མ་བྱེད་ཆོས་ལ་འབུངས༔
ནམ་འཆི་ངེས་མེད་འཆི་བ་མི་རྟག་བསམས༔
དགེ་སྡིག་ལས་འབྲས་མི་བསླུ་འདོར་ལེན་དཔྱོད༔
རིགས་དྲུག་སྡུག་བསྔལ་སུས་ཀྱང་བཟོད་དུ་མེད༔

KYE MA RIN CHEN LUE DI U DUM VA RA TAR
NYED KA CHI NAE MI THOB TSE DIR NYED
DAL JOR TONG LOG MA JED CHOE LA BUNG
NAM CHI NGE MED CHI WA MI TAG SOM
GE DIG LAE DRAE MI LU DOR LEN CHO
RIG DRUG DUG NGAL SUE KYANG ZOD DU ME

*Alas! I now have this precious body so rare like the udumbara lotus, so difficult to get and which will not be gained again by me in the future. I must not go empty-handed from this life which has the freedoms and opportunities, but must strive at the dharma. I do not know when I will die so I must always think about death and impermanence. That virtuous and sinful actions have consequences (of happiness and sorrow) is definitely true so I must clearly examine and know what is to be abandoned and what is to be adopted. There is no-one who can bear the sufferings of the six realms of samsara.*

These thoughts are the basic reflections which are used in the hinayana tradition to give people the strong sense that samsara is a dangerous and difficult place. Our normal tendency and wish is to make our life as easy and comfortable as possible. But if your house is burning down, painting the inside walls will not be very helpful. Very often we don't want to look at the actual situation we find ourselves in. In psychoanalysis there is talk of ego defences, of repression, dissociation and so forth, all being ways in which we seek to avoid looking at reality because reality is painful. If you're very good at repression and dissociation and so on, you can convince yourself that actually life is not painful, so you can believe, "Oh, basically I'm very happy, and every now and then some bad things happen to me." At this level, what buddhism wants to say is, "This is nonsense. Basically you're really fucked-up, but every now and then you're happy." This human life that we have is rare, like an *udumbara* flower. It means that you don't get it very often. If we look on the hillside, and open the earth underneath, we find millions of little insects, many, many millions of insects, but very few human beings.

In the first teaching that the Buddha gave, in the Deer Park in Sarnath, he set out the Four Noble Truths of suffering, the cause of suffering, the ending of suffering, and the means to end suffering. A key aspect of the cause of suffering is the non-recognition of the three marks of conditioned existence: impermanence, absence of inherent self-nature, and suffering. These three work together to reinforce each other. Much of our suffering arises because things are impermanent, and things are impermanent because they have no inherent self-nature. Being clear about impermanence and death is enormously important. Although, at first, it may make you feel a bit sad and shaky, later it makes you very happy. When you get used to it, the thought of impermanence and death becomes like flushing the toilet. All the shit of your life is just washed away. Then, because it's not going to last, you don't need to get so involved.

In the sadhana, it's talking about eighteen aspects of a precious human birth:

**KYE MA RIN CHEN LUE DI U DUM VA RA TAR
NYED KA CHI NAE MI THOB TSE DIR NYED
DAL JOR TONG LOG MA JED CHOE LA BUNG.**

*Alas! I now have this precious body, so rare like the udumbara lotus,
so difficult to get and which will not be gained again by me in the future.
I must not go from these freedoms and opportunities empty-handed,
but must strive at the dharma.*

It gives a lot of details concerning this in the notes:

> *There are eight freedoms and they refer to not being born in any of the following states: hells, insatiable ghost, animal, long living gods, uncivilized tribes, among those having wrong views, barbarian border country, an idiot. There are ten opportunities, the five coming from oneself are to have a perfect human body, to be born in a country to which the dharma has spread, to have the five sense organs free of fault, not having done any of the five boundless sins, and to have faith in the pure dharma. The five coming from others are that a complete perfect buddha has come in the world, that he has taught the dharma, that the doctrines he taught are still preserved, that there is the holy arya sangha practising the dharma, that there is a compassionate guru who teaches the dharma to his devoted disciples.*

What is really important in this is to recognise that to come into the dharma can radically transform your life. Of course many evangelical christians will say the same: "When Jesus came into my life, suddenly everything was different." On one level it doesn't really matter what comes into your life, as long as it's something that takes you out of the preoccupation with your own very limited needs and desires and fantasies. In that moment you can start to look at other people and see just how awful it is not to have any purpose in your life. To take refuge and come into the dharma is to get some map of existence so that even when the winds of karma and life circumstances blow you this way and that way somehow, after the storm, you can have the map and you can re-track your life and think, "Well, anyway, I want to do this." It gives meaning and depth and purpose. That's really what's important.

What it's trying to say is, although capitalist consumerism is concerned simply with people's purchasing power and is equating everybody with their buying power, actually people are very different. Buddhism itself is not at all against — certainly in its tantric form — money and riches. You can be a millionaire and practise tantra, that's not the problem. The problem with consumerist capitalism is that it tells people, "If you buy these certain things and put them on you, and around you, your life will be guaranteed good, you will be safe," and this is a lie! Real benefit comes from the effort *not* to rely on objects. That's how it is.

## B. Preparatory Practice

**NAM CHI NGE MED CHI WA MI TAG SOM
GE DIG LAE DRAE MI LU DOR LEN CHO
RIG DRUG DUG NGAL SUE KYANG ZOD DU ME**

*I do not know when I will die, so I must always think about death and impermanence (in order to increase my diligence). That virtuous and sinful actions have consequences (of happiness and sorrow respectively) is definitely true, so I must clearly examine and know what is to be abandoned and what is to be adopted. There is no one who can bear the suffering of the six realms of samsara.*

Virtue and bad things develop from causes and have effects; this principle is never wrong, it doesn't cheat you. So you should be very careful to stop doing bad things, and try to do good things. Then, finally, it says, everywhere you go in these six realms, you only get suffering. The purpose of these verses is to generate fear, a deep fear and anxiety.

Nowadays many people trade on the stock exchange. They buy shares, equities, but of course it's just gambling. Sooner or later some prediction is that prices will come tumbling down. Life is like that. When things are going up, people smile, and when the same things come down then people look very sad. You don't have a choice because, due to the power of your own attachment, you react to situations. A bad thing happens to you — you don't have a choice — you get unhappy. If we die now and we're reborn in some horrible realm, and we're born as a pig, we'll be very unhappy or perhaps too stupid to even know we should be unhappy at this sad limitation of our potential. If you've ever heard a pig being killed, it's not happy, not happy at all. Many, many situations in life are not happy. Not only will we not continue to live very long in this body, but in our next life we could be anywhere. That's why they say you should practise dharma, because dharma, in some way, tries to buy you a ticket to a better place.

Earlier in the year I was listening to a *bon* lama giving some dzogchen teachings, and he said at the end of it, "Yes, but of course, you western people, you have too much food and you never will practise these things." I think we have to take this seriously, because we use our money and our power to change the world, to alter the object side, the situation side, in order to make our lives easy. Indeed, if you live in a city almost everything you see is made by human beings, and can be changed by human beings, but for a

Tibetan, living in a small village surrounded by huge mountains and howling winds, human beings are very, very small. The world is very, very big and powerful therefore shifting one's own habits makes more sense than acting to change external factors.

On the level of ordinary happiness in this life, of course it's wonderful that you can have central heating and electric light, and good hospitals, it makes life wonderful in many ways. It's not that we need to get rid of that but in terms of buddhism, coming along with these wonderful new developments is a new kind of stupidity, a new kind of dulling of ourselves, where we buy into this fantasy that we are in control of the world, that we can make things happen the way we want to. There is an omnipotent fantasy deep in the heart of western rational science. On a cold night, if you drive your car down the road maybe it's a little bit slippy and dangerous but inside it's warm, you can put on some music. If you have to walk down through the snow in the dark, through the forest, stumbling and falling and your shoes are completely wet, you get a different feeling about death. In that way it's very easy for us to forget that we will die. Even if we have good friends who have died, maybe terribly, *they* died, *we* didn't die, and there is a particular kind of satisfaction that someone else dies, and not you. You feel sad at the time, but you know where death's gone: it's gone next door, it's not come here. One of the great blessings of being a therapist is that I sit all the time with people who are suffering, and I'm not suffering. In fact, I'm paid because they're suffering. It's a wonderful diversion. In psychotherapy they talk about 'empathic attunement', so if Robert is suffering then I *really feel* what he is suffering, but this is nonsense, because *he* is suffering, and I'm feeling close to what he is suffering. It's not the same thing and that's important, because we are very stupid as people. Terrible things happen in the world, in Kosovo, East Timor, and so on. You can watch it on television. You feel a bit sad, but then you go to have your dinner, and you think, "Oh well, anyway, my life is okay." That's why, although these *Four Reflections* can be very simple and we often think we know what they are, they're actually important tools to use, because they're designed to turn your mind around, to open up a gap, and in this gap you can put a new dharma view.

## b. Refuge and Developing an Enlightened Attitude

**HRI RANG DUN CHOE YING PADMA NYI DAI TENG
KYAB KUN DAG NYID RIG DZIN PADMA JUNG
DRUB NYE TSEN CHOG GYE DANG RIG DZIN TSOG
TSA SUM GYAL WAI KYIL KHOR DZOG PAR SAL**

*Hri. In the vast space before me, on top of lotus, sun and moon, is the embodiment of all the refuges, the vidyadhara Padmasambhava with the eight excellent forms who gained siddhis and the hosts of vidyadharas. Thus I clearly meditate on the complete Buddha's mandala of the three roots (guru, gods, dakini).*

**NA MO DAG DANG THA YAE SEM CHEN GYI
LU MED KYAB NAE NAM LA KYAB SU CHI
JANG CHUB SEM KYE DRO LA THUGJE ZIG**

*Adoration. I and all the limitless sentient beings take refuge in the unfailing refuge places. We develop the altruistic intention to help others. Please look with compassion to all those who move in samsara and help us.*

We take refuge because we're frightened. If you're not frightened, you don't need any refuge. That's very important. That's why people's dharma practice can become very slow, because they lose contact with the fear so then they just do it when they feel like it, rather than because they need to do it. Just as with Chhimed Rigdzin Rinpoche, he had quite bad diabetes, and his blood sugar level used to go up and down all the time, so that he had to adjust it with injections. We are the same. Our pancreas, our dharma pancreas, is not working, and our hopes and fears are going up and down all the time. Unless we give ourselves this dharma injection properly, we become very sick. But I think we all know that Chhimed Rigdzin was a very bad patient and he didn't like to pay very much attention to his blood sugar level. Whenever he could, he would eat something else, and then Gudrun had to shout at him. Rinpoche didn't want to know that he had diabetes. He knew: "I like this food," that's what he knew, but he didn't want to know about diabetes, and in that he shows us exactly what we do. We don't want to know about samsara. We want to know about the things we like. We want to do the things we like, and then we get very surprised when we get disturbed. It's very important to watch our own state. Taking refuge sets a marker of our intention to change our lives. This will be discussed more fully later.

### c. Seven Branch Practice

ན་མོ་ཕྱི་ནང་གསང་བའི་མཎྜལ་བཀོད་དེ་འབུལ༔

ཕྱག་འཚལ་མཆོད་འབུལ་ཉེས་བཤགས་རྗེས་ཡི་རངས༔

ཆོས་གསུང་སྐུར་བཞུགས་དགེ་བ་ཡོངས་ལ་བསྔོ༔

མཆོག་དང་ཐུན་མོང་དངོས་གྲུབ་དེང་འདིར་སྩོལ༔

ཚོགས་ཞིང་རང་ལ་ཐིམ་པས་སྐྱེ་སྒྲིབ་བ་དག༔

རང་རྒྱུད་རྡོ་རྗེ་སེམས་དཔས་བྱིན་གྱིས་རློབས༔

**NA MO CHI NANG SANG WAI MANDAL KOD DE BUL
CHAG TSAL CHOD BUL NYE SHAG JE YI RANG
CHOE SUNG KUR ZHUG GE WA YONG LA NGO**

## B. Preparatory Practice

**CHOG DANG THUN MONG NGOE DRUB DENG DIR TSOL
TSOG ZHING RANG LA THIM PAE DIG DRIB DAG
RANG GYUD DORJE SEM PAE JIN GYI LOB**

*Adoration. We clearly imagine and offer the outer, inner and secret mandalas. We make prostrations and offerings, confess and purify our sins and faults and rejoice at the happiness and virtues of others. We request dharma teachings, beseech our refuges to remain and dedicate all virtues to the complete enlightenment of all beings. Please grant us supreme and ordinary real attainments. The assembly of gods dissolves in light and is absorbed into us, purifying all our sins and obscurations. May our natures be blessed by Dorje Sempa.*

The mandala offering that we have here is designed to generate merit. This, again, is an aspect of a particular historical moment in the development of the dharma, where there was the idea that enlightenment is something you achieve after a journey, and in order to go on the journey, as for any journey, you have to have the necessary resources. For enlightenment these are the two accumulations of merit and wisdom. Looking at this from the Tibetan point of view (and the Tibetans are very practical people) they are very concerned with cause and effect. Generally speaking, in a christian prayer we say, "Oh, dear God, we ask you humbly to give this to us." And we don't know if God will give us what we want, because we are very bad children, and maybe daddy won't let us have what we want. That's the structure of christian prayer.

With a mandala offering it is completely different. You give this mandala to the Buddha, and he gives you something back. It's a very straightforward exchange. The Buddha doesn't need your mandala, but he is happy to receive it. You give him the mandala, and he gives you something back. This is a very important thing for us to really understand. This is a different view from the kind of anxious father-child relationship of christianity. This is a contractual, causal, interactive relationship. If you offer something, you will get a clear reply. You offer, so you get a clear reply. There is no question of doubt or chance involved in this. We make the offerings to all the buddhas, bodhisattvas, gods and so on. They are happy. They dissolve into light and then into our bodies. This is the first level of purification, and through it we are blessed by Vajrasattva.

Vajrasattva is a very important god in Tibetan buddhism. Vajrasattva means 'indestructible being' or 'indestructible nature', and he represents the manifestation of our own buddha-nature in an unchangeable form. Our nature is really Vajrasattva, but due to karma, due to these habits and tendencies, we have lost touch with our nature as Vajrasattva, so we pray to Vajrasattva to remind ourselves that we are Vajrasattva.

For example, if you have a teenage girl who has *anorexia nervosa*, and you invite her to look at herself in the mirror, she will always see herself much thinner in the reflection than anyone else will see her. What we have to try to do is to help the girl to look at herself as she is, and to see reality, phenomenological reality — what is there — to see that that is more real than this fantasy perception that she is cooking inside. It's the same for us. We look in the mirror of ourselves and we see our faults, our confusions, our limitations. When we do this practice we look in the mirror, and we try to see the image of Vajrasattva. Vajrasattva is our real nature, and if we really see Vajrasattva, we wake up, we are Vajrasattva, and then the fantasy and illusion, "I'm a bad person, I can't do this, I wish I was more like that," all of these stories that we go on and on with, are washed away.

The gods in Tibetan buddhism are methods. They are there to be used. We worship these gods as a method for recognising who *we* are. It is not about establishing some absolute hierarchy in the world, but it is to try to make use of our own tendencies to idealise, and to focus the idealisation on a pure form of emptiness in order to recognise our own nature. This Dorje Sempa meditation, Vajrasattva meditation, is very short, but it has the essence of all tantric practice in it.

### d. Dorje Sempa Meditation

ཧཱུྃ༔ རང་གི་སྤྱི་གཙུག་པད་ཟླ་འཛིན་འོད་གྲོང་༔

བླ་མ་རྡོར་སེམས་རྡོ་རྗེ་དྲིལ་འཛིན་དཀར༔

བོངས་སྐུའི་རྒྱན་རྫོགས་ཕྱགས་གར་བླ་སྟེང་གྱུ༔

ཡི་གེ་བརྒྱས་བསྐོར་པར་བདུད་རྩིའི་རྒྱུན་བབས་ནས༔

ཚངས་བུག་ནས་ཞུགས་སྡིག་སྒྲིབ་དག་པར་བསམ༔

## B. Preparatory Practice

**HRI RANG GI CHI TSUG PAD DA JA OD LONG
LA MA DOR SEM DORJE DRIL DZIN KAR
LONG KUI GYEN DZOG THUG KAR DA TENG HUNG
YIG GYE KOR WAR DUD TSII GYUN BAB NAE
TSANG BUG NAE ZHUG DIG DRIB DAG PAR SAM**

*Hri. In the midst of rainbow light upon a lotus and moon on the top of my head is my guru in the form of Dorje Sempa who is white in colour holding a vajra and a bell. He wears all the sambhogakaya ornaments and in his heart upon a moon disc is the letter Hung around which the hundred syllable mantra revolves. From it a stream of amrita descends which I visualize as entering through the hole in my cranium and completely purifying my sins and obscurations.*

In the heart of the god is his seed syllable, the *hung*, and around this syllable the mantra is rotating.

**OM VAJRA SATO SA MA YA   MANU PA LA YA
VAJRA SATO TE NO PA   TI SHTA DRI DHO ME BHA WA
SU TO KYIO ME BHA WA   SU PO KYIO ME BHA WA
A NU RAKTO ME BHA WA   SAR VA SIDDHI MA ME PRA YA TSA**

```
SAR VAR KAR MA SU TSA ME   TSI TAM SHRI YAM KU RU HUNG
HA HA HA HA HO
BHA GA WAN SAR VA TA THA GA TA   VAJRA MA ME MUN TSA
VAJRA BHA WA MA HA SA MA YA SA TWA AA
```

*The five pristine cognitions. Dorje Sempa with the power of being strong in your vows. You must protect me and all who follow after you and rely on you! Dorje Sempa, you must hear me! You must keep me! You must think of me! Please purify all my sins. You must think strongly of me. You must stay with me and not separate from me.*
*Grant me all real attainments. You must do all necessary deeds.*
*All subtle karmic traces living in the heart must become emptiness. Give me the dharmakaya, sambhogakaya, nirmanakaya and svabhavikakaya. Victorious one, you are like all the tathagatas.*
*Dorje Sempa, please keep me strongly. Dorje Sempa. Great vow. We must get attainments. We must get fulfilment of our vows.*

The mantra is rotating in a spiral coming out of the *hung,* so it comes out at the top, spirals round, and then goes back in the bottom. As it is rotating, rays of light are coming out, turning into *dud tsii,* purifying nectar, which fills the body of Vajrasattva and then flows into our body.

Then there is a request for forgiveness, and the short mantra of Vajrasattva:

ༀ་ས་མ་ཡཿ ཨཱཿས་མ་ཡཿ ཧཱུྃ་ས་མ་ཡཿ བཛྲ་ས་མ་ཡཿ
བདག་གཞན་གྱི་ཚེ་རབས་འཁོར་བ་ཐོག་མ་མེད་པ་ནས་བསགས་པའི་
སྡིག་སྒྲིབ་ཉེས་ལྟུང་དྲི་མའི་ཚོགས་ཐམས་ཅད་རྩ་བ་ནས་
བྱང་ཞིང་དག་པར་བྱིན་གྱིས་བརླབས་ཏུ་གསོལ༔

```
OM SA MA YA   AA SAM MA YA   HUNG SA MA YA   BENDZA SA MA YA
DAG ZHAN GYI TSE RAB KHOR WA THOG MA ME PA NAE SAG PAI
DIG DRIB NYE TUNG DRI MAI TSOG THAM CHE TSA WA NAE
JANG ZHING DAG PA JIN GYI LAB TU SOL
```

B. Preparatory Practice

Dorje Sempa

*Body vows: forgive my lapses. Speech vows: forgive my lapses. Mind vows: forgive my lapses. Vajra vows: forgive my lapses. I, and all beings, in all our countless previous lives have collected sins, obscurations, faults, stains and causes for falling into states of sorrow; all these we beg you to cleanse from the root and so bless us with purity.*

ཨོཾ་བཛྲ་སཏྭ་ཧཱུྂ་ཨཱཿ

**OM BENDZA SATWA HUNG AA**

*Om. Indestructible being, purify me!*

Some people can visualise or imagine things very clearly. They can see things in three dimensions, with many colours, with movement. Other people can't see anything at all. In the level of tantra practice called *mahayoga*, accuracy of visualisation is seen as being very important. But the practice that we do, this whole practice, is not a mahayoga practice. It is a mixture of mahayoga, anuyoga and dzogchen styles. In anuyoga the feeling-tone is more important than the accuracy of the perception. Mahayoga is concerned with purifying an object, and anuyoga with purifying the subject, dzogchen is purifying with respect to both. This means that even if you can't visualise anything, it doesn't matter, you just believe. You just have some idea, some feeling. The feeling is important, because it's a feeling that goes into you, and then your muscles tighten, your bowels come up. Without knowing anything about the *tsalung* practice, and all the complex breathing techniques involved, you yourself will do tsalung here. Your awareness will go into the central channel, and you will get a blessing. It is feeling that comes close to us; perception is more distant. If you visualise Padmasambhava very clearly but you have no feeling, it doesn't benefit you, and it doesn't benefit Padmasambhava. He doesn't need you to look at him. Even if you can't see Padmasambhava clearly, if you have some feeling, you get the benefit, because the feeling brings you into contact.

The explanation of the practice itself is very straightforward. Clearly the important thing is to have faith. You have to believe that something is happening. It's very like theatre. When you go to a theatre or to a cinema the most important thing is that you suspend disbelief. People will come on stage and they will present themselves as being something-or-other. They are not that, they are actors, but you have to believe that they *are* that. The more you allow yourself to enter into what you see in the theatre, the more impact it has on you. Sometimes you will go to see a comedy and you find yourself laughing at something completely stupid. It's not even real, but you find yourself laughing. It's the same here: now we do Dorje Sempa theatre! Here is Dorje Sempa. He is very bright, has a little bell: *dingle dingle ding, nga nga nga* — that's theatre! You know that if you read a play it's very different from going to the theatre and seeing it. That's why it's very nice to do the puja with C R Lama, because he's a master of theatre. Theatre is wonderful. It's not an insult to say tantra is theatre. Theatre is perfect. All life is theatre. In Sanskrit they say it is *leela*, it is a play. Just as you have Krishna *leela*, so here we have Dorje Sempa *leela*. This is the play of Dorje Sempa, a drama in which something is enacted, and...nothing takes place. Theatre is real, illusion is real. What we live as our everyday life is theatre. Our reality is illusion.

You may know the play *Hamlet* by Shakespeare. In this play use is made of the theme of 'the play within the play'. It's something you find in many kinds of drama, but in this play it's very nice.

Briefly, the beloved father of Hamlet, has died, he has been poisoned. Hamlet is sure that his mother has arranged the poisoning of his father because she is in love with someone else. The family is dysfunctional. Hamlet himself is falling apart. He's acting mad, he's shouting at people, and his mother keeps saying, "Oh, calm down, calm down. Life's changed. Never mind, you'll get over it," but he says, "Something is rotten here. Something smells very bad!" When some theatre players come to the castle Hamlet speaks to them, and he writes a little play for them to perform in which a king is poisoned. So the queen and the new king are sitting watching this play and suddenly this new king gets very angry and disturbed. "What is this?" He feels very insulted. Hamlet is looking at him. "Ha ha, now we see." So, inside this play by Shakespeare we have a play in which the mother and the stepfather are trying to pretend nothing has happened, and then the third play, this dramatic enaction, shows the falsity of the second play, and brings dramatic life to the first play.

Similarly with dharma, or this puja in particular, what we have is a theatre text. Inside this text, our drama, the drama of being James or Robert, is disturbed by having to enter into the drama of being Vajrasattva. But in order for the drama to work, you have to believe in it, you have to enter into it, because if you really believe the script of being James, or Robert, or Rainer or whoever, and you are reading your own script all the time, so that you are just mouthing these words from the puja, on the outside, as it were, while you really feel, "I am James, I am James," then nothing will change. That's why, of course, in Tibetan monasteries they set the stage very beautifully. They have many paintings and banners hanging, they have beautiful statues, they have lights, they have colour, they have music, they have bells and drums for audience participation. You have the whole thing.

What you have is a double move. The theatre of the puja takes you out of yourself in order to return you to yourself. This is why faith is very important. Faith is a method. It's not that you are signing away your freedom, that you're becoming enslaved into a cult, but you are using faith, which is a very intense focusing of attention, as a means of entering into this dramatic movement, which brings about a profound psycho-spiritual transformation. This is because faith is an attitude that allows possibilities to come alive. It's not faith that some big Papa is going to save you. Rather, faith is something that you do, to shift your relationship with yourself, so that you can understand something new. Faith is a mixture of openness and confidence. For example, if somebody is going to ski down a slope, which is quite difficult for them, maybe with a jump in it, they have to let go, they have to just think, "Oh, I can do it."

This relates to something we looked at earlier, namely the relationship between anxiety and control. Usually when we become anxious we try to take care of it by controlling. Either we hold back on ourselves or we try to control what is going on outside. But a good skier, going on a slalom, cannot be in a tight control. They have to be in a very relaxed control. They have to be able to work with what arises. You can know the same kind of thing through dancing, where you have to lose yourself in order to find yourself. You have to abandon control and definition of self in order to open a space in which you are revealed to yourself in a new way. That really is the purpose of faith in this kind of practice, it's a way of transforming experience.

Dorje Sempa practice is very, very important, because the end result of doing Dorje Sempa practice is that you should believe that your nature is pure. And not only do you believe that it is pure, but you start to get the experience that your nature is pure.

What does 'pure' mean here? In the view of dzogchen, which informs this text, there are two levels of purity. There is the purity which is there from the very beginning, *kadag* in Tibetan, and the purity which is the freedom from obscurations, *drime dagpa*. That is to say, from the very beginning our own real nature, the buddha-nature, has always been pure, it has never been covered in any way, but due to the power of ignorance and grasping and confusion we have been wandering in samsara, accumulating karma, being obscured, reacting, being full of funny ideas about ourselves, hopes and fears, many, many things tumbling around in us. All of these obscurations can be removed. When these are removed, what is revealed is this original purity. When you realise original purity, you realise that it has never been obscured. This is a drama of paradox, things are not what they appear to be.

One of my teachers, Jatral Rinpoche, explained to me that it's as if you're lying in bed having a nightmare, and in the bed is your brother, who is awake, and trying to shake you to wake you up. The reality is that the person is just lying in bed. The bed is warm and safe. The brother is the guru, shaking, saying, "Wake up, wake up! Nothing to worry about. Safe in bed." Samsara is the drama of the nightmare, that's what it is. In it many things seem to be happening which are real and important and powerful and which take you over, but in reality, like in a dream, like a nightmare, there's nothing really there, they have no substance. However, just like somebody who is deep in sleep, when they are woken up, they go back to sleep again. This is what we do. We get the initiation, but we are very addicted to our dream, to our drama. And why? Because we are the star of our own drama. In our own drama, the world turns around us. When we wake up a little bit and we have more awareness, our drama is still running, but it's running in a world of other people's dramas as well. And yet, again paradoxically, it is by recognising that we just have a bit-part in the whole show that we become centred in our own ground, right at the centre of everything. So it's important to catch the flavour of practice for these Tibetan pujas. It's not worried, anxious, serious. It's relaxed, confident, open, with a sense of entitlement to make use of these methods that will return you home.

Generally speaking, the view that we try to realise in tantra and in dzogchen, is that of non-duality. Non-duality means that we are not concerned with two separate things, for example, subject and object, self and other, hot and cold, samsara and nirvana. All the opposites are realised, because they have no inherent self-nature, to actually be freed from any basis for causing opposition. For example, if you take an ordinary idea, of hot and cold: here is hot and there is cold. We can say, "Hot is the opposite of cold," we put them back-to-back, they're going in different directions. You taste something and you think, "It's not so hot". If it's not so hot it's going in the other direction. What's in the other direction? Cold. So instead of them being back-to-back they seem to be somehow linked. All opposites are connected. In this way, 'hot' has no meaning by itself. You cannot have an idea of hot without having an idea of cold. In summer, when you're hot, you have ice cream. Ice cream is like snow. In winter, when you're cold you have heating on, which is like summer. The view of non-duality is not something very sacred and high in the sky. It's very ordinary. Just as hot and cold are connected and there is a movement between these polarities, so, instead of being turned back-to-back as separate things, they are more like points on the movement of a wave, hot/cold, hot/cold.

In the same way, from the hinayana tradition, certainly in the Tibetan view of that, samsara and nirvana are set back-to-back. We don't like samsara, we want to get to nirvana. We want to get to nirvana because it's not like samsara. If samsara and nirvana were the same, you would be very disappointed. If you go to India, you don't really want to have *wurst* and *kartoffel*. Generally speaking, we want there to be difference.

But in the mahayana view, especially with a madhyamika understanding of the nature of emptiness as absolute absence of any kind of inherent self-existence, what we take to be the inherent existence of anything is simply a series of names which are applied to an appearance, a concept, an experience. Through this we come to see that there is no inherent self-existence in samsara, and there is no inherent self-existence in nirvana. That is to say, everything is empty. When you recognise everything is empty, your experience is called nirvana. When you don't realise everything is empty, your experience is called samsara. In that way, both samsara and nirvana have the same ground, or the same basis, which is emptiness, and they reveal themselves entirely dependent on whether you recognise the real nature, or you don't recognise the real nature. All the methods which are employed in buddhism could be set out along a continuum, according to how much absolute belief and identity with emptiness they manifest.

For example, you may want to acquire some merit, and you think, "In my next life I'm going to go to hell because I'm a bad person, so every day I will burn one butter lamp in the hope that I get some merit to make my experience in hell not so bad." Hell is real, the butter lamp is real, the merit is real, put them all together and you get a little bit of benefit. So that's at one end. On the other hand, if we really look into the nature of our own mind, and we recognise from the very beginning nothing has been there, our own mind has no inherent nature, everything which arises in the mind has no inherent self-nature, with the confidence of that, there is no obscuration at all to be removed. It is we ourselves who construct, for ourself, a vision of how our world is, and what is real and what is false. According to the view of non-duality, which is the basic view of dzogchen and the higher tantras, from the very beginning nothing has ever been born.

For example, we are sitting in a room. That's a sentence which is easy to understand, because you look around and you think, "Yes, we're sitting in a room." What is the status of the room you're sitting in? Clearly the good evangelical people, who have built this room, expect that when we leave on Sunday afternoon the building will still be here. If, when we leave, some part of the building goes with us, they will write a very angry letter and want some money. Clearly the ordinary perception is that this room exists. But when we look around, we can see planks of wood. All of these pieces of wood can be taken apart. This linoleum can be removed from the floor. Due to the juxtaposition, the placing together, of the various elements here, we experience 'the room'. This experience of being in a room makes us feel safe, but the room exists as an idea, it exists as a concept. The concept brings the manifestation of the room into a particular shape. If a dog comes in here again, he doesn't think, 'This is a room.' The dog *is* in the room, but he doesn't think he's in a *room*. That's not because the dog is stupid. No, it's because it doesn't have a concept of room. The *concept* of room creates the room. We bring this information together because we've all been in many rooms in the past, so when we come in here our perceptual field is organised in terms of this concept, which we already carry inside us. What we actually have here is some pressure on our buttocks, some pressure on the ankles, a certain visual experience, a slightly stale smell, because we're all breathing in the same enclosed space. This is what we experience. Under my bum I feel a little, kind of, "Oh, it's getting a bit sore." On the basis of that sensation I say to myself, "This floor is hard." 'Hard' is some concept in my head, which I put onto what is under me on the basis of some sensation I feel.

But if, instead of going to the level of conceptualisation and labelling, I simply stay with the sensation, what is it? In the same way, we look out. We see some things. We see outlines, we see bits of wood, other things, and then we say, "Oh, this is a person. This is a wall. This is wood." This is the meeting of perception and conception. We construct the experience of being in the room while we are in the room. Although we construct it, we layer our construction with the belief that the construction is actually the revelation of something which is existing by itself. This is the main difference in the perception of samsara and of nirvana. The constructions of samsara are really constructions, but they confuse themselves by appearing as if they are revelations. And then, sometimes, the experiences that we can have of opening, or nirvana, although they are really revelations of our true nature, we think that they are a construction created by our own meditation. So it is very, very important, to keep examining again and again, what role our own assumptions have in creating the world in which we exist. That's why, in buddhism, we say that this experience that we have is a dimension of karma, it is a manifestation of our karma. From that point of view, the reason that we are able to agree that we are sitting in a room is because we have sufficient shared karma to have the same kind of experience. In this way, what appears to be existing in-itself-as-a-room, we begin to see is actually a process of co-production between manifestation and the movement of our own mind. It makes quite a difference if we do that, because then we see that the concept of 'room' is just floating on the top, like a cork on the water. The waves of experience keep moving.

In dzogchen we speak of one ground with two pathways. One is the way of samsara, the other is the way of nirvana. Spaciousness is present moment-by-moment in which we can relax and open to the pulsing dynamic quality of experience but which, for beginners, creates anxiety. Or, we can try to stay with the security of conceptualisation, which allows us to predict the nature of the world we are experiencing. The cost of that, however, is that we lose experience itself, and we find ourselves moving in a world of conceptual organisation, construction, anxious prediction, and so forth. Clearly the key issue here is anxiety, and the key aspect of the practice of dzogchen is relaxation. The urge that the ego has, this centralised sense of organisation, is always that in order to be safe, I need to organise my world. I need to control it, and structure it and shape it. In order to practise dzogchen and this higher tantra we have to put ourselves in a state of relaxation.

Relaxation is a quality of faith. By faith here I don't mean a particular belief in something, but more an open-hearted faith, or trust, which is a gesture out. For example, a small child falls off its bicycle and hurts itself. It runs into the house and says, "Oh, papa, papa, (or mama, mama), look! look! look!" and the parent picks the child up, holds it, calms it. The child's trust, that the parent will be able to take the pain away, is fulfilled. The child feels better, and if you're holding the child, you feel them relaxing. You feel the tension of holding back the pain being released, so that the painful event passes and the child is free to move on, in other words, is open and available. Then it goes off and does something else. As the child relaxes, it is returned to itself. This is the function of these higher tantric meditation practices, and dzogchen meditation practices. The more we relax, the more we give up the burden of trying to construct ourselves and allow ourselves to be held by the practice, by the view. We relax, and we are returned to ourselves, and we manage to stay more and more in that state.

In terms of the guru yoga, we use entering into a culture of praising the teacher, seeing the teacher as being very special, very wonderful, having achieved all good things, in order to allow our capacity for idealisation, hope and confidence to move outwards.

The cause of suffering is attachment to entities. I attach myself to entities. That is a process of duality. I am separate from these things, I want these things, so I grasp these things. Then I feel good because I have the things I want. That is the structure that causes suffering in samsara. We have been in samsara for a very long time, and all the time we've been in samsara we've been using that structure. That means we are all experts at attachment. Absolutely perfect. Therefore the Buddha taught the path of tantra. Tantra makes use of our capacity for attachment to bring us liberation. That is why it is called a very skilful method, and that's why they say that a tantric yogi is able to make use of things for liberation which would tie an ordinary person into samsara. The reason that attachments in samsara bring us pain is because when we attach to something, the thing that we attach to, especially if we attach to a person, is likely not to be going to do exactly what we want.

Many of us are very surprised when we meet someone and we have a sweet love story, that this person, although we love them, turns out not to do what we want. I'm always surprised at this. You see this most clearly with children. They're always very surprised when their parents don't do what they want. "But I want to! Yeah, let's go to the swings! They're nice, the swings. You like to swing! Come, papa! What could be more interesting?" So clearly we have a lot of ability in this direction.

In the practice of guru yoga, as in this text, we establish the guru as the focus of our attachment. All the things that we want from anyone else in our life, we put onto the guru. "You are the sole source of my happiness. You are the wish-fulfilling gem. You are the one who will make all my dreams come true." So we say that our own guru is the same as Padmasambhava, and Padmasambhava is the essence of all the buddhas. This is similar to the sort of things people say in a romantic way. All one's hopes and dreams become concentrated in one point.

The reason that Padmasambhava will never cheat you, as it says in the first prayer we do in the main practice, *kyab nae lu me kon chog rin po che* (you are the unfailing refuge), is because he doesn't exist. This is really true. And because he doesn't exist, when he gives us his blessing, we don't exist either. Through this merging with the guru figure we are returned to the unborn ground of our own real nature in which, clearly, manifestation is there, clarity is there, experience is there, but nothing comes together as a separate entity having true inherent existence.

So the guru yoga starts with a description. In front of us here is Padmasambhava, and he's looking good. Saturday night, all slicked up, looking very shiny!

## e. Guru Yoga

ཧྲཱིཿ རང་མདུན་ཆོས་དབྱིངས་པདྨ་ཉི་ཟླའི་སྟེང་ཿ
སྐྱབས་ཀུན་བདག་ཉིད་རིག་འཛིན་པདྨ་འབྱུང་ཿ
གྲུབ་བརྙེས་མཚན་མཆོག་བརྒྱད་དང་རིག་འཛིན་ཚོགས་ཿ
རྩ་གསུམ་རྒྱལ་བའི་དཀྱིལ་འཁོར་རྫོགས་པར་གསལ་ཿ

**HRI RANG DUN CHOE YING PADMA NYI DAI TENG
KYAB KUN DAG NYID RIG DZIN PADMA JUNG
DRUB NYE TSEN CHOG GYE DANG RIG DZIN TSOG
TSA SUM GYAL WAI KYIL KHOR DZOG PAR SAL**

*Hri. In the vast space before me, on top of lotus, sun and moon
is the embodiment of all the refuges, the vidyadhara Padmasambhava
with the eight excellent forms who gained siddhis,
and the hosts of vidyadharas. Thus I clearly meditate
on the complete Buddha's mandala of the three roots.*

Then we say the lineage prayer, starting with the gurus of the nine levels of transmission.

## Lineage Prayer

ཨེ་མ་ཧོ༔ རྒྱལ་བ་དགོངས་བརྒྱུད་རིག་འཛིན་བརྡ་བརྒྱུད་དང༔
གང་ཟག་སྙན་བརྒྱུད་སྨོན་ལམ་དབང་བསྐུར་བརྒྱུད༔
བཀའ་བབ་ལུང་བརྒྱུད་མཁའ་འགྲོ་གཏད་རྒྱའི་བརྒྱུད༔
ལས་འཕྲོ་གཏེར་བརྒྱུད་ཤོག་སེར་ཚིག་གི་བརྒྱུད༔
བཀའ་བབ་ལུང་ཟིན་ཡི་དམ་ཞི་ཁྲོ་དང༔
མཁའ་འགྲོ་ཆོས་སྲུང་བཅས་ལ་གསོལ་བ་འདེབས༔
གུས་པས་ཕྱག་འཚལ་མཆོད་འབུལ་སྐྱབས་སུ་མཆི༔
རྩ་བ་ཡན་ལག་དམ་ཚིག་སྡོམ་ལས་འགལ༔
ཉམས་ཆག་ཉེས་ལྟུང་བཤགས་ཤིང་བྱིན་གྱིས་རློབས༔

**E MA HO GYAL WA GONG GYUD RIG DZIN DA GYUD DANG
GANG ZAG NYEN GYUD MON LAM WANG KUR GYUD
KA BAB LUNG GYUD KHA DRO TAD GYAI GYUD
LAE THRO TER GYUD SHOG SER TSIG GI GYUD
KA BAB LUNG ZIN YI DAM ZHI THRO DANG
KHA DRO CHOE SUNG CHE LA SOL WA DEB
GUE PAE CHAG TSAL CHOD BUL KYAB SU CHI
TSA WA YAN LAG DAM TSIG DOM LAE GAL
NYAM CHAG NYE TUNG SHAG SHING JIN GYI LOB**

*Wonderful! The lineage of the jinas' deep understanding, the vidyadharas' symbol lineage and the lineage of those who heard teaching, the lineage of aspiration and initiation; the lineage of the permitted ones and the lineage of the entrusted dakinis. The lineage of fortunate treasure finders and the lineage of those who first saw the new treasure books. Those who were instructed to do practice, and the peaceful and fierce wishing gods, and the dakinis and dharma guardians: to all of them we pray. With devotion we prostrate, make offerings and take refuge. Our straying from the firm promises of our root and branch vows, our lost vows, faults and falls we confess. Please bless us with purity.*

The nine lineages are very clearly described in this prayer. They are the ways in which the dharma teaching transmission comes into the world. Remembering the transmission reminds us of our dependence on the kindness of others. Without them we would remain sealed in the bubble of our pseudo-autonomy and self-concern. Remembrance and gratitude link us to something greater than ourselves and through this we are introduced to our own nature, so we make prostrations to them, we make offerings, we purify our vows. We ask for purification, and then we sing this prayer.

### Imploring the Guru

ཨེ་བླ་མ་མཁྱེན་ནོ༔    ཆོས་སྐུ་སྣང་བ་མཐའ་ཡས་མཁྱེན་ནོ༔
ཨེ་བླ་མ་མཁྱེན་ནོ༔    ལོངས་སྐུ་ཐུགས་རྗེ་ཆེན་པོ་མཁྱེན་ནོ༔
ཨེ་བླ་མ་མཁྱེན་ནོ༔    སྤྲུལ་སྐུ་ཤཱཀྱ་ཐུབ་པ་མཁྱེན་ནོ༔
ཨེ་བླ་མ་མཁྱེན་ནོ༔    གུ་རུ་པདྨ་འབྱུང་གནས་མཁྱེན་ནོ༔
སྐྱེ་དྲིན་ཅན་རྩ་བའི་བླ་མ་མཁྱེན་ནོ༔ མཁྱེན༔

**EH LA MA KHYEN NO CHOE KU NANG WA THA YAE KHYEN NO**
**EH LA MA KHYEN NO LONG KU THUG JE CHEN PO KHYEN NO**
**EH LA MA KHYEN NO TRUL KU SHAKYA THUB PA KHYEN NO**
**EH LA MA KHYEN NO GU RU PADMA JUNG NAE KHYEN NO**
**KYE DRIN CHEN TSA WAI LA MA KHYEN NO  KHYEN**

*Oh! Guru, think of us! Dharmakaya Nangwa Thayae: think of us!*
*Oh! Guru, think of us! Sambhogakaya Chenrezig: think of us!*
*Oh! Guru, think of us! Nirmanakaya Shakyamuni: think of us!*
*Oh! Guru, think of us! Guru Padmasambhava: think of us!*
*Oh! Most kind root guru: think of us! Think of us!*

What this means, what it's trying to do, is like writing a love letter, you forget everything else. "Oh, baby, where are you? I need you so much." Like that. You go into a little spiral in which only this object has any meaning. This is being used for a very specific purpose.

The most common problem for meditators is distraction, that we find it difficult to put all our attention into one thing. So if we're doing a basic meditation, like trying to keep the focus of your attention on your breath, that's quite difficult because the breath is, for most of us, not very sexy. The thoughts and dreams that come in our heads while we're supposed to be focusing on our breath, on the other hand, these are very sexy. They take us to all sorts of nice, interesting places. So like a very clever parent, Padmasambhava decides, "Well, if they want to have something sexy, we'll give them something sexy to look at, then they will be interested." It's just that simple, and that's why you have this whole range of gods, because different people have different fetishistic interests. You have dancing boy-gods, like these little boy-bands that are very popular with twelve-year-old girls, and then you get the kind of Barbie ones. You get any kind of thing that will get you going. The main thing is that it gets you going. This is a method. If the method doesn't work, there's no benefit. If you're a gay man, you're probably not so interested to go to bed with Marilyn Monroe. You might be interested to talk about dresses with her, but you probably don't want to have sex with her. It's exactly the same in the dharma. There is no point in going and taking initiations in a practice that you're never going to do because you don't find it sexy. Nowadays in the West very few people have arranged marriages, where the family, the parents, decide who you will marry. That is to say, duty and obligation no longer provide a containing intention — individuals tend to feel that the value of what is chosen is inseparable from the feeling of making a free choice.

People used to go to C R Lama and say things like, "Oh, Rinpoche, should I do Dorje Drolo?" Rinpoche would say, "If you want to do Dorje Drolo, you do Dorje Drolo." "Ooh, I have this problem, what should I do?" "What would you like to do? Oh, you like to do that, then you do that." He said to me, "You know, if I tell people what to do, they never do it, so now I just say...." And this is important, because in more traditional cultures people were trained in their education to want what they got, but in our culture we are trained to get what we want, so it's very important to really work out what kind of practice is going to make sense for you. You need to read different kinds of practices and see, because if you commit yourself to doing it, you should try to stay in there. The divorce rate is very high, in ordinary life and in dharma practice. That is really important.

It's exactly *this* practice, when we do this *eh la ma khyen no* that we are doing. We are trying to bring up libidinal energy, the energy of desire, of sexual desire as well, for union. In tantra we see a boy and a girl doing kissy-kissy, that's what we see. It's not an illusion. One of the big traumas of my childhood was that I had a little doll, and between her legs there was just some round plastic, and I was always very surprised, "Why does this little doll not have anything there?" It's very, very confusing, and you could have the same idea about these Tibetan gods. Maybe you imagine it's all just smooth, but no, no, no, no! Sexual energy, desire, desire for union which brings opening in the heart, heating in the body, the longing, this is very, very important. Our own real nature is androgynous, we are both male and female, so you can pray to the same sex, to the opposite sex, it doesn't matter, devotion is going there. We can have union with our own opposite because we are both anima-animus, whatever, however we choose to describe it.

So when you recite this prayer to the guru, you can recite it a hundred times, a thousand times. Recited with devotion, you can do it with a crying voice, you can do it with an angry shouting voice, you can do it with anything, the main thing is to be there, doing the practice. This is a practice of passion.

As you are saying this, you believe, just as it says later in the text, that light is coming from the three places of the guru, from the forehead, the throat and the heart, flowing into your body.

### Requesting the Four Initiations

བདག་གཞན་ལུས་ངག་ཡིད་གསུམ་སྨིན་ཅིང་གྲོལ༈
དབང་བཞི་བསྐུར་ཐོབ་སྒྲིབ་བཞི་ཀུན་དག་ནས༈
གནས་ངན་ལོག་པའི་ལམ་ནས་དྲངས་ནས་ཀྱང༈
སྐྱེ་དང་ཚེ་རབས་ཀུན་ཏུ་རྗེས་བཟུང་ཤོག༈

**DAG ZHAN LUE NGAG YID SUM MIN CHING DROL**
**WANG ZHI KUR THOB DRIB ZHI KUN DAG NAE**
**NAE NGEN LOG PAI LAM NAE DRANG NAE KYANG**
**KYE DANG TSE RAB KUN TU JE ZUNG SHOG**

*I and all other beings request the four initiations which will ripen and liberate our body, speech and mind. Gaining these, the four obscurations will be purified. Please guide us from the wrong path of the states of woe and in this and all future lives, please hold us firmly!*

You, and all other sentient beings, are filled with this rainbow light. You gain these four initiations. You have a condensed form here of a later part of the practice. *(See Section E:k)*

At this point, if you have time, just after the *nae*, you can then do the dissolving. The guru comes to the top of your head and dissolves into a ball of light. The ball of light is absorbed into your heart. Your body dissolves into the ball of light and then, united, the ball of light dissolves down into nothing. Then we have the final two lines, *nae ngen log pai lam nae drang nae kyang/ Kye dang tse rab kun tu je zung shog*, saying, 'Please protect us from these bad ways, and in all my future lives may I be born close to you'.

The view of enlightenment contained in tantra is quite social. This is because the general idea is that when you get enlightened you go and live in someone else's buddhaland, until you get your own buddhaland, but anyway, there are always people hanging around. Generally speaking, most lamas always have lots of people around them. That's both a sign of status, just as it is with a king — the bigger the king, the more servants they're allowed to have. You may know the story of King Lear and the tragedy of the shrinking number of his retinue, but it's also stressing that enlightenment is not something you get for yourself. Enlightenment is simply shifting the articulation that you have in relation to others. Because we are social beings we are always living in connection with other people, and so enlightenment won't be any different. One way of saying this is that dharmakaya is for us and samboghakaya and nirmanakaya are for other people. By recognising our own nature we become free. Then we manifest out for the sake of others, doing whatever they require.

One of the difficulties of these long practices is that they take a long time to do. If you really go into that, they put you in a slightly altered state, which means, if you've got to go back into your work-reality, that can be quite difficult. But if we understand that the central principle is that we use the practice in order to transform our own state and our experience of the world, then we can do it in a very condensed way. If somebody is interested in football, and you mention to them the name of a good, famous, footballer they will become excited very quickly. It's the same principle. If you study the dharma, and you practise the dharma regularly, you will be able to have very rapid mobilisation into the meditation. Our job is to do the dharma for us, not to do the dharma for the dharma, or the lama, or anybody else. The dharma needs to be in a form that we can use it.

You can do the *Big Rigdzin* from time to time. If you can, you do it every day. Otherwise you do the *Short Rigdzin*. But you can also do this practice in which, without any preliminaries, you can just in an instant visualise in front of you Padmasambhava. If you can't visualise clearly, as I said before, you just imagine he is there. Then you can recite. Depending on what time you have available, you could do the Seven Line Prayer, if you like. You could do the *Bendza Guru Mantra*, if you like. Or, more quickly, you can just do *Om Ah Hung, Om Ah Hung, Om Ah Hung, Om Ah Hung*, and as you say the *Om Ah Hung* you have the white, red and blue lights coming into you. You take these initiations in an instant. You immediately feel an identification. And you can do a sudden dissolving. You can just absorb the Guru straight into your heart. You can take him to the top of your head and then straight down. You can do this practice all through the day. You can do it in three minutes.

So if you have the time, you can start the day with the *Short Rigdzin* practice, and then in the day, whenever you get a bit lost or confused or you find you have a moment, you can do this brief focus practice and it will bring you back. The main thing is to keep the connection with the practice because the practice keeps you established in the view, which transforms your experience. Just as a proper, professional, alcoholic will start the day with a nice glass of whisky, and at work will go to the toilet from time to time to take out a little bottle, and then in the evening do the full-bottle practice, so we should also seek to achieve this state of total immersion in Padmasambhava. You should get to such a state that between this big drink, and the next big drink, you must have a little something. This is real devotion. This is the way in which the tantric vision comes alive, in which the mantra is never gone from your lips, the visualisation is never gone from your awareness, and you find yourself living in a transformed reality.

# C. SADHANA:
# Introductory Part

### The Introductory Invocation of Padmasambhava

སྐྱབས་གནས་བསླུ་མེད་དཀོན་མཆོག་རིན་པོ་ཆེ།
ཐུགས་རྗེ་མངའ་བའི་ཨུ་རྒྱན་པདྨ་ལ།
བདག་གི་ཇི་ལྟར་གསོལ་བ་བཏབ་པ་བཞིན།
མྱུར་དུ་འགྲུབ་པར་བྱིན་གྱིས་བརླབས་དུ་གསོལ།

**KYAB NAE LU ME KON CHOG RIN PO CHE**
**THUG JE NGA WAI U GYEN PAD MA LA**
**DAG GI JE TAR SOL WA TAB PA ZHIN**
**NYUR DU DRUB PAR JIN GYI LAB DU SOL**

*To the precious jewel who is my unfailing refuge, Ugyen Padma who has compassion, I pray for the blessing that whatever I request may be quickly accomplished.*

FROM A WESTERN POINT OF VIEW this is a very interesting verse because it's saying, 'Precious Padmasambhava, you're the essence of compassion, the unfailing refuge, come and give me what I want.' It's not 'Come and give me what you want', not *thy* will be done, but *my* will be done. It is very important that in tantric practice we include ourselves within this. This kind of text in Tibetan is often called a *trinley*, which means activity.

One of the big battles that often happens in monotheistic religion is the battle against magic. In monotheism, because power resides in God, God will decide what is good for you. God is the father, and father knows best. Whereas according to the principles of magic, in almost all countries I think we can say, in Africa, Asia and in the old days in Europe, there is a much more clear-cut correlation or connection between an activity that an individual performs and an effect in the world. If you do a particular kind of activity, a certain kind of result will arrive. Just as if you put water in a pan and you put it on the fire, it will boil. And if you put milk in a pan and you put it on the fire, and don't watch it, it will boil over. The water will never boil over, but the milk will boil over. If you know the qualities of the materials you are working with, you will be able to see how you get different results from doing different things.

In Tibetan buddhism there are many different kinds of gods, many different local gods, spirits, and so forth, each of them having some special qualities. By learning about the qualities of the different gods you can make use of them for particular purposes. This is a technical relationship but the mood has to be one of respect and proper attention to detail.

If you go to the dentist, the dentist has many tools and, hopefully, he knows what to do with them. Hopefully, again, the mood is respectful and polite but nonetheless he's going to *ssssss* and *rrrrrr* and then: "Now pay me money!" But when you go to the dentist it's not just the dentist who does something, because *you* have to keep your mouth open. It's not a usual thing to open your mouth. You're lying there, very quiet, you don't move too much, this also is participation. Very often when we conceptualise a situation we think we're being passive, but actually we're doing something. It's easy to fall into a master/slave way of thinking where it's as if the master does everything: "The King built his palace in five years." Oh, yeah? Who built it? The workers! But their role, their effort, becomes invisible in the discourse of hierarchy. This obscures the participatory nature of our dimension. What is really important is to see that this world is a dialogue, it's an ongoing exchange.

And so *you* ask Padmasambhava to do something. In fact, you can also tell Padmasambhava to do something. Then you have to know what you want. If you don't know what you want, then it won't be very helpful. If you know what you want, but you're rather shy, that also won't help. If you say (very low and shy), "Padmasambhava, I want to be a buddha so I can save all beings," it's very important to think through what you want because you may actually get it, and then what? Because although in the mahayana tradition there developed the idea of buddha-lands so that when you die you can be born in a buddha-land, next to be the big Buddha, that's not the whole story. It's the question of your view. When you die you go to heaven, if you're lucky, and you can just sort of hang-out near a big god up there. Then you have all these others, cherubim, seraphim, and then there's you there also. You don't have to do anything except praise god: "You're great, you're great." If you remember Elvis Presley, he also had many people around him saying, "You're great, you're great. Thousand dollars, thousand dollars." Of course we know it wasn't very good for Elvis Presely to have these people around him. Psycho-fans are very dangerous. Much better for a buddha to have someone around who can take the piss. You need to maintain the view of emptiness and not be seduced by any environment, otherwise the non-dual integration will be hidden by your own dharma practice.

This is important because otherwise everything becomes very holy, very sacred, and completely separated from ordinary life. All of this means that we need to know what we want. Humour and happiness and laughter have a big place in Tibetan buddhism, but at the same time the basic task is serious, because there is something to be understood, which is the nature of your own mind, and with that a commitment to help other people recognize their nature too.

### a. Seven Line Prayer

ཧཱུྂ༔ ཨོ་རྒྱན་ཡུལ་གྱི་ནུབ་བྱང་མཚམས༔

པདྨ་གེ་སར་སྡོང་པོ་ལ༔

ཡ་མཚན་མཆོག་གི་དངོས་གྲུབ་བརྙེས༔

པདྨ་འབྱུང་གནས་ཞེས་སུ་གྲགས༔

འཁོར་དུ་མཁའ་འགྲོ་མང་པོས་བསྐོར༔

ཁྱེད་ཀྱི་རྗེས་སུ་བདག་བསྒྲུབ་ཀྱིས༔

བྱིན་གྱིས་བརླབ་ཕྱིར་གཤེགས་སུ་གསོལ༔

གུ་རུ་པདྨ་སིདྡྷི་ཧཱུྂ༔

HUNG UR GYEN YUL GYI NUB JANG TSHAM
PE MA GE SAR DONG PO LA
YAM TSHEN CHOG GI NGOE DRUB NYE
PE MA JUNG NAE ZHE SU DRAG
KHOR DU KHAN DRO MANG POE KOR
KHYE KYI JE SU DAG DRUB KYI
JIN GYI LAB CHIR SHEG SU SOL
GU RU PAD MA SID DHI HUNG

*Hung. In the north-west corner of the land of Urgyen, upon the stem and stamen of a lotus, are you who have the marvellous and supreme attainments, Padmasambhava of great renown, with a retinue of many dakinis around you. Following and relying on you I do your practice, therefore, in order to grant your blessings, please come here! Guru Padmasambhava, give me the real attainment of buddhahood.*

This is a very, very famous prayer, and there are many, many commentaries on it. C R Lama said many times that all proper collections of *terma*, of treasure texts, will have this prayer inside them. This prayer, in itself, you can use as your whole practice. Tulku Thondrup has already published Mipham Rinpoche's commentary on the text in *Enlightened Journey*[6], and that's a very helpful thing to read.

Generally speaking, this verse has the basic structure of the practice. That means, first of all we say this object is very good, is very high, is very special. Then we say, "I'm with you," and then, "You must do something for me." That's the deal. We believe that it's very effective because Padmasambhava wants to help people. But as we saw earlier, it's not polite to help people if they don't want to be helped. You can't actually help people, anyway, if they don't want to be helped because the goal of buddhism is not changed behaviour, but changed understanding, out of which a change in behaviour arises.

When the muslims came into India, one of the things they did a lot was to kill a cow in order to get some hindu people involved in eating, or even touching, cow meat. They would kill a cow and scatter the blood in hindu temples. This would pollute the temple and anyone who came in touch with

---

[6] Tulku Thondup: *Enlightened Journey : Buddhist Practice as Everyday Life* (Shambhala, 1995)

the blood. They would force the hindus to become covered in cow blood, and then other, more strict, hindus would say, "Now you've lost your caste, you can never get out of this." Having lost their hindu identity they were outcastes, and thereby more open to conversion to islam. Thus these people were forced out of one dogmatic structure and into another. This example shows the vulnerability of religious identity built on ritual practice, embedded in a sharp differentiation of good and bad, pure and impure. Everything which is created will collapse in time, every compounded construct has its own destruction built into it.

Enlightenment, however, is not a case of believing in a dogmatic system, it is a transformation of the nature of experience. You can't transform the deep structure of someone else's experience by doing something to them, if they don't want it to happen. We ourselves have to make the effort, and that's why this prayer is very important because it's saying these two forces come together: Padmasambhava, who is already enlightened, and we, who want to be enlightened. On an outer level Padmasambhava is this powerful presence, an enlightened person who is other than us, and through this prayer, we ask him to come and give us this blessing. On a more inward level, Padmasambhava is our own true nature, which is hidden from us. As is often explained, in the first line, *ur gyen yul gyi nub jang tsham*, the north-west corner is where samsara and nirvana meet, and the country of Urgyen is dharmadhatu. The true nature of actuality is precisely this point where samsara and nirvana are connected.

The *pema gesar dong po* (in the second line), the lotus, as we know, always represents purity. The natural purity, *kadag*, and the purity which develops through practice, these two are united in infinite purity. Then, in the third line, *yam tshen chog gi ngoe drub nye*, indicates that all good qualities are present at that place. That is to say, if you realise this stage, if you truly integrate with this stage, everything you need will be there.

One of the things about living in our world is that we go through many stages of progression. Often, as we come to a stage, it feels as if that stage is the final one of our life. Small children can be very proud when they can sit on the potty and go to the toilet themselves. Then they look down and say, "Oh, I'm finished!" We go like this through life, through all these stages. Maybe you go to university and you think, "Oh, now I've got my degree, finished!" But then you have to get a job. Then you have to learn something more. There is always something more, and something more. It's the very nature of our world that we never come to a safe, final point while we're alive. You see that with Bill Clinton, probably the most powerful man in the world at the time, who was completely humiliated. Many wealthy people, we know, have a very difficult time. People with many great qualities have a very difficult time. But here it says *yam tshen chog gi ngoe drub nye*, you have got all these qualities and they don't seem to change. Why is this? Well, in our world we always put ourselves into the picture thinking, "I have these qualities. This is me." This identification creates a false notion, as if we can sustain something forever as a possession. Whereas for Padmasambhava, his qualities arise effortlessly, beyond appropriation, free of being the objects of ego-identification. He does not rest on his achievements, he does not rest on anything. Integrated into the pure ground nature, all qualities become his ornaments.

For example, if the river is flowing along, you can put your hands in the water and say, "Oh, now I have some water." But the water is moving through. Everything is impermanent, and it is impermanent because it's flowing. We cannot own it, or tame it, or make it ours. That's why our qualities always go and change. The qualities you have when you are young change as you get older. And as you get very old, your body changes a lot, and you get different qualities again. These qualities, that we see as being *our* qualities, have actually arisen according to the principle of dependent co-origination. For example, I have a friend, who recently got a bit sick and she said, "But I never get sick. I'm a really healthy person." But this is an illusion because she is talking as if she has somehow made her own body and made it completely healthy and is fully identified with that. But she has no idea what is going on inside. Her health is the luck of some genetic inheritance, of her present karma.

This attachment to a sense of self, to a self-identity, such as occurs where we make the statement "I am this body, I am me, I am like this, I am like that," is called *dagdzin* in Tibetan. *Dag* means 'I' while *dzin* means 'to hold' or 'to grasp'. I can say, "I have this watch," but this is because I am holding it. If I stop holding it, it falls down. To have something, in that sense, involves effort. When I put the watch down, my body is no longer holding it but my mind is, for I continue to think this is my watch. All appropriation requires certain resources. You may think you have many resources but actually you really only have access to resources for a period of time. After a while your relation to the things around you changes. Colleagues leave or retire, possessions are broken or lost, and your own interests change, so that what was once held precious is now put out as garbage.

So when it says here *yam tshen chog gi ngoe drub nye*, *nye* means 'to have' in Tibetan, but Padmasambhava doesn't have these good qualities in the way in which I have a watch, because the watch will break or get lost or something, or I'll die and go somewhere else. His qualities are woven directly into the nature of his dharmakaya realisation. Just as the rays flow naturally out of the sun, so the tradition tells us that these qualities of Padmasambhava arise effortlessly out of the nature of dharmakaya, which is his unchanging true nature, which is the recognition of emptiness. Of course, this is very difficult to represent in language, because our language is all about material attachment. Padmasambhava is a path of realisation. Padmasambhava is a way of understanding the teaching.

The next line says *pema jung nae zhe su drag*. *Pema* refers to the dharmakaya, and *jung nae* means 'a source'. Having a lotus as the place where you arise represents the form kayas, the samboghakaya and the nirmanakaya. These two aspects of the form kaya, these two kinds of manifestation, together with the dharmakaya, are the unification of the nature of all the buddhas. This is the nature of Padmasambhava.

This brings us to the fifth line, *khor du khan dro mang poe kor* which indicates that 'around these three kayas everything is manifesting'. In the Indian tradition dakinis are low village goddesses who cause trouble. What is very important, always, in understanding dharma, is to recognise these different views. If you mix everything together you will have a very bad soup. When we try to understand this verse in terms of the view of the practice, *dakini* does not here refer to some female principle, some girl flying around. *Kha* is the sky, it means the space, it means emptiness, dharmakaya and *dro* means 'to go, to move'. What is going on inside this *kha*, this space of enlightenment? All the thoughts, the feelings, the sensations, the experience, the experiences that arise for us, including the experience of being someone having the experience.

On the roads there are many car crashes because the road is very narrow but you don't get so many plane crashes, because the sky is very big. It's like that. In your head, ordinarily, you have a lot of car crashes. You drive on the narrow road of your karma with your thoughts, your feelings, your sensations, your habitual directions, your obsessions. Thoughts and feelings band together. You worry. You think you made mistakes. But in the big sky of dharmakaya there's plenty of space. There's no road, no road in the sky, so there is enough space for thoughts and feelings and sensations to arise and pass. This is the basis of the meditation. In dzogchen practice you call it *rangdrol*, which is the self-liberation of everything that arises. It means that you maintain space as the medium you work in, and not this narrow road of your own self-identity volition. Very often, when a thought or a sensation arises for us, it is followed immediately by a feeling: we don't like to have that thought or we very much like to have that thought, and in that way these thoughts become like a big pile-up on the motorway. Life stops, while you stay stuck in some repetitive movement. This is the structure for states like depression, agoraphobia, some of the psychotic disorders and so forth, where you're simply running the same thoughts. There is no movement in life but the cars are just banging together again and again.

The text says *khor du khan dro mang poe kor* which means, 'in this state of dharmakaya, your mind can be very busy, you can have a lot of experience'. Someone like C R Lama had many, many things going on. All day long he'd be doing many, many different things. As we have seen earlier, in the hinayana kind of meditation we tend to see the disturbance of the world as very severe and difficult, and so we try to avoid all that disturbance by making our minds very calm and peaceful. We try to cut off from mental activity. In the practice of tantra, however, we try to experience all the kinds of mental arisings, physical arisings, interactive arisings which would normally disturb us, we try to experience these as the dakini, or as the free movement out of the ground of dharmakaya.

Then we say *khye kyi je su dag drub kyi,* 'by following you, by doing your practice', which means, 'by integrating our understanding into the state of dharmakaya.' That is how you follow Padmasambhava. You don't follow Padmasambhava by buying a statue of Padmasambhava. We follow him by becoming like him, inseparable from him. We follow Padmasambhava by merging into Padmasambhava, by identifying with him. This is the meaning of the seventh line, *jin gyi lab chir sheg su sol*, please come here and give your blessing. The blessing is not a thing we get, but an experience we enter into. If you hold Padmasambhava at a distance then that will be not so helpful. The purpose of gaining enlightenment is to be useful to other people. If you just say to Padmasambhava, "You are very great", that's not making very much use of him. For example, say you meet someone and you like them, and you think, "Oh, they're very nice," and every day you say to this person, "Oh, you are such a beautiful woman. Oh, I really admire you and look at you." Then, at a certain point, the woman might think, "Well, why don't you kiss me?" Padmasambhava is available for sex, this is absolutely sure. As we have already seen, union, merging, fusion is the symbol, a sexual symbol for non-duality, for bringing together that which is separate. If you respect someone, you can allow their qualities to manifest out into the world. It's not a question of just putting them up on a shelf somewhere. I do your practice. That is to say, I will visualise you and do this dissolving practice, and you come here and give me the blessing. This is a practice of union. We use the power of devotion to create a kind of magnet situation, in which this very powerful force is there and our longing is here, and when these two come together we have a one-pointed attention in the practice.

One of the commonest male sexual problems is premature ejaculation. It's normal for all men from time to time to ejaculate quite quickly, but sometimes the man gets a bit caught up in this, and then predicts that next time it's going to happen again. That anxiety then ensures that it does happen. In a similar way, you can have a premature meditation. So you do the puja, and you get to the point where you dissolve, and it….."Aaah, now it's all…Oh! Next bit!" You do a hundred and twenty pages of foreplay, and then…all gone! This is not very satisfying for you, nor for Padmasambhava. This is, "Oh, they ring these bells, I come down, I'm ready, I've got all dressed up, I've put on my robes, I'm in a good mood, and then they forget about me! They rush on down the text without really saying "Hello", let alone getting to know me." That's why it's very important to understand what the real principle of tantric practice is. It is transformation of your sense of self-identity through the use of identification with the deity. That is the principle of all tantra, and it requires time.

At the end, we say *Guru Pema Siddhi Hung*. This is the mantra, and it gives a particular validation of what has been described. If we do it in a dualistic way we are saying, "Please give me this now." If we do it in a non-dual way then this *Guru Pema Siddhi Hung* is…here it is! We just enter….it's there.

It's very helpful to have a lot of faith. You can pray in the manner of a desperate child that's lost its parent. You can be lonely. You can cry. You can bring a lot of passion into it, but that is only the first half. You are using this intensification to bring about the merging, and the merging, at the point of merging, requires you to be calm and deep and clear, otherwise the emotion will drive you straight past the opening.

Generally speaking, nyingmapas believe that this prayer has a lot of blessing power in it, that it is a true expression of the energy of Padmasambhava, and that by saying this prayer the resonance, which is inherent in it, helps to bring us into alignment with the nature of the three kayas. As you know, C R Lama believes in this prayer very much. He always encourages people to do as many recitations of the Seven Line Prayer as possible.

## b. General Prayers for the Lineage

ཀུན་བཟང་རྡོར་སེམས་དགའ་རབ་ཤྲི་སིང་།
ཨུ་རྒྱན་པདྨ་རྗེ་འབངས་ཉི་ཤུ་ལྔ།
བཀའ་གཏེར་བརྒྱུད་ལྡན་རྩ་བའི་བླ་མ་སོགས།
འདྲེན་མཆོག་ཡབ་སྲས་ཡོངས་ལ་གསོལ་བ་འདེབས།

KUN ZANG DOR SEM GA RAB SHI RI SING
UR GYEN PADMA JE BANG NYI SHU NGA
KA TER GYUD DEN TSA WAI LA MA SOG
DREN CHOG YAB SAE YONG LA SOL WA DEB

*To Kuntu Zangpo, Dorje Sempa, Garab Dorje, and Shri Singha, to Padmasambhava and his twenty five disciples, to my root guru who possesses the lineages of kama and terma, and to all the supreme guides, both gurus and disciples, we pray.*

རྣམ་དག་སྐུ་མངའ་མཆོག་ཏུ་གཟུགས་བཟང་བ།
ཡེ་ཤེས་རྒྱ་མཚོ་གསེར་གྱི་ལྷུན་པོ་འདྲ།
གྲགས་པ་འཇིག་རྟེན་གསུམ་ན་ལྷམ་མེ་བ།
མགོན་པོ་མཆོག་གྱུར་ཁྱེད་ལ་གསོལ་བ་འདེབས།

NAM DAG KU NGA CHOG TU ZUG ZANG WA
YE SHE GYAM TSO SER GYI LHUN PO DRA
DRAG PA JIG TEN SUM NA LHAM ME WA
GON PO CHOG GYUR KHYE LA SOL WA DEB

## C. SADHANA: Introductory Part

*Whose perfectly pure body possesses a supremely excellent form,*
*with a colour like that of the Golden Mountain (Sumeru), and*
*whose knowledge is like the ocean, whose fame illuminates the three*
*worlds, we pray to you who are the supreme protector.*

རྒྱལ་བ་ཉིད་ལས་ལྷག་པའི་ལུང་མངའ་ཞིང་།
ཕྲིན་ལས་མཛད་པ་བསམ་གྱིས་མི་ཁྱབ་པ།
བསྟན་དང་འགྲོ་བའི་རྩ་ལག་མཆོག་གྱུར་པའི།
ཨུ་རྒྱན་རིན་པོ་ཆེ་ལ་གསོལ་བ་འདེབས།

**GYAL WA NYID LAE LHAG PAI LUNG NGA ZHING**
**THRIN LAE DZE PA SAM GYI MI KHYAB PA**
**TEN DANG DRO WAI TSA LAG CHOG GYUR PAI**
**UR GYEN RIN PO CHE LA SOL WA DEB**

*You whose teachings are more excellent than those of the Jina himself,*
*who perform activities beyond the reach of thought, most excellent cause*
*for the growth of both the doctrine and sentient beings,*
*Padmasambhava, we pray to you.*

All of these prayers are designed to create a mood of devotion and security, and the confidence that in the past people have done these kind of practices and got some kind of benefit. They're there for getting you in the mood and helping to furnish your mind with the images and stories of these great heroes so that they remain with you as an inspiration and support, creating a sense of belonging.

### Prayer to the Three-Kaya Guru

ཧཱུྃ༔ མ་བཅོས་སྤྲོས་བྲལ་བླ་མ་ཆོས་ཀྱི་སྐུ༔
བདེ་ཆེན་ལོངས་སྤྱོད་བླ་མ་ཆོས་ཀྱི་རྗེ༔
པད་སྡོང་ལས་འཁྲུངས་བླ་མ་སྤྲུལ་པའི་སྐུ༔
སྐུ་གསུམ་རྡོ་རྗེ་འཆང་ལ་གསོལ་བ་འདེབས༔

**HUNG MA CHOE TROE DRAL LA MA CHOE KYI KU**
**DE CHEN LONG CHOE LA MA CHOE KYI JE**
**PE DONG LE TRUNG LA MA TRUL PE KU**
**KU SUM DOR JE CHANG LA SOL WA DEB**

*Hung. The guru without artifice, free of all relative positions is the dharmakaya. The guru of great happiness, the lord of dharma, is the sambhogakaya. The guru born from the lotus stem is the nirmanakaya. We pray to the three-kaya vajradhara.*

This is considered to be a very powerful prayer. It describes the three-kaya nature of Padmasambhava and our own guru. It is the blessing of these three kayas which are the most important thing to understand. When we recite it slowly, we use it to integrate with the state of dharmakaya described in the first line. Giving up mental effort, not adopting any intention or position, we stay present with whatever is occurring, without adopting or rejecting. It's the prayer that C R Lama himself used for offering his food when he was at home, so it has an intimate place in our lineage. You can recite it to make a food offering before each meal. If you do it for food, then at the end of it, instead of saying *sol wa deb* you say *choe pa bul*, 'offer'.

## C. SADHANA: Introductory Part

**General Prayers**

རིག་འཛིན་བྱང་ཆུབ་སེམས་དཔའི་དགོངས་པ་ཡིས༔
གང་ཟག་ལས་ཅན་རྣམས་ལ་བྱིན་བརླབས་ཏེ༔
དུས་མཚོད་འདི་ནས་ལྔ་བརྒྱ་ཐ་མའི་བར༔
གསང་སྔགས་བཀའ་བཞིན་སྒྲུབ་པའི་དམ་ཚིག་ཅན༔
གང་ཟག་སྙན་ཁུང་བརྒྱུད་པ་ལ་གསོལ་བ་འདེབས༔

RIG DZIN JANG CHUB SEM PAI GONG PA YI
GANG ZAG LAE CHAN NAM LA JIN LAB TE
DUE TSOE DI NAE NGAB GYA THA MAI BAR
SANG NGAG KA ZHIN DRUB PAI DAM TSIG CHAN
GANG ZAG NYEN KHUNG GYUD PA LA SOL WA DEB

*By the mind of the vidyadhara bodhisattvas the fortunate ones got blessing.*
*Due to this, from that time on until the final five hundred years, those*
*vow keepers will practice according to the instructions of the tantras.*
*We pray to the lineage of those who heard teachings.*

The power of the original blessing has maintained the teaching until the final five hundred years, during which period the dharma starts to fade and become mixed with false teachings. This is the current period of time and so there is an even greater need to maintain the correct traditional practice.

འདས་པའི་སངས་རྒྱས་རྣམས་ཀྱི་ཕྱག་ཀྱི་སྲས༔
ད་ལྟར་བཞུགས་པའི་སངས་རྒྱས་རྣམས་སྐུ་ཡི་མཆོད༔
མ་འོངས་སངས་རྒྱས་རྣམས་ཐམས་ཅད་འདས་པའི་དཔལ༔
ཡོན་ཏན་ལྡན་གྱིས་གྲུབ་པའི་བླ་མ་མཆོག༔
རྡོ་རྗེ་ཐོད་ཕྲེང་རྩལ་ལ་གསོལ་བ་འདེབས༔

DAE PAI SANG GYAE NAM KYI THUG KYI SRAE
DA TAR ZHUG PAI SANG GYAE KU YI TSAB
MA ONG SANG GYAE THAM CHAE DUE PAI PAL
YON TAN LHUN GYI DRUB PAI LA MA CHOG
DOR JE THOD THRENG TSAL LA SOL WA DEB

*The heart's son of all the former buddhas, the representative of all the buddhas who are staying at present, the assembled power of all the future buddhas, most excellent guru with the very great qualities effortlessly arising, Dorje Thod Threng Tsal, we pray to you.*

This verse praises one of the wrathful forms of Padmasambhava by highlighting that he is inseparable from all the buddhas of the three times, and that his teachings and practices cannot be surpassed.

TAE PA TSAM GYI DRO NAM WANG DU DUD
DIG PA TSAM GYI DE GYED DRAN DU KOL
SAM PA TSAM GYI GOE DOD CHAR TAR BEB
UR GYEN GYUD PAR CHE LA SOL WA DEB

*By your mere glance all beings are gathered under your power.*
*By your mere command the eight classes of spirits attend you as servants.*
*By your mere thought all we need and desire falls like rain,*
*Padmasambhava with your lineage, we pray to you.*

This prayer highlights Padmasambhava's mastery of the four activities: pacifying, increasing, overawing and destroying.

## C. SADHANA: Introductory Part

རྗེ་བཙུན་པདྨའི་བྱིན་བརླབས་ཉེར་ཐོབ་ཅིང་།
སྦས་ཡུལ་གནས་སྒོ་འབྱེད་ཅིང་ཟབ་གཏེར་བཏོན།
གྲུབ་པའི་དབང་ཕྱུག་ནུས་ལྡན་རྡོ་རྗེ་ལ།
གསོལ་བ་འདེབས་སོ་བདག་རྒྱུད་བྱིན་གྱིས་རློབས།

**JE TSUN PAD MAI JIN LAB NYER THOB CHING**
**BAE YUL NAE GO JED CHING ZAB TER TON**
**DRUB PAI WANG CHUG NU DAN DOR JE LA**
**SOL WA DEB SO DAG GYU JIN GYI LOB**

*He fully gained the blessing of Padmasambhava, and opening the door of a secret land he revealed the profound treasures. The lord of the siddhas, Nuden Dorje, we pray to you to bless our minds.*

This prayer to C R Lama's first incarnation highlights his having previously been one of the twenty-five close disciples of Padmasambhava, in other words, Khe'u Chung Lotsawa, and that through that connection he went on to reveal an important collection of terma.

ཡེ་ནས་རང་རིག་གདོད་མའི་ཆོས་དབྱིངས་སུ།
ཆོས་ཀུན་རྣམ་པར་གྲོལ་བའི་སྒྱུ་འཕྲུལ་གྱིས།
མཐའ་ཡས་རྒྱལ་བའི་འཁོར་ལོའི་མགོན་གཅིག་པུ།
དབང་བསྒྱུར་གྲུབ་པའི་བླ་མར་གསོལ་བ་འདེབས།

**YE NAE RANG RIG DOD MAI CHOE YING SU**
**CHOE KUN NAM PAR DROL WAI GYU THRUL GYI**
**THA YAE GYAL WAI KHOR LOI GON CHIG PU**
**WANG GYUR DRUB PAI LA MAR SOL WA DEB**

*In the unchanging dharmadhatu of his mind's original nature*
*all phenomena were fully liberated as magical illusions and thus*
*he became the sole lord of the endless Jina's doctrines.*
*We pray to the powerful siddha guru.*

This verse is to Nuden Dorje's incarnation:

སྐལ་ལྡན་སྨིན་གྲོལ་ཨུ་རྒྱན་གླིང་མཆོག་ཏུ།
བདེ་སྟོང་ཟུང་འཇུག་འོད་གསལ་ཆོས་ཉིད་དོན།
མངོན་སུམ་སྟོན་མཛད་རོལ་བའི་རྡོ་རྗེ་ལ།
གསོལ་བ་འདེབས་སོ་མཆོག་ཐུན་དངོས་གྲུབ་སྩོལ།

**KAL DAN MIN DROL URGYAN LING CHOG TU**
**DE TONG ZUNG JUG OD SAL CHOE NYID DON**
**NGON SUM TON DZAD ROL WAI DOR JE LA**
**SOL WA DEB SO CHOG THUN NGO DRUB TSOL**

*The fortunate one who in the excellent ripening and liberating realm of Padmasambhava understood the union of happiness and sunyata, the clarity of the natural condition and could demonstrate this to others. Dechen Rolpai Dorje, we pray to you to grant us supreme and general siddhis.*

དམ་པ་དེ་དག་ཀུན་གྱིས་རྗེས་བཟུང་ཞིང་།
དུར་སྨྲིག་འཛིན་པ་བཅུ་ལ་ཞུགས་དམ་པ་ཡིས།
རྒྱལ་བསྟན་ཉིན་མོར་བྱེད་པའི་ལྷག་བསམ་ཅན།
ཆོས་ཁྲིམས་བཟང་པོའི་ཞབས་ལ་གསོལ་བ་འདེབས།

**DAM PA DE DAG KUN GYI JE ZUNG ZHING**
**NGUR MIG DZIN PA TUL ZHUG DAM PA YI**

## C. SADHANA: Introductory Part

**GYAL TAN NYIN MOR JED PAI LHAG SAM CHAN
TSUL THRIM ZANGPOI ZHAB LA SOL WA DEB**

*You who are held as a disciple by all the holy ones, most excellent determined practitioner dressed in red; you whose superior thoughts bring about the daytime of the doctrines of the Jina, Tsulthrim Zangpo, at your feet we pray.*

This verse is to Tulku Tsorlo, the main teacher and root guru of C R Lama.

**DO GYUD TAN CHOE MAN NGAG ZAB MO YI
CHOE NAM GANG LA ZHUE PAI TSA WA DANG
GYUD PAI LA MA MA LUE THAM CHE LA
TAG TU GUE PAI YID KYI SOL WA DEB**

*The possessor of all the profound dharmas of sutra, tantra, shastras and secret instructions, my root guru, and all the lineage gurus without exception, to you I pray always with a devoted mind.*

Khe'u Chung Lotsawa

Nuden Dorje

Tamdrin Wangmo

Padma Donsal

Gonpo Wangyal

Tulku Tsorlo

## C. SADHANA: Introductory Part

**GANG ZHIG DAE PAE LA MAI TSOG NAM LA**
**TSIG DI TAG TU SOL WA DEB JED NA**
**DAG SOG GYUD LA LA MA KHYE NAM KYI**
**YE SHE ZIG PAI JIN LAB JUG PAR SHOG**

*If to you, the hosts of gurus, with these words we pray always with faith*
*may there enter into our minds the blessing of being looked after*
*by the supreme knowledge of the gurus.*

Then we come to the lineage prayer. Once again it starts by addressing the dharmakaya in the first line, in the next line it addresses the sambhogakaya, and then Padmasambhava as nirmanakaya in the third line is the inseparability of all three kayas.

### Lineage Prayer

ཨེ་མ་ཧོ༔
རང་བཞིན་སྐྱེ་མེད་ཆོས་སྐུ་སྣང་མཐའ་ཡས༔
རང་མདངས་འགགས་མེད་ལོངས་སྐུ་སྤྱན་རས་གཟིགས༔
གཉིས་མེད་རང་བྱུང་སྤྲུལ་སྐུ་པདྨ་འབྱུང༔
གསོལ་བ་འདེབས་སོ་མཆོག་ཐུན་དངོས་གྲུབ་རྩོལ༔

**E MA HO**
**RANG ZHIN KYE ME CHOE KU NAN THA YAE**
**RANG DANG GAG MED LONG KU CHEN RAE ZIG**
**NYI MED RANG JUNG TULKU PADMA JUNG**
**SOL WA DEB SO CHOG THUN NGOE DRUB TSOL**

*Wonderful! Nangwa Thayae, the real nature of the unborn dharmakaya;*
*Chenresi, the natural radiance of the unceasing sambhogakaya;*

*Padmasambhava the non-dual, self-existing nirmanakaya: we pray that you will bestow supreme and general real attainments.*

Nangwa Thayae, (Sanskrit: Amitabha), is the buddha of the western paradise, Dewa Chen (Sanskrit: Sukhavati). The principal bodhisattva of that realm is Chenrezig (Sanskrit: Avalokitesvara). Padmasambhava was born from the letter Hri in Amitabha's heart.

**LAE CHEN DAG PAI KHOR NGA DROG BAN JE
ZAB TER NGA DAG NUE DAN DRO PHAN LING
SANG WAI DZOD DZIN TAM DRIN WANG MOI ZHAB
SOL WA DEB SO CHOG THUN NGOE DRUB TSOL**

*The fortunate pure circle of five and Drogban Je, and the one who has the profound treasure, Nuden Drophan Ling, and Tamdrin Wangmo who holds the secret treasure trove, at your feet we pray that you will bestow supreme and general real attainments.*

## C. SADHANA: Introductory Part

GYAL WAI NYU GU PADMA DON SAL ZHAB
SANG DZIN PA WO GYE RAB DOR JE TSAL
BI MA LA NGOE TSUL THRIM ZANG PO DANG
KA DRIN KHOR MED TSA WAI LA MA LA
SOL WA DEB SO CHOG THUN NGOE DRUB TSOL

*To Padma Donsal, the Jina's offshoot, and Sangdzin Pawo Gyerab Dorje Tsal, and the actual Vimalamitra, Tshultrim Zangpo, and my root guru whose kindness can never be repaid, we pray that you will bestow supreme and general real attainments.*

ཀུ་གསུམ་ཀུན་འདུས་རིག་འཛིན་པདྨ་འབྱུང་༔
ཡི་དམ་རྒྱལ་བའི་དཀྱིལ་འཁོར་ལྷ་ཚོགས་དང་༔
ཟབ་གཏེར་ཆོས་སྐྱོང་སྲུང་མ་ཐམས་ཅད་ལ༔
གསོལ་བ་འདེབས་སོ་མཆོག་ཐུན་དངོས་གྲུབ་སྩོལ༔

TSA SUM KUN DUE RIG DZIN PADMA JUNG
YI DAM GYAL WAI KYIL KHOR LHA TSOG DANG
ZAB TER CHOE KYONG SUNG MA THAM CHE LA
SOL WA DEB SO CHOG THUN NGOE DRUB TSOL

*Padmasambhava, the vidyadhara who encompasses all the three roots, and the wishing gods of the hosts of gods of the Jina's mandala and all the dharma protectors and guardians of the profound treasure, we pray that you will bestow supreme and general real attainments.*

དེ་ལྟར་གསོལ་བ་བཏབ་ཚོམས་ཉིད་རྗེན་པར་དོགས༔
སྣང་རིག་གསལ་སྟོང་འཛིན་འོད་ཕྱག་ཨེའི་ཁམས༔
ཕུག་མཚན་སྐུ་དང་ཡེ་ཤེས་མངོན་གྱུར་ནས༔

ག་དག་ལྷུན་གྲུབ་གདོད་མའི་རྩལ་རྫོགས་ཤོག།

**DE TAR SOL TAB CHOE NYID JEN PAR TOG
NANG RIG SAL TONG JA OD THIG LEI KHAM
CHAG TSEN KU DANG YE SHE NGON GYUR NAE
KA DAG LHUN DRUB DOD MAI TSAL DZOG SHOG**

*In accordance with what I have just prayed for, may the natural condition be realized just as it is, with appearances/ideas, fundamental awareness, lucidity, and emptiness, the sphere of balls of wisdom's rainbow light, with god's symbol, kayas and pristine and supreme knowledges becoming clearly manifest in and for me, I must truly become the primordially pure, effortlessly-arising, original and genuine flow of energy.*

With the blessing of the lineage our own nature is revealed to us, and just by this all the other aspects of teaching and practice become clear, without effort, in the great non-duality of stillness and movement.

The important thing about a practice like a lineage prayer is that it is setting out the authenticity of the production of the teaching. This means that one can have confidence that it hasn't just been invented as a fabrication of someone's mind, but it is part of a process in which many people have done the practice. So, it both carries the essence and all the power of their practice, but also it has been proved to be effective, because people wouldn't do it unless it has some benefit. This brings us to the end of the introductory part.

# D. SADHANA:
# Preparatory Practices

We're then going to the main part of the practice, which begins with

ཨོཾ་བཛྲ་ས་མ་ཡ་ཛཿ

**OM BENZA SA MA YA DZA**

*Five pristine cognitions. Keep your vajra vows. Come here!*

USING THIS MANTRA will bring an immediate identification into the state of Padmasambhava, into the state of these three kayas. What you will find in this kind of meditation text is that there is a shifting pulse, like a wave, that goes through it. At one moment we have the practice of immediately identifying with the state of Padmasambhava and then, in the very next moment, we're visualising him in front of us, and better than us. And this pulsing goes all the way through. This is very important because in our ordinary experience in daily life, sometimes we can be clear, sometimes we can be confused. Often when we get confused we then start thinking, "Oh, now I'm confused," and we dig ourselves deeper and deeper into that mood. Allowing oneself to pulse between separation and unification stops these moments being placed back-to-back as two different states and one starts to experience them more as a pulse of energy.

## a. The Visualisation

ཧྲཱིཿ རང་མདུན་ཆོས་དབྱིངས་པདྨ་ཉི་ཟླའི་སྟེང༔
སྐྱབས་ཀུན་བདག་ཉིད་རིག་འཛིན་པདྨ་འབྱུང༔
གྲུབ་བརྙེས་མཚན་མཆོག་བརྒྱད་དང་རིག་འཛིན་ཚོགས༔
རྩ་གསུམ་རྒྱལ་བའི་དཀྱིལ་འཁོར་རྫོགས་པར་གསལ༔

**HRI RANG DUN CHOE YING PADMA NYI DAI TENG**
**KYAB KUN DAG NYID RIG DZIN PADMA JUNG**
**DRUB NYE TSEN CHOG GYE DANG RIG DZIN TSOG**
**TSA SUM GYAL WAI KYIL KHOR DZOG PAR SAL**

*Hri. In the vast space before me, on top of lotus, sun and moon
is the embodiment of all the refuges, the vidyadhara Padmasambhava
with the eight excellent forms who gained siddhis and
the hosts of vidyadharas. Thus I clearly meditate
on the complete Jina's mandala of the three roots.*

## b. Refuge and Bodhicitta

ཧྲཱིཿ གདོད་མའི་རང་མདངས་སྐུ་གསུམ་བླ་མ་རྗེ༔
སྐྱབས་ཀུན་འདུས་པ་རང་རིག་པདྨ་འབྱུང༔
རིག་རྩལ་སྤྲུལ་པ་དཀྱིལ་འཁོར་ཡོངས་རྫོགས་ལ༔
རང་དོ་ཤེས་པའི་ངང་དུ་སྐྱབས་སུ་མཆི༔

**HRI DOD MAI RANG DANG KU SUM LA MA JE**
**KYAB KUN DUE PA RANG RIG PADMA JUNG**
**RIG TSAL TRUL PA KYIL KHOR YONG DZOG LA**

## D. SADHANA Preparatory Practices

**RANG NGO SHE PAI NGANG DU KYAB SU CHI**

*Hri. The primordial radiance of the reverend three-kaya guru,*
*the encompasser of all the refuges, my own awareness, Padmasambhava:*
*to the complete mandala, the emanation of the energy wave of awareness,*
*in the state of knowing my own nature, I go for refuge.*

ཧོཿ བདག་གཞན་ཀུན་བཏགས་འཁྲུལ་པས་བཅིང་པའི་འགྲོཿ
མཐའ་མེད་འཁོར་མཚོར་བྱིང་བའི་སེམས་ཅན་རྣམསཿ
ཟུང་འཇུག་རང་ངོ་ཤེས་པ་རྒྱལ་བའི་ཞིངཿ
སྨོན་འཇུག་དོན་དམ་བྱང་ཆུབ་སེམས་བསྐྱེད་དོཿ

**HO DAG ZHAN KUN TAG THRUL PAI CHING PAI DRO**
**THA ME KHOR TSOR JING WAI SEM CHEN NAM**
**ZUNG JUG RANG NGO SHE PA GYAL WAI ZHING**
**MON JUG DON DAM JANG CHUB SEM KYE DO**

*Ho! I, and all others, are the beings who are bound by the confusion of*
*reified discrimination, the sentient beings sinking in the limitless ocean of*
*samsara. The jina's realm is knowing our own nature of complete union.*
*We develop its enlightened altruistic attitude of intention*
*and practice and enter absolute bodhicitta.*

Refuge is a very important practice in buddhism. All the different buddhist traditions have some kind of refuge practice and, generally speaking, you can say the difference between a buddhist and a non-buddhist is whether they have taken refuge or not.

Now, there are formal ways of taking refuge and actual ways of taking refuge. When we recite this refuge prayer that's a formal way of doing it. We say, "This is the reality. This is the view, or this is the person, on which I rely, in which I take refuge. I use you for my protection." But that is a statement. To actually have refuge in buddhism, or in the Buddha and the dharma, and the various things we have been talking about, means that when you have a problem in your life you use the dharma to help yourself with the problem. On one level you can say, "The world is very difficult. Bad things come from the world to me, so I want to have refuge in the Buddha. Please put some wall of perspex between me and these horrible things." Unfortunately, when we start to do meditation we realise that the problems are not coming from outside. they're coming from inside. So then we say, "Please Buddha, take one piece of perspex and stick it up my ass. Separate me from all these bad things." Then we have to keep moving it around when problems come, because dharma is a wedge which at first we have to drive between ourselves and the objects of our attachment. We get hooked up on the things that we desire, the things that we want, the things that we don't want. We get hooked into pride, jealousy, and so forth. We can't put something on the outside to protect ourselves from that. We have to hold this awareness of dharma inside and use it moment-by-moment to deal with what is arising. *That* is taking refuge in the dharma.

Otherwise, we have a story: "Oh, I went to this lama and I took refuge, and he gave me a Tibetan name, and now I do this practice and so I'm a buddhist." This is not refuge. This is a new kind of identity to which you can get attached. The best refuge is to recognise the nature of your own mind. This is how we take refuge in Padmasambhava. We use him in the practice of meditation as a means for us to recognise the nature of our own mind, so that, on a relative level we can use the external form of Padmasambhava that we visualize as a means of having refuge, because he reminds us that there are some other possibilities. On an infinite level we integrate into the state of Padmasambhava. We transform ourselves through full identification with Padmasambhava, and that then gives us the direct refuge of this dharmakaya state.

We could say, to put it in western terms, that Padmasambhava is a signifier which carries many, many messages. Sometimes Padmasambhava can be a Central-Asian hero. There are many heroes in the world. He is a hero figure. He has all the features of the archetypal hero. You can see him as the person, the historical figure, who brought tantric buddhism into Tibet. You can see him as this great, powerful yogi figure, a manifestation of the sambhoghakaya who has the eight aspects, and we can also see him as this form of our own nature. It's usually helpful to be aware of the whole range of possibilities that are present in a reading of Padmasambhava, and then, according to your own situation, you can focus on the view which is going to be most helpful to you at that moment. So, if you feel sad and lonely you can pray to a papa-figure, if you want inspiration you can identify with the heroic, energetic figure, and if you want to recognise yourself, you can do the dissolving practice and stay in that state. In this refuge, it is to the lama who has the three kayas as a primordial manifestation, a primordial display, that we go for refuge. That's to say, the guru is the one who is always showing the integration of the ground wisdom and manifestation.

Maybe we need to say, just briefly, what these three kayas are, because they're often quite difficult to understand. There are many readings of the three kayas. They are not one thing but have many different understandings and interpretations. In reality, the three kayas are experience, a kind of experience. But in order to describe that experience, in order to learn about it, we have to use language, and language takes us into another world. A map is not the same as a territory, and language is not the same as experience, but we need some clarity in language in order to get the experience. However, until we get the experience, the language won't be very meaningful. When you're new to these ideas often you can end up with bit of a headache, because it just does seem very abstract and complicated.

Dharmakaya is said to be like the sky. It's open, it has no form, no shape, no taste, no colour. When we do the dissolving practice and we go into this state of light, and then all the light dissolves out, if we manage to keep our attention fully in this point of light, as we get smaller and smaller, we are merged in this object, and then it's gone. At that point your attention has nothing to rest on, but it doesn't vanish. It's there, but it's not resting on anything. You have an opening sense of awareness, present in nothing. In that state, nothing is going on.

And then, something arises. This is a very, very important point for meditators and if you don't understand the view well, you can make yourself very stupid at this point. Some people imagine that this open state of dharmakaya, because it's described in the text as being their true nature, is something they should remain in for a very long period of time without anything else happening, and so they think that having no thoughts or sensations or feelings is a good achievement. But if you have no thoughts at all, this is simply a state of the absence of arising of consciousness and, on a polemical level, this is what buddhists say that Shiva does on top of Mount Kailash. Shiva is the big enemy in buddhist tantra. Quite a few buddhist gods are dancing on top of Shiva. Not because buddhists don't like hindus, but because in the buddhist system they think that Shiva's understanding involves a state of absenting consciousness, a kind of big nothing which is the result of yoga. Yoga involves holding back, pulling back, no excitation, calming everything down, which is then held. But sooner or later, thoughts come back. Because, of course, we believe in rebirth, so even if you die, thoughts come back. That's why samsara is so horrible. You can't get out of it by cutting your wrists. You can't get out of it by an overdose. Buddhists would say Shiva tried to overdose, he overdosed on meditation. Then, when he wakes up in the accident and emergency department, "Mahadev, what are you doing here?!"

In the buddhist view, because we are concerned with non-duality, we don't hold emptiness or openness apart from manifestation, they are inseparable. Of course, at first, we know a lot more about manifestation than we do of emptiness, so we have to try to practise a lot to get the experience of emptiness. But the goal is not emptiness, it's the integration of the emptiness with manifestation. This is realised through the dharmakaya state in which, when our awareness rests in emptiness and when thoughts arise, we are directly able to experience that the thought arises out of emptiness. The big problem is, if you hold your mind calm and a thought comes, if you then experience the thought as coming at you from somewhere else, your meditation will go nowhere. This is really the big problem. This is what happens most of the time in our meditation. We are disturbed by thoughts, and we try to control the thought.

This is why they say in dzogchen there is one ground and two paths. The ground is the inseparability of emptiness and awareness. Everything arises from this ground of emptiness. If you recognise the ground of emptiness, this is the experience of nirvana. If you think, at the moment when manifestation arises, that it's coming from somewhere else or it is self-existing and is separate from the ground, this is samsara. When one has understood the difference, then the meaning of samboghakaya and nirmanakaya become clearer. Samboghakaya is the richness of the manifestation. It comes in the form of sound, and rays, and light, and this is developed in the meditation as the five-coloured rays of light coming out into the seed syllable, as we shall see later.

The second line of taking refuge is saying Padmasambhava is *rang rig*, the nature of our own mind, self-existing awareness, which is the unification of all the refuges. We have to remember that buddhism, this tantric buddhism, arose in India in a basically hindu, late upanishadic, culture. That was a culture with many, many gods, and so buddhism developed many gods and many methods. We, on the other hand, are from a monotheistic culture. We see again and again in this text the phrase *kyab nae kun due pa*, 'all the refuges are there in one form'. That's because Tibetans have many, many refuges. We don't have so many refuges, but Tibetans have many, many, many, many,

many gods, and things that they use for different purposes. What the text is always trying to say is, "Don't disperse your energy. Don't create entities out of these different deities. Their nature is all the same. If you pray to one, you get the blessing of all the others." Tibetans themselves developed the saying, that in India the yogis do one practice and get enlightened, and in Tibet we do a hundred practices and don't get enlightened. That's why, if you hang around Tibetan lamas you get many, many, many, many practices, because that's what they have, and because all the practices are good, nobody can throw them away. But the main thing is to understand the nature of your mind.

Then it goes on to say in the text, 'we take refuge in the state of recognising our own nature in this infinite mandala, which is the manifestation of the energy of our own mind.' If you had no mind, you wouldn't be worried about Padmasambhava. You have a mind, and then you learn something about Padmasambhava. Where is Padmasambhava? You can say he's in Zangdopalri. Where is Zangdopalri? Where is Freiburg? That way. Where is that way? Oh, it's just over the hill. Where is the hill? That is the most important question. If you think the hill is outside your mind you have a problem in understanding this practice. As we can see, the hill is both a concept and an experience. On the level of the concept, the hill is out there covered in snow, and I'm nice and warm in here. On the level of experience, the hill is in my mind. That's turned around, isn't it? Normally we think, "Oh the hill is a concept in my mind, but the actual experience of the hill is out there."

This second version comes because we don't understand our own experience. We don't look at the nature of the phenomenology of our own being. When we look into the nature of our mind, we find that there is no other source for experience than the nature of the mind itself. If you really understand this then it's very interesting to be in a motorcar, because the motorcar is moving in your mind. This is not an idealistic philosophy. It's not saying everything is just a phantom idea. It's saying that the mind is also the site of the manifestation of material, because material is the energy of the five elements. In these two lines it's saying this mandala of Padmasambhava is the energy of our own mind. Padmasambhava is an aspect of us. We are an aspect of Padmasambhava. That's the refuge that we take, as it says in the last line, we take this view and this is how we take refuge — in the view.

For example, I can say I will sit on this mat by sitting on it. I take refuge in the nature of my own mind by being in my own mind. How else will you take refuge in your own mind? Once your bum is on the mat there is nothing else for your bum to do. You don't need to keep getting up to see whether you're sitting down. There is a certain simple givenness to having your bum on the mat. This is the same with recognising the nature of your own mind. But if you have imagined that your mind is going to be different from how it is, even when you get to it, you keep looking for something else. That's why they say it's very difficult for scholars to get enlightened. Yet all the great nyingma lamas are scholars. C R Lama was a very great scholar. What one needs to do is to know when to bring knowledge and when to go into awareness, and that the two (until you have a lot of experience) are very difficult to bring together. So the heart of this refuge is trusting that you yourself, at this moment now, have all that is required for enlightenment. You don't have to go anywhere else to find enlightenment. You don't have to dig it up in the garden, buy it in a shop, pray to somebody else for it. It is there.

Now, just as a final point on this: that can appear a very nice idea, "Oh, it's already here." But we have been moving for a very long period of time, so we have an intention, we have a momentum. We are off-balance. And if somebody says, "It's just here" it's very hard to stop, because we want to go on. This set of impulses or momentum is what is traditionally called karma. That is why, although what we have here is the view of dzogchen, we use a practice of tantra, which is to say visualisation, prayers, music, bells and mudras, because these activities allow us to keep the momentum of wanting to do things, of being dynamically embodied, and to direct this movement in the direction of the realisation of the three kayas now. If you're driving along on the ice and the car starts to slip, the impulse can be to put on the brakes, but that's not going to work. What you have to do is to keep the car going but to direct it more forcefully, even accelerate to get a bit more energy. So we use the practice of tantra to mobilise all the energies which could knock us off-course. By skilfully managing them, we use their energy to keep us going in the right direction.

Now we turn to a brief consideration of bodhicitta. Bodhicitta itself means an enlightened mind, an awakened mind. The enlightened mind has as its quality, a movement outwards, a gesture into the world which we can call compassion. It's this mind that we try to develop. What helps us to help other people is to have some rapid understanding of why they suffer. Generally speaking, from a buddhist point of view, all suffering arises from attachment. If somebody comes and tells you, "Oh, my mother has just died, and I feel very unhappy," it's not very useful to just say, "Oh, you shouldn't be attached." Attachment is what makes us human. From a buddhist point of view being human is not such a great thing. In the christian tradition, God makes the world, and gives it to the human beings as the lords of creation.

But from a buddhist point of view, you're born human because of a mixture of pride and desire. To be human is simply some temporary hotel you're staying in. Being a good human being is not what life's all about, being enlightened is what life is all about. People who get enlightened are not human because really *we're* not human. The big spaceship of Zangdopalri has sent us all here. It's like that. We live not only in the remnants of a christian culture but in a very strongly humanistic culture, and humanism is very, very powerful. It's the basis of our liberal bourgeois democracy. It's the basis of free education and so forth. It says that all human beings have certain basic rights and entitlements, and human beings are these incredibly wonderful beings. In buddhism that's really not how we see it because we are seeing everything as manifesting according to causes, and the cause of having a human birth is certain virtue done in the past, but also a lot of attachment, and it's accompanied by confusion.

The Buddha is able to do two things well: he can comfort and he can wake up. That's also what a good therapist tries to do. He has to, or she has to, comfort the patient, give them a sense of safety and security, but at the same time wake them up a little bit. Too much comforting and it just becomes sleepy, too much waking up and it can just be a bit harsh and confusing, and then there is a reaction to it. This is what we try to develop in this practical approach, to have both a warm heart, tenderness towards people, but also a very clear reading of the structural impediments which keep people tied in their attachments and the power of the five poisons, and so forth. That's why in Tibetan buddhism there are many nice, sweet, stories about what Tara will do for you, and how everything is very sweet and nice. We all need some comforting stories sometimes! But we also need to practice some real meditation, looking into the nature of our own mind. We can only do that if we are wakened and quite sharp, and we know what we are doing. So here it's saying, 'I and all other beings who wander under the power of, and relying on, concepts have been bound in this painful dimension of samsara for a very long time, for infinite time. This is our situation.' And what this is also saying is that concepts tie us into samsara. You cannot get liberated by a concept. But concepts can be useful. You can use the concept, and then it will start to cut some freedom for you. Tibetans say that you can use butter to soften leather. You can ease it into the leather, and use it for treating it, but if you keep butter in a leather bag, the leather bag will become hard and brittle. This is an example for the dharma. If you keep the dharma inside you as a mass of concepts and knowledge it will make you hard and brittle, you will want to score points with other people and be the one who knows. Rather we should be using dharma to rub into our daily life so that it softens our nature, so that when we find ourselves becoming rigid or full of assumptions, this dharma understanding makes us more flexible, more tender, more responsive.

In the bodhicitta prayer, it says *zung jug rang ngo she pa gyal wai zhing: zung jug* means 'union', and is used to describe sexual union, inseparability. With this union we recognise our own nature. That is to say that subject and object need to become joined together. As long as we exist as a subject which is relating to objects as something separate from us, we cannot recognise our own nature. It's only when we bring together subject and object into one point, and allow that point to dissolve, then we start to see. Then we want to bring that understanding to all sentient beings, and that's why we develop this intention to awaken all beings.

The best way to help other people is to do meditation, because you are toxic, or in ordinary English, we say you're full of shit. We're all full of shit. This is what the five poisons mean. Poison is not sweet. You don't go to a patisserie to buy poison. You know, we're quite nice people. We can even have some friends, and we might find people who like us, and so forth, and we can do something to help other people, on the basis of which we can think, "Oh, I'm okay, not such a bad person." But from the point of view of dharma, when we do meditation and we look in our own mind, we see how distracted we are, how confused we are. These five poisons of stupidity, desire, anger, jealousy and pride are very powerful in all beings and we have become very good liars and cheaters because we're able to disguise from ourselves, and sometimes from other people, just how full of shit we are. One of the things that C R Lama used to say a lot about himself is, "I am liar number one, cheater number one." If we want to say this *kye gi je su da drug kyi* and we want to do like Rinpoche, then we should also say this and even have an asshole competition, because if you make friends with your own shit then you can start to recycle it, you can become a little bit ecological. This is what tantra is about. But if you don't know what is shit, you won't try to recycle it; you'll think its flowers and put it on the dining table.

Always, the first principle is to do no harm, then the second principle, try to help others. In fact, these are the same thing. If you tidy yourself up, if you stop being full of these poisons, if you develop some clarity, effortlessly you will help other people.

Many of you will know of Milarepa, who later in his life had many students around him. They were living in some caves, high up above a valley. The students came to Milarepa and said, "Oh master, down in the valley many, many people are suffering and we have been practising a long time. Shouldn't we go to help these people?" And Milarepa said, "Oh, do you think if you spend another five years doing meditation, by the time you finish there'll be no one left in the valley?" There are always people who are suffering. The fact that people are suffering doesn't mean that we should rush to help them if we don't know what we are doing.

A friend of mine was driving in Switzerland and there was a car crash in front of him. He ran over, and found there was a little girl in the front. The window had smashed, and a windscreen wiper had gone through her throat. He took out his Swiss army knife and cut her free. Luckily he was a research zoologist who was used to sticking ridiculous things into the necks of monkeys. It helps if you know what you're doing. I think, me, with a Swiss army knife, I would probably faint and stab her. It's a very important principle to work on yourself first and gain clarity. People are very, very interested to help, everybody wants to help and do something, but first of all we have to understand what the structure of the problem is. If you just get a map of the problem, you can come up with a very quick solution, "Oh, you do that and that and that," but once you start to look in yourself, you realise that this map doesn't show you very much. You realise just how fucked-up you are, how confused you are, how easily you get distracted. Then you become a little bit more humble about thinking that you can help other people. So that's important.

### The Gathering of the Accumulations of Merit and Wisdom

HRI RIG DZIN GYAL WAI LHA TSOG CHEN DREN SHEG
CHOD BUL NYE SHAG YI RANG CHOE KHOR KOR
MI DA TAG TEN GE WA YONG LA NGO
DRO KUN RIG DZIN GYAL WAI SA THOB SHOG

*Hri. We invite the divine gathering of all the vidyadhara jinas. Please come here! Presenting offerings, confessing our faults, rejoicing at the virtue of others and requesting dharma teachings, beseeching the refuges to always stay without dying, and giving away the virtue to all, by this all beings must gain the stage of the vidyadhara jinas.*

This is the seven-branch method of rapidly accumulating virtue. It is based on the method of practice developed by the bodhisattva Samantabhadra. If you have time you can say it slowly and do each part of the practice in detail. It is very wholesome and balancing.

### c. Cutting the Boundary

**HRI DAG NYID YE NAE RANG JUNG HE RU KA
TSAM CHOD THRO CHUNG TRUL PAI BAR NANG GANG
DI NA GYU ZHING TSE WAI NOD JED GEG
CHOD JIN DOD YON TOR MAI TSIM GYI LA**

*Hri. From the very beginning I have been the self-existing heruka, and I emanate boundary setting small fierce forms, filling the sky. The troublesome yakshas and obstructors who move about here I satisfy with the sacrificial object manifesting offerings and gifts having all desirable qualities.*

## D. SADHANA Preparatory Practices

མི་འགྲོ་འདུག་ན་ལྷ་སྔགས་ཏིང་འཛིན་གྱིས༔
མཚོན་ཆ་མེ་ཡིས་རྡུལ་དུ་བརླག་པར་བྱེད༔
ཧྲཱིཿ བཛྲ་གུ་རུ་ཌཱཀྐི་ཁྲོ་རྡོ་རྗེ་གནོད་བྱེད་འབྱུང་པོ་མ་ར་ཡ་ཕཊ་ཕཊ༔

NAE DIR MA DUG RANG NAE DE WAR DENG
MI DRO DUG NA LHA NGAG TING DZIN GYI
TSON CHA ME YI DUL DU LAG PAR JED
HRI BENZA GU RU DAK KI KROTA RA DZA
NOE JED JUNG PO MA RA YA PHAT PHAT

*Therefore you must not stay here but should proceed happily to your own places. If you do not go away but remain here, then with god's form, mantra and samadhi, by weapons and fire I will grind you down to dust. Hri. Vajra guru, dakini, fierce form king — yakshas and bhutas must be killed. Cut! Cut!*

With this, we move into really tantric territory. In a christian church, if it's a catholic church, up in front of the altar you have the rail, and that marks the difference between the sacred space where the priest is, where the descent into the host occurs and where the priest takes the host up to the barrier, and the other side where the ordinary people, after confession, come up to the barrier to receive the host. When we do a visualisation of the mandala what we are doing is establishing a sacred space and so we need to mark out a boundary to say, "Bad things outside, holy things inside." Luckily we are included in the holy things!

We start with the visualisation: *from the very beginning I have been the self-existing heruka*. A heruka is a wrathful form of the Buddha. That is to say that the sharpness and the clarity of wisdom is being mobilised with energy to make a difference, and by manifesting in this form we are going to frighten and bully the demons. That's why we have to have flames and wings and be covered in elephant skins, tiger skins, blood and so forth. When I was a child I used to like watching wrestling on television, and very often they would wear very big black masks so that's what we do here. It's much better if you can frighten people so they run away, than if you say, "Please go," and then they punch you. That's the reality.

The principle here is to be so full of this energy that there is no question, there is no doubt. It's like being the bouncer in a club. He just whispers, "Oh, I don't think you're coming in," and then the shoulders go up. This is what we have to see. Tantra operates on human principles. We understand what this means. You aren't polite in this. You'll be very firm, very direct, it's not for discussion. No, this is an instruction: "Fuck off!" Out of you radiate many, many of these little angry people, and they push everybody back. Also we're giving them a little *torma*, we give them a little cake. "You can't come to the party, but here's a little something for you."

This is the outer form. What is important in this is that here again we have a drama, but it is a different kind of theatre. In this you're arising as a very dangerous person. I could imagine, looking around, that many people here find it quite difficult to be dangerous. Probably quite a few of you have the experience of being nice and nice and nice and nice, and then suddenly pissed off. What this kind of practice is doing, is to help us to instantly manifest clarity, very sharp, effective clarity. To make a situation simple, and to do it early, not to wait until these people have come in and spoiled the party. They're in a corner drinking all the booze, they're touching someone's bum. That's difficult. Better to keep them outside. That's a basic principle in life, isn't it? But we also know that we often leave it too late, and then it all gets complicated. It gets mixed-in. So this is very good for mobilising energy, and that is what tantra does. It shows us ways of mobilising into different moods, different attitudes, with wholly different ways of being, very quickly, and then we can use this energy in an intentional way, with some kind of clarity about the issue, rather than in a reactive way. For, once we've been cooked-up inside by a situation where we're a little bit out of control, to avoid this we say to them, "Listen, don't stay here. Go somewhere else. If you stay here, I'll beat the shit out of you." That is what it says. This is how life is. Clarity and distraction need to be kept apart.

Monasteries in Tibet have big dogs outside, and they have high walls, because bandits come. When the bandits come, they kill people. Robbers in Tibet were murderers, you know. They would take your clothes off, on a cold winter like this in the middle of nowhere, they just take your clothes off and leave you to wander naked. There are bad people in the world and in Tibet there wasn't any police force. You couldn't just phone up, "Hello, come quickly." This is the problem. Especially because the demon is not out there. The demon is already in here. You're trying to get it from inside you, here. There's no policeman in the world can do that for you, so that's what we do here.

## D. SADHANA Preparatory Practices

### The Four-Hung Mantra

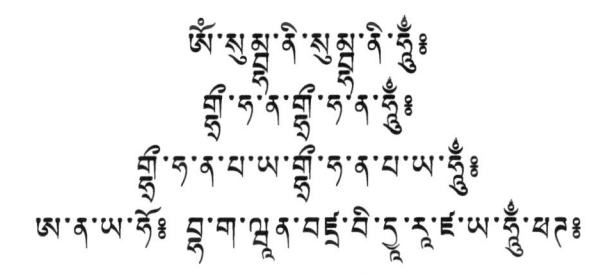

ༀ་སུམ་བྷ་ནི་སུམ་བྷ་ནི་ཧཱུྂ༔
གྲི་ཧ་ན་གྲི་ཧ་ན་ཧཱུྂ༔
གྲི་ཧ་ན་པ་ཡ་གྲི་ཧ་ན་པ་ཡ་ཧཱུྂ༔
ཨ་ན་ཡ་ཧོཿ བྷ་ག་ཝཱན་བཛྲ་བི་དྱ་རཱ་ཛ་ཡ་ཧཱུྂ་ཕཊ༔

OM SUM BHA NI SUM BHA NI HUNG
GRI HA NA GRI HA NA HUNG
GRI HA NA PA YA GRI HA NA PA YA HUNG
A NA YA HO BHA GA WAN BENZA BI DYA RA DZA YA HUNG PHAT

*The five pristine cognitions. Beat and burn, beat and burn! Catch and crush, catch and crush! Catch others, press them down and bind! Catch others, press them down and bind! Do to others! Bhagavan, indestructible natural awareness king, do this!*

In tantra there are many practices which are cutting practices, that are hard and sharp. For example, in the practice of *chod* we use the syllable *phat* a lot. Also in dzogchen teaching we use *phat* a lot. It is designed to cut, to cut a gap in the stream of your thinking so that you have some space. When we do this bit of the practice, it really helps if we can take it seriously. If we realise how demonic we are, and how demonic other people can be and how, maybe, there are dangerous spirits in the world, then we move into this practice in a powerful way. If you were living in Groznyi, in Chechnya, at this moment you would love to be able to turn yourself into a heruka. This is the situation. We should think, "We are now trying to get out of samsara. Samsara is a very difficult and dangerous place, and these people are coming to cause us trouble. If they cause us trouble, we will become disturbed, then we'll never get out of samsara. This is our last chance! This is important!" Unless it becomes important and powerful, how will it transform anything?

Now we've got these bad people out there. They've gone away, but we talk together and we say, "Listen, darling, I think we should get an electric fence put up and some of these nice bright lights. Then we'll be safe." That's why we do the protection circle. We say, "Above and below, all around us, there is this very powerful tent, made of different kinds of weapons, which can never be destroyed, and which manifests in a very powerful way to keep out all kinds of demons."

ཧྲཱིཿ སྟེང་འོག་མཚོན་ཆ་ལྔ་ཡི་གུར་ཁང་དུ༔
གཞོམ་མེད་བསྲུང་བའི་འཁོར་ལོར་ལྷུན་གྱིས་གྲུབ༔
ལྷ་འདྲེ་མིང་མེད་མཉམ་ཉིད་ཆོས་དབྱིངས་ཀློང༔
འཁོར་འདས་རོལ་པ་ཆེན་པོར་མཚམས་གཅོད་དོ༔
བཛྲ་རཀྵ༔

**HRI TENG OG TSON CHA NGA YI GUR KHANG DU
ZHOM MED SUNG WAI KHOR LOR LHUN GYI DRUB
LHA DRE MING MED NYAM NYID CHOE YING LONG
KHOR DAE ROL WA CHEN POR TSAM CHOD DO
BENDZA RAKSHA**

> *Hri. Above and below there is a complete canopy of the five weapons forming the indestructible protective circle which is effortlessly arising. In the perfect equality of the dharmadhatu where there is not even the name of local gods and demons I cut the boundary of the identical illusory nature of samsara and nirvana. This protection is very strong!*

I think it would be fair to describe this aspect of the practice as dualistic. That is to say, at this moment you are not trying to integrate the demon into your own nature, you are trying to keep it out. Again, we can see this movement in the practice between non-duality and duality, and it's just pulsing back and forth. Having put these external demons outside and made this wall to make the place safe, we have to then deal with the internal demon, so we do purification practice.

# D. SADHANA Preparatory Practices

## d. Confession

HRI RANG RIG RANG JUNG RIG DZIN KYIL KHOR DU
RANG NGO MA SHE LOG TOG NYE TSOG KUN
RANG ZHAG NYAM PA CHEN PO CHOE KUI LONG
RANG DROL DZIN MED NGANG DU ZOD PAR SOL
BENDZA SA MA YA SHUDDHE AH

*Hri. In the self-existing vidyadhara's mandala of my own genuine awareness, for all the accumulated false understandings and faults arising from not knowing my own nature, within the naturally abiding great equality of the dharmakaya, in the state of self-liberation free of grasping I ask to be excused. My vajra vows are pure in sunyata.*

གུ་རུ་པདྨ་སཱུ་བྷ་མ་ནུ་ས་མ་ཡ་ས་ཏུ་ཨཱུཿཧཱུྃ་ཕཊཿ

OM GURU PADMA SA MA YA MA NU PA LA YA
GURU PADMA TE NO PA TI SHTA DRI DHO ME BHA WA
SU TO KYIO ME BHA WA SU PO KYIO ME BHA WA
A NU RAKTO ME BHA WA SAR VA SIDDHI MA ME PRA YA TSA
SAR VA KAR MA SU TSA ME TSI TAM SHRI YAM KU RU HUNG
HA HA HA HA HO
BHA GA WAN SARVA TA THA GATA GURU PADMA MA ME MUN TSA
GURU PADMA BHA WA MA HA SA MA YA SA TWA AA HUNG PHAT

*The five pristine cognitions. Guru Padma with the power of being strong
in your vows. You must protect me and all who follow after you
and rely on you! Guru Padma, you must hear me! You must keep me!
You must think of me. Please purify all my sins. You must think strongly
of me. You must stay with me and not separate from me.
Grant me all real attainments. You must do all necessary deeds!
All subtle karmic traces, living in the heart must become emptiness.
Give me the dharmakaya, sambhogakaya, nirmanakaya and
svabhavikakaya. Victorious one, you are like all the tathagatas.
Guru Padma, please keep me strongly. Guru Padma. Great vows.
We must get attainments. We must get fulfilment of our vows.*

ཨོཾ་ས་མ་ཡ༔ ཨཱཿསམ་མ་ཡ༔ ཧཱུྃ་ས་མ་ཡ༔ བཛྲ་ས་མ་ཡ༔
བདག་གཞན་གྱི་ཚེ་རབས་འཁོར་བ་ཐོག་མ་མེད་པ་ནས་བསགས་པའི་
སྡིག་སྒྲིབ་ཉེས་ལྟུང་དྲི་མའི་ཚོགས་ཐམས་ཅད་རྩ་བ་ནས་
བྱང་ཞིང་དག་པར་བྱིན་གྱིས་བརླབས་ཏུ་གསོལ༔

OM SA MA YA AA SAM MA YA HUNG SA MA YA BEN DZA SA MA YA
DAG ZHAN GYI TSE RAB KHOR WA THOG MA ME PA NAE SAG PAI
DIG DRIB NYE TUNG DRI MAI TSOG THAM CHE TSA WA NAE
JANG ZHING DAG PA JIN GYI LAB TU SOL

## D. SADHANA Preparatory Practices

*Body vows: forgive my lapses. Speech vows: forgive my lapses.*
*Mind vows: forgive my lapses. Vajra vows: forgive my lapses.*
*I, and all beings, in all our countless previous lives have collected sins,*
*obscurations, faults, stains and causes for falling into states of sorrow.*
*All these we beg you to cleanse from the root and so bless us with purity.*

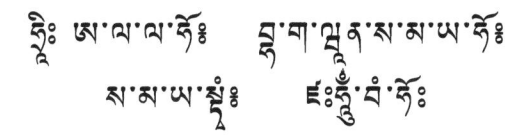

**HRI AA LA LA HO BHA GA WAN SA MA YA HO**
**SA MA YA STOM DZA HUNG BAM HO**

*Hri. Wonderful. Bhagawan, keep your vows. Give us blessing*
*according to your vows! Come! Come!*

We do a confession in which we become aware of the various faults and bad things that we have done. But here, this is a very nice confession, because it's giving an explanation of why we do things. We don't do bad things because we are bad. We become bad through doing bad things. That's important, because if we then understand why we do bad things, we will stop creating this felt sense, "I *am* bad!" Our inner nature, our real nature, is pure. We want to dissolve all the false, misleading thoughts which arise from not recognising our own nature of dharmakaya, and in this state of the recognition of the quality of the dharmakaya, we want to self-liberate all these obscurations, by remaining without attachment to them. What is really important here is the idea of self-liberation. We don't have to push away our faults, because the general principle is, if I push against the surface, unless the surface falls over, it will be exerting an equal and opposite pressure back on me. We learn that in school, in physics. It's the same principle with these emotions. If you try to push your emotions away, you become involved in them, and they become strengthened by your interest in them. The more one tries to control and constrain oneself, the more pressure builds up inside. Do you think that's real? That is a solution that only works in the short term, because sooner or later this energy of the repression will bounce out. Like a boomerang or like a spring, it will come back.

In buddhist practice we don't beat ourselves up and say, "Oh, I'm a very bad person. I have done all these terrible things." It's not because we have no discrimination and we can't tell the difference between good and bad but because blaming is a very inefficient way of trying to purify the stream of manifestation. It's paradoxical that if you just leave the very negative impulses in your mind, if you don't try to correct them, they will go free by themselves. So the best way to purify yourself is not to attempt to purify yourself but to remain relaxed and spacious.

That's because when we say, "I am a bad person," although it may be true (and a lot of things we've done are not so great) what we do in that moment of saying, "I am a bad person," is we then construct ourself according to a patterning of concepts, and give to these concepts the sense of having an inherent self-nature: I know who I am. This, according to buddhist understanding is the root of suffering and it's the form of ignorance. It is attachment to self as a concept which continues to extend itself and influence our behaviour. From the very beginning our true nature has been unborn. That is to say, it has no substantial existence.

In this cup there is some tea. If I pour it out of the cup onto the paper, the paper will become stained with tea and I will be upset, because this is my book. But when I pour it from the cup onto the book, it goes through the air. It doesn't stay in the air. This is how reality is. When we construct ourselves as an entity, we become like the book and we become stained, we become marked by the interaction. When we go into the state of recognising our own nature, we are like the space. The space takes no stain, there is no mark in the space. You put your hand through the space, it doesn't mind.

This is a very profound text. The view in this *Big Rigdzin* text is the view of non-duality, that everything is pure from the very beginning. If we really understand that, first of all as a belief and then, through the practice, as an experience, we gain the confidence to self-liberate behaviour. This takes both awareness and courage. For example C R Lama, I believe anyway, completely lived this. He was very spontaneous. He did what he liked. Sometimes he stepped on people, and he made them unhappy. On one level you can say he didn't care, because he remained in the practice. If you care what other people think you are caught in duality. But, I think, if you did an audit to count up the kind of experiences that you had around someone like C R Lama, although sometimes he made you unhappy, probably you'd end up with a general feeling that the impact of his being on our lives was quite helpful.

But if you live in a spontaneous way you have to learn how to deal with the consequences of your actions. There's no point to get a little drunk and be

## D. SADHANA Preparatory Practices

"Ha-ha-ha-ha-ha," and then after think, "Oh God, what did I say?" It's about maintaining a state of awareness whatever arises, so one manifests in the world. This has consequences. People like it or they don't like it or whatever, and you stay open to working with the consequences of that, without being conditioned by them.

From this point of view of dzogchen, real purification comes from moving beyond control. We're not trying to control ourselves and the world. We're not trying to be good and avoid being bad. We're being present in existence and moving to maintain this state of existence with the understanding that that, in itself, is not harmful to beings. Even if you have very wonderful parents, and you go to a nice kindergarten, as a child it's very difficult to grow up without getting some sense that you have to control yourself in order to be acceptable. When we try to move into this practice of dzogchen, we're having to deconstruct, to move beyond these deeply embodied feelings that unless I hold it together, unless I'm very careful, unless I'm very watchful, everything is going to go wrong. There's a lot to understand in this practice.

Then there's the hundred-syllable mantra of Dorje Sempa. This mantra, as I'm sure you know, is considered to be very, very powerful. It contains the energies of the peaceful and wrathful gods and can deal with any forms of obscuration we have.[7]

Then in the text it says:

**OM SAMAYA, AH SAMAYA, HUNG SAMAYA, BENDZA SAMAYA.**

In tantra, the way to gain entry into any kind of tantric practice is through initiation. The general structure of an initiation is that there are four initiations. There is a description of roughly the structure of these four initiations later in the text, when we have the practice of receiving the light. *(See Section E:k)*. Here it's referring to the same thing. *Om samaya* is from the first initiation, the *bumpa* initiation, or purification of the body. The meaning is, having received the initiation, we need to keep the practice.

The practice keeps the connection, and that connection is called the *samaya*. Samaya is a vow whereby we bind ourselves into the practice, onto the deity. If that is maintained, this bridge which has been constructed between the god, (here it's Padmasambhava or Dorje Sempa, they are not separate), and ourself, becomes a basis for our own recognition of our purity.

---

[7] See Chapter 4 of *Simply Being* for a detailed description of purification by C R Lama

The biggest problem for people, maybe particularly for western people, is to believe that we have buddha-nature, to believe that our real nature is pure, that essentially we are good, that we are, in our heart, in our essence, Kuntu Zangpo. Kuntu Zangpo, Samantabhadra, is the founding deity of dzogchen within the nyingmapa tradition, whose name means 'Always Good'. This is what the initiation is designed to do. The purpose of tantric initiation is to allow you to be connected with the god, and the god is nothing but the three-kaya presence, which is your own true nature. So, on the basis of saying this *om samaya, ah samaya, hung samaya, vajra samaya*, when we say these four, we reconnect. "My body is pure, my speech is pure, my mind is pure, the integrated presence of these three is pure," and then we say, "I confess, and want to have purification of all these faults that I've done." Again, if I take the tea and I pour it on my book, and the tea sinks into the paper and stains it, we think, "Oh, that's very sad." Then I take my book and I go to the tap and I put the water on and I rub my book, and it then becomes not very nice. But if I take the tea, and I pour it onto the linoleum, it sits there, it doesn't really soak in or maybe just stays on the surface, and then I can bring some water and wipe it, and it's gone. What is really important is that we have some idea of what our own nature is. Most of the time we experience ourselves as quite absorbent. We react to situations. We take things on. People say things and upset us. We live like a sponge. If we are like a sponge, or like paper, it will be very difficult to purify ourself. If we are really like linoleum, at one level, then we can wipe it off the top. This is why believing in and then realising the dharmakaya nature is very important. Our commitment to our belief, our vows and our practice makes us less permeable to the stains of samsara.

Clearly, over these days, we've had a lot of words, and it's not something that we are very used to nowadays. In Tibet the tradition of transmission of dharma involved a lot of talking. Explanations of texts would go on for months, and part of the task is to enter into a shared meditative state as you do it. The person explaining the text tries to stay close to the feeling and the realisation of the text, and those listening to the explanation of the text attempt to maintain a focused attention on what is being said. This involves both sides trying to practise non-distraction and that, of course, is hard. It's very exhausting to give sustained attention to something for a long period of time but it's quite useful for developing this ability, which we can then take into the meditation practice. Distraction is, as we've seen before, very important for us. We use distraction to try to edit and maintain our ordinary sense-of-self state. When we give focused attention we can't practise distraction, and therefore we're faced with many of the feelings and tendencies that we would normally try to get rid of. Then it goes on:

**AA LA LA HO   BHA GA WAN SA MA YA HO
SA MA YA STOM   DZA HUNG BAM HO.**

In this we take identification with the nature of both Dorje Sempa and Padmasambhava. We can do it with *mudra* and so forth, but the essential point is we relax into the state of purification. We believe this has actually happened. That's one of the functions of having mudras and mantras, to give this extra sense of almost magical, powerful truth to something, because up here in our heads, habit is a little bit thick and stupid, so you have to hit it with a hammer. If you think back to the lineage prayer, when it talks of the lineage of the nine levels of transmission, at the first level of transmission the *gyalwa gong pai gyud*, one buddha sits in meditation, and another one picks up what he's feeling. And then those who don't get it quite on that level get it on the next level, this *rigdzin da'i gyu* where somebody just makes a little sign. Then gradually the message gets more and more crude. Because we are at this sort of thick, stupid level we need a lot of reminding of something that's fairly simple, and that's why it's useful to do all the bits of the practice, because they reinforce each other and that helps the essential meaning to seep through.

## e. Invitation

HUNG UR GYEN YUL GYI NUB JANG TSHAM
PE MA GE SAR DONG PO LA
YAM TSHEN CHOG GI NGOE DRUB NYE
PE MA JUNG NAE ZHE SU DRAG
KHOR DU KHAN DRO MANG POE KOR
KHYE KYI JE SU DAG DRUB KYI
JIN GYI LAB CHIR SHEG SU SOL
GU RU PAD MA SID DHI HUNG

*Hung. In the north-west corner of the land of Urgyen, upon the stem and stamen of a lotus, are you who have the marvellous and supreme attainments, Padmasambhava of great renown, with a retinue of many dakinis around you. Following and relying on you I do your practice, therefore, in order to grant your blessings, please come here! Guru Padmasambhava, give me the real attainment of buddhahood.*

### The Descent of Blessing

## D. SADHANA Preparatory Practices

གནས་འདིར་བྱིན་ཕོབ་བསྒྲུབ་པའི་རྟགས་མཚན་སྟོན༔
མཆོག་ཐུན་དངོས་གྲུབ་སྩོལ་ལ་བར་ཆད་སོལ༔
ཨོཾ་བཛྲ་གུ་རུ་པདྨ་ཐོད་ཕྲེང་རྩལ༔
ཧ་རི་ནི་ས་ཀྲི་ཀྲོ་ཏ་སརྦ་
ས་མ་ཡ་ཕེམ་ཕེམ་ཛ་ཛཿ

HUNG HRI RANG NANG OG MIN SANG CHEN NGA YAB ZHING
NGE PA DON GYI RIG DZIN PAD MA JUNG
TSAN CHOG GYAD DANG JE BANG DAK KI TSOG
NAL JOR DAD DUNG LO YI CHEN DRANG NA
THUG JE TSE WAI NYAM NANG U RU RU
NA TSOG ROL MOI DRA YANG SI LI LI
MI KANG LING BUI DA BOD LHANG SE LHANG
DRI ZHIM POE KAR DUD PA THU LU LU
KHAN DRO GYE PAI GAR TAB SHIG SE SHIG
YI DAM LHA TSOG HUNG LU DI RI RI
CHOE KYONG DAM CHEN LAE JED KHYUG SE KHYUG
NAE DIR JIN PHOB DRUB PAI TAG TSEN TON
CHOG THUN NGOE DRUB TSOL LA BAR CHE SOL
OM BENZA GU RU PAD MA THOD THRENG TSAL
HA RI NI SA DAK KI KRO TA SARWA
SA MA YA PHEM PHEM DZA DZA

*Hung. Hri. In the natural state of Akanishta, the very secret realm of Ngayabling, is Padmasambhava, the vidyadhara of the certain original nature, with the eight excellent forms, the twenty-five disciples and the hosts of dakinis. When we yogis invite you with faithful, devoted minds your compassionate thoughts and feelings flow down, u-ru-ru. The melodies of many instruments are blending, si-li-li. The symbolic call of human thigh-bone horns is rising up, lhang-se-lhang. The smoke of fragrant white incense billows, thu-lu-lu. The dakinis dance happily, swaying shig-se-shig. The song of Hung flows powerfully from the host of wishing gods, di-ri-ri. The dharma-protectors, vow-keepers and workers rush quickly, khyug-se-khyug. Give blessing and show us the signs and symbols of practice. Grant us supreme and general real attainments and clear away all obstacles. Om. Indestructible teacher Padma Thod Treng Tsal with the vajra, ratna, padma, and karma dakinis and all fierce forms: keep your vows! Come! Come! You must really come here!*

There are many, many different kinds of invitations to the gods. Sometimes when you do this kind of invitation you can get up and dance, you can wave banners, you can burn incense. It's very sweet. Sometimes it's done with the women holding arrows with five-coloured ribbons on them and moving. We can imagine that coming out of Zangdopalri is Padmasambhava, and the others, and they're moving in a great line, and they sway. Their robes are moving and you can smell the incense. They're smiling because they're coming to a party. When we sing this, especially if you sing it on your own, you can sing it many, many times, and you can sing it very sweetly and very softly. You can cry. You can smile that they're all coming, and at the end, when it comes, you should really be trembling a little, because it's coming to *you*. As they come, they all dissolve into you — very beautiful. You can have them in front of you as well. You can have both. It's non-dual and it's dual. It's not a difference.

### f. Purifying and Blessing the Offerings

## D. SADHANA Preparatory Practices

**OM AA HUNG**
**DAG NANG TRUL PA YING KYI KYIL KHOR DU**
**THAB SHE CHI NANG SANG WAI CHOD PAI DZAE**
**ZAG MED KUN ZANG ROL PA CHOD PAI TRIN**
**TSA SUM RIG DZIN NYE PAI DZAE SU GYUR**
**OM AA HUNG**
**SARVA PANTSA AM RI TA RAK TA BHA LING TA HUNG HRI THA**

*Om, Aa, Hung. In the mandala of the dharmadhatu, the emanation of pure vision, are the outer, inner and secret offering articles of method and wisdom. They form countless magical offering clouds, pure and undefiled like those of Kuntu Zangpo and become whatever articles are pleasing to the three roots and vidyadharas. Om, Aa, Hung. All five liberating elixirs, rakta and torma must become full.*

**OM BENZA ARGHAM PHADYAM PUEPE DHUPE ALOKE GENDHE NE WI DYE SHABDA AA HUNG**

*Om. Vajra drinking water, feet bathing water, flowers, incense, lamps, perfumed water, food and sound — these offerings are pure in sunyata.*

We're asking for a kind of blessing to purify the offerings that are here, on the basis that all we experience is the actual nature of the offering. *Dag nang* means the simple nature of my experience, what's happening when I free myself from the thrall of partiality and appropriation. Every aspect of our own experience we offer. If you're sitting in the practice, and you have a sore back, and you need to pee, offer that as well. We shouldn't make discrimination between good experience and bad experience. Everything is offered as a beautiful offering. Needing to pee is wonderful because then you can have a pee and that's also very nice. If you didn't have to pee you would miss out on that whole range of sensation in your life. Sensation is just this tickling, shining edge of experience, of existence, of being alive, so this is what we offer. We offer the magical or the wonderful quality of our ordinary existence in its inseparability from its own infinitely open ground.

We offer with the mantra the five *amritas*, blood and torma. Amrita is the transformation of all the things that would usually be disgusting into things which are blissful. We need to do this because as long as we have strong reactions to certain phenomena we will be maintained in a dualistic state with them. You get different lists of the ingredients, but usually it's things like human flesh, dog flesh, shit, piss, and so forth. It's not that we should become mad, like dogs, and just run around eating anything, but there are certain experiences in the world which make us a little frightened or ashamed or fearful in some way, and these kind of experiences bring us back to our narrow sense of self. If we can have a better relationship with these liminal, these threshold articles, which would frighten us, we open to accept the world as it is. *Rak ta* is blood, two bloods: the blood of birth and the blood of death. Birth blood is the blood of menstruation, and this blood represents the shining quality of the possibility of manifestation into the world. *Bha ling ta, torma*, means killing. *Bha ling* is the thing that you kill. Traditionally in Bengal it's a goat.

When I lived with C R Lama in Shantiniketan we used to go every year several times to a little shrine nearby, where one finger knuckle joint of the goddess Parvati had fallen. After she died, Shiva kept dancing with her in his arms. Her body started to decompose and parts of it fell all over India. These sites were believed to be rich in the energy, the *shakti*, of the goddess, and so many yogis would go there. We would have a big picnic, and do some practice there. And there, there were many wooden posts, shaped like a letter Y, with a metal pin across the top. They put the goat's neck in the frame, put the pin on, and then with a big sword cut its head off. Sometimes we went to visit a Bengali brahmin family, and the old grandfather would very proudly bring out a beautiful wooden box, open it, and inside was a huge, curved knife. It was very nicely made, with silver on the top and carvings of Kali.

The village that Rinpoche used to live in, Shantiniketan, has a local train station three kilometres away which is called Bolpur. *Pur* indicates place, and *bol* is linked to *bali*, sacrifice, as *bha ling ta*. It got this name because it's said that the king of that area used to kill a thousand goats every day, so it's a killing town. In buddhism, the idea of killing is used to represent killing the demons of ignorance, stupidity, pride, jealousy, and so forth. Again, it's about taking something which is a strong, powerful human tendency, the tendency to murderous aggression and paranoid placation which we can see in every child — as adults we've usually learned to cover it over a little bit more but it's still cooking beneath the surface a bit — and use that as a metaphor in the dharma for something powerful and useful. We transform the base quality of the desire to annihilate someone into opening a space in which we can recognise our own nature. It's a central point that because tantra is working with energy and creativity and dynamic manifestation, the real enemy in that process is repression. We don't want to repress sexual tendencies, tendencies of desire, nor angry, murderous tendencies, but to mobilise both of these in the task of enlightenment. By this their rough dualistic form is softened and dissolved into the flow of non-dual energy.

Then we make another jump, because we say *om bendza argham padyam puepe dhupe aloke gendhe ne wi dye shabda aa hung*, meaning we offer these sweet, pure things, the things typical of a hindu puja. It works on the basis that if a guest comes to your house you treat them nicely. You invite the Buddha or Padmasambhava to your house and you offer some nice things, drinking water, flowers and so forth. That's a big jump from killing and blood, so you can see again the moving pulse of the puja. One minute it's all very open, raw, then it's very calm, very sweet. This is nice in life, isn't it? A good symphony has many movements in it. Tantra is training us to be dancers. Even the gods in tantra, many of them, have to get up and dance.

Clearly, life is a dance, and if we are able to dance with the various aspects of our life, it becomes easier. It's always the same: if you go to a party, someone puts on a track and everybody is dancing, then another track comes, but it's different. "I don't dance to this," people think, and they sit down. Then another track comes, people get up again. You know, most of us have just a few tunes we can dance to. We can't dance to every tune. This is very important because what that means is, we step back from life. Life sends us some little tune and we say, "I don't dance to that. I know me, and I just don't do that." In that way we betray ourselves, but we also betray other people, because maybe *they* need us to do this kind of activity. Through this practice, through identifying with these different moods and moves, we increase the repertoire of responses we can make in the world, and so we find that we have a more continuous articulation with the various profiles that day-to-day experience brings to us.

Padmasambhava

Padmasambhava and his 8 Manifestations 121

Tsokye Dorje

Padmasambhava

Loden Chogsae

Padma Gyalpo

# Padmasambhava and his 8 Manifestations

Nyingma Odzer

Shakya Senge

Senge Dradog

Dorje Drolo

# E. SADHANA: Main Part

## a. Visualisation of the Mandala and the Deity

WE RECITE *HUNG HRI, AND RELAX* in the state of emptiness, just very open, not doing anything, not busy. Then out of that state, we start the visualisation.

**HUNG HRI  CHI NANG CHOE KUN MI MIG KA NAE DAG
MA SAM DZOD PA DRAL WA DE ZHIN NYID
MA TOG DRO LA TSE WAI THUG JE DENG
LHUN DRUB RANG DANG SANG CHEN GYAL WAI ZHING
NGA YAB ZANG DOG PAL RI PAD MA OD**

*Hung. Hri. All outer and inner phenomena are pure from the very beginning and are beyond being dualistic objects. In the actuality, beyond speech, thought and expression, towards the beings who do not realize this, sympathetic compassion arises as the effortlessly appearing natural radiance of the very secret Buddha's realm, Ngayab Zangdopalri Padma Od.*

Everything which is outside, everything which is inside, is pure from the very beginning. This is the natural condition, *de zhin nyid*, which is free of, or beyond any kind of possibility of conceptualisation or expression. If you're doing the meditation by yourself, this is a very good time to stop. Do really go into this meditation, because it is a meditation instruction. In the first line *mi mig* means not to think about anything. *Mi mig* is the same as Migme, the name of C R Lama's eldest son. *Mig pa* means to focus the mind on an object. In this first line we have to free our mind from relationships with objects, external objects, as it says, then internal objects. You will need to do some extra meditation, at this point, to help yourself. For example, if you know how to do *phat*, you could do some *phat* here. If you know how to do the three *ah* practice, you do the three *Ah* practice. If you want to do a quick dissolving with the ball of light and *Om Ah Hung*, you could do this practice at this point. The point is to use any method you can to bring yourself into this state. But please, don't do *phat* when you're doing the puja with C R Lama, and especially, if you do do *phat*, don't tell him that I said that doing *phat* would be a good idea — I already have enough problems in my life! But it's very important. If you understand the principle of the puja, then you have to do what *you* need to do to support yourself, to really go into this state.

Then, there is the third line beginning *ma tog*, meaning 'towards sentient beings who have not realised this state, compassion arises.' Spontaneously, there's a radiance out of which there arises the palace of Padmasambhava, Zangdopalri. In Tibetan descriptions like this, it usually doesn't make it very clear whether you're doing this as a *dag khye*, with you yourself as the god, or as a *dun khye* with the god visualised in front of you. But as it makes it clearer later, when you come to the mantra recitation, this is really in the form of a *dag khye*. This is you, you are this. You have to imagine that out of the state of openness rays of light manifest, forming as Zangdopalri. Then you have the description of the palace, then inside the palace, Padmasambhava, and then around him these different shapes, and it's all manifesting in emptiness, free of real entities, fixed positions, relative qualities.

The first two lines embody wisdom, and out of wisdom comes compassion. That's why we should really get a little flavour of wisdom, otherwise it's only *blah blah*, and the text says, don't do *blah blah*. The text says, *mi mig ka nae dag*, not resting on objects, pure from the very beginning. If you are simply reading this text subject/object style, you are not doing what the text says and that's very bad, for you would be like a sad, depressed person with a big box of chocolates, eating them, and watching an exercise programme on television. If you want the benefit you've got to participate directly, not just think about it.

## E. SADHANA: Main Part

༄རྵེལ་ལྷོ་ཕྱོགས་བེ་དཱུརྱ་ནུབ་རཱ་ག༔
བྱང་ཕྱོགས་གསེར་དང་བ་གམ་མུ་མིན་མཛེས༔
གྲུ་བཞི་སྒོ་ཁྱུད་ཏ་བབ་རིན་ཆེན་ཏོག༔
ཚད་དང་མཚན་ཉིད་ཡོངས་རྫོགས་དེ་དབུས་སུ༔

**SHAR SHEL LHO CHOG BEDURYA NUB RA GA**
**JANG CHOG SER DANG BA GAM MU MIN DZE**
**DRU ZHI GO KYUD TA BAB RIN CHEN TOG**
**TSAD DANG TSAN NYID YONG DZOG DE WUE SU**

*The east side is of crystal, the south is malachite and the west is ruby.*
*The north side is gold and the balconies are a beautiful lapis lazuli.*
*It is square with portico, walled steps, and a jewel pinnacle,*
*and has all measurements and symbols complete and perfect.*

པདྨ་ཉི་ཟླ་ཟུང་སྦྱོར་གདན་གྱི་སྟེང་༔
རང་རིག་ཧྲཱིཿཡིག་འཕྲོ་འདུས་འོད་ཟེར་གྱུར་ལས༔
རྒྱལ་བ་ཀུན་འདུས་རིག་འཛིན་པདྨ་འབྱུང་༔
དཀར་དམར་མདངས་ལྡན་བཅུ་དྲུག་ལང་ཚོ་རྒྱས༔

**PAD MA NYI DA ZUNG JOR DAN GYI TENG**
**RANG RIG HRI YIG THRO DUE YONG GYUR LAE**
**GYAL WA KUN DUE RIG DZIN PAD MA JUNG**
**KAR MAR DANG DEN CHU DRUG LANG TSO GYE**

*In the centre, on top of cushions of lotus, sun and moon joined together*
*is my natural awareness, the letter Hri, from which rays of light*
*spread out and gather together again, completely transforming it into*
*the encompasser of all the buddhas, the vidyadhara Padmasambhava.*
*With a pink complexion, he is relaxed and youthful as a sixteen year old.*

The description is straightforward, setting out the structure of the mandala palace. It is useful to study the many depictions you can see in thangkas. The palace comes into manifestation before the figure. The situation comes before the being. One of the functions of this description is rebirth. According to the general Tibetan idea, after you died in your previous life, you entered a process of complex experience in the bardos, and then found yourself to be moving down a long, dark tunnel. You see a situation where two people are having sex, and you become very interested in their genital contact. You jump into the middle. Then conception takes place. Then you're born. Now here in the visualisation, instead of coming out of the narrow, black, tunnel driven by the winds of karma, we have a relaxed, open space in which manifestation occurs. So we are giving a new birth to ourselves, out of emptiness, in the divine form of Padmasambhava.

As you probably know, there are four kinds of birth according to buddhism: birth from an egg, birth from a womb, birth from heat and moisture, and lotus birth. Here, you get a chance for a lotus birth, *pad ma nyi da zung jor dan gyi teng*. The lotus has on top of it a sun and then a moon disk. They are joined together, and on that seat — ha! — there you are. We are born from a lotus here. We have a lotus flower with the sun and moon on top. The sun and moon on top, united together, are important.

Generally speaking, in our body we say that we have one central channel, and on either side we have two main supporting channels, out of which many, many branch channels come. For women, right side is a white channel, left side is a red channel; for men, the right hand side is a red channel, the left hand side is a white channel. Now, at the moment of conception, when the travelling consciousness comes to the site of genital contact and fertilisation takes place, this is described as the union of the white and red essences. Then the essences separate, with the white essence of the father going up and the red essence of the mother going down, and they are separated by the central channel. The foetus then develops around this.

If the white and red essences can connect in the heart, through the central channel, there is integration, but this is usually blocked until death by the turbulence of the karmic winds. The symbolism is that we exist as polarised opposites with the possibility of integration. What we have here is a structure of duality. If we can bring these two forces together into a collaborative movement then we have deep relaxation and the whole system is transformed. But as long as, if you like, the male and the female, the wisdom and compassion, are oppositional, you have no integration.

In this description we have the lotus flower and then on top of it we have the sun and moon disk. They are touching, that's what it says, *zung jor*, and because they are touching, this is the unification of wisdom and compassion. The lotus symbolises purity. The unity of wisdom and compassion are symbolised by the sun and the moon. And on top of this you manifest as the letter *Hri*, out of which rays of light go out to all the buddhas, all the wishing gods, all the yidams and so forth, making offerings. They accept the offerings and they return it, potentiated with their wisdom and their compassion. So it all comes together and transforms into the form of Padmasambhava which we are. This is why we can say he is — or we are — now the unification of all the refuges, of all the buddhas and so forth. That's why it says *gyal wa kun due*, essence of all the buddhas, *rig dzin*, person with great understanding, Padmasambhava. He is white and red in colour. He is pink in colour, but in Tibetan you have to make it by putting the white and the red together in this way, which again is the integration of the wisdom and compassion. And he's just sixteen. We're young again, young at heart!

## b. Padmasambhava and his Manifestations

ཞལ་གཅིག་ཁྲོ་འཛུམ་སྤྱན་གསུམ་འགྲོ་ལ་གཟིགས༔
གཡས་པས་རྡོ་རྗེ་རྩེ་ལྔ་སྡིགས་མཛུབ་གདེངས༔
གཡོན་པས་བྷན་དྷ་ཚེ་བུམ་ཉི་ཟླའི་མཛེས༔
ཐེག་གསུམ་ཆས་རྫོགས་སྐུ་ལ་གསང་གོས་དང༔
ཆོས་གོས་རྣམ་གསུམ་ཟ་འོག་བེར་ཆེན་གནབ༔

**ZHAL CHIG THRO DZUM CHEN SUM DRO LA ZIG**
**YAE PA DOR JE TSE NGA DIG DZUB DENG**
**YON PAE BHAN DHA TSE BUM NYI DAI DZE**
**THEG SUM CHAE DZOG KU LA SANG GOE DANG**
**CHOE GOE NAM SUM ZA OG BER CHEN NAB**

*He has one face which smiles yet displays a little anger and three eyes which look on all beings. His right hand brandishes a five pointed vajra in the subduing gesture. His left hand holds a skull cup with a long life pot beautified with a sun and moon. With the complete dress of the three yanas, on his body he has the white secret gown, and the dharma robes and a very fine great gown.*

These items indicate that he embodies all possibilities: he is a yogi, a monk, a king and has power in all domains. Being unimpeded, he links all manifestation.

དབུ་ལ་མཉེན་ཞུ་གོད་སྒྲོ་དར་སྣས་བརྒྱན༔
རིན་ཆེན་རྒྱན་སྤྲས་ཁ་ཊྭཱཾ་གྲུ་མོར་བསྟེན༔
སག་ལྷམ་གསོལ་ཞིང་སྐྱིལ་ཀྲུང་ཏིང་འཛིན་མཉེས༔
སྐུ་ལ་སྒྲུབ་པ་བཀའ་བརྒྱད་དཀྱིལ་འཁོར་རྫོགས༔
རྒྱལ་ཀུན་གསང་གསུམ་མི་བསྐྱོད་ཐུགས་རྡོ་རྗེ༔
ཕྲིན་ལས་ནུས་སྟོབས་རྫོགས་པའི་དོ་བོར་གསལ༔

**WU LA NYEN ZHU GOD DRO DAR NAE GYEN**
**RIN CHEN GYEN TRAE KHA TAM DRU MOR TEN**
**SAG LHAM SOL ZHING KYIL TRUNG TING DZIN NYE**
**KU LA DRUB PA KAB GYAD KYIL KHOR DZOG**
**GYAL KUN SANG SUM MI KYOD THUG DOR JE**
**THRIN LAE NUE TOB DZOG PAI NGO WOR SAL**

*On his head is the nyenzhu hat decorated with a vulture feather and five coloured silk. Adorned with jewel ornaments he holds a khatvanga in the crook of his elbow. Wearing shoes with curled points he sits in samadhi in lotus posture. Within his body are the complete mandalas of the eight heruka sadhanas. His mind vajra is the unchanging body, speech and mind of all the jinas. Meditate clearly on his nature having the complete effective powerful activities.*

The following description of the meaning of Padmasambhava's symbols comes from Rigdzin Godem in the Byangter lineage:

> 'Hung. Padmasambhava having the three kayas of body, speech and mind, you are the active representative of the jinas who stops the troubles of samsara. Due to your great compassion you incarnate in order to lead out all those who move in samsara — salutation and praise to the guide of all beings.
>
> You have a vulture's feather on top of your hat, the sign of the vast spreading of supreme and pristine knowledge with the completion of sadhana practice. You wear a very powerful and splendid hat, the sign that you understand the mahayana view. The hair on your head is piled up and tied in a bun, the sign of your encompassing all the buddhas of the three times within yourself.
>
> With your three eyes you look strongly on those who move in samsara, the sign of your guiding all beings to liberation by means of great compassion. Your smiling face is attractive with a good colour, the sign that you lead those who move in samsara to salvation by means of love and compassion.
>
> On your body you wear a great gown of luxurious brocade, the sign that in your body the gods of the eight great practices are complete and clear. You wear the very red dharma robes, the sign of your having the ethical practice of very pure vows. On your body you wear a very splendid and imposing gown, the sign that you overwhelm those who move in the samsaric states of gods, nagas and humans.
>
> In your right hand you hold a golden vajra, the sign that with the five supreme and pristine knowledges you destroy those who seduce you with false views. In your left hand you hold a skull of liberating elixir, the sign that you bestow real attainments upon practitioners. You hold a three pointed khatvanga against your body, the sign that with you method and superior knowledge are always united.

*Your two feet are seated in the unchanging posture, the sign that you are
never separate from the dharmakaya. You sit on cushions of lotus,
sun and moon, the sign that you put an end to the troubles of samsara's
afflictions. You make the powerful sound of the long and short Hungs,
the sign that you put the goddesses and dakinis under your power.*

*Around you is a rainbow aura from which rays of light come out,
the sign of your leading those who move in samsara to liberation
by the method of compassion. Padmasambhava, the Jina's son,
you who encompass all the buddhas within yourself, you who with many
different methods lead those who move in samsara to liberation,
Padmasambhava, to your body we make salutation and praise'.*

གཡས་སུ་ལྷ་ལྕམ་མནྡ་ར་བ་དཀརཿ
གཡས་པས་མདའ་དར་གཡོན་པས་ཚེ་བུམ་བསྣམསཿ
འཆི་མེད་ཚེ་ཡི་ལྷ་མོའི་དོ་བོར་བཞུགསཿ
གཡོན་དུ་ཡེ་ཤེས་མཚོ་རྒྱལ་སྐུ་མདོག་སྨུགཿ
ཕྱག་གཉིས་ཐོད་པའི་བདུད་རྩི་གཙོ་ལ་སྟོབསཿ
གཉིས་ཀ་ཆེད་སྐྱིལ་དགྱེས་པའི་ཉམས་སུ་བཞུགསཿ

**YAE SU LHA CHAM MAN DA RA WA KAR
YAE PAE DA DAR YON PAE TSE BUM NAM
CHI MED TSE YI LHA MOI NGO WOR ZHUG
YON DU YE SHE TSO GYAL KU DOG MUG
CHAG NYI THOD PAI DUD TSI TSO LA TOB
NYI KA CHED KYIL GYE PAI NYAM SU ZHUG**

*On his right side is princess Mandarava, white in colour with an arrow
with silk tassels in her right hand and a long-life pot in her left. She has
the nature of the goddess of immortal life. On his left is Yeshe Tsogyal
whose body is maroon. With her two hands she serves Padmasambhava
with a skull-cup of liberating elixir. Both are sitting with a happy feeling.*

# E. SADHANA: Main Part

དེ་ཕྱིར་པདྨ་འདབ་བརྒྱད་ཡངས་པའི་སྟེང་༔
ཤར་དུ་མཚོ་སྐྱེས་རྡོ་རྗེ་སྐུ་མདོག་མཐིང་༔
རུས་རྒྱན་སྐྱིལ་ཀྲུང་རྡོ་དྲིལ་ཐུགས་ཀར་བསྣོལ༔
ལྷ་ལྕམ་བདེ་བའི་ཀྐྲི་མཉམ་པར་འཁྲིལ༔

**DE CHIR PAD MA DAB GYAD YANG WAI TENG
SHAR DU TSO KYE DOR JE KU DOG THING
RUE GYEN KYIL TRUNG DOR DRIL THUG KAR NOL
LHA CHAM DE WAI DAK KI NYAM PAR THRIL**

*Beyond them on top of the eight spread-out petals of a lotus
are the following figures: to the east is Tsokye Dorje with a blue body.
He wears bone ornaments and sits in lotus posture holding a vajra
and bell crossed at his heart. He is fully joined in union
with his consort, the happy dakini.*

ལྷོ་རུ་པདྨ་སམྦྷ་སྐུ་མདོག་དཀར༔
སྐུ་ལ་དར་དམར་ཆོས་གོས་གཡས་པ་ཡིས༔
སྐྱབ་སྦྱིན་གཡོན་པས་མཚོག་སྦྱིན་བྷནྡྷ་བསྣམས༔

**LHO RU PAD MA SAM BHA KU DOG KAR
KU LA DAR MAR CHOE GOE YAE PA YI
KYAB JIN YON PAE CHOG JIN BHAN DHA NAM**

*To the south is Padmasambhava with a white body.
He wears the red dharma robes and with his right hand he grants
protection while with his left he holds a skull cup in the offering gesture.*

ཉུབ་ཏུ་བློ་ལྡན་མཆོག་སྲིད་སྐུ་མདོག་དཀརཿ
སྐུ་ལ་བེར་དཀར་དབུ་ལ་དར་ཐོད་གསོལཿ
གཡས་པས་ཌཱ་རུ་གཡོན་པས་བྷན་དྷ་བསྣམསཿ

**NUB TU LO DAN CHOG SE KU DOG KAR
KU LA BER KAR WU LA DAR THOD SOL
YAE PAE DA RU YON PAE BHAN DHA NAM**

*To the west is Loden Chogsae who is white.
On his body is a white gown and on his head he wears a turban. With
his right hand he holds a damaru and with his left he holds a skull.*

བྱང་དུ་པདྨ་རྒྱལ་པོ་སྐུ་མདོག་དམརཿ
སྐུ་ལ་བེར་དམར་དབུ་ལ་ལྭ་ཐོད་བསོལཿ
ཕྱག་གཡས་ལྕགས་ཀྱུ་གཡོན་པས་བྷན་དྷ་བསྣམསཿ

**JANG DU PAD MA GYAL PO KU DOG MAR
KU LA BER MAR WU LA LA THOD SOL
CHAG YAE CHAG KYU YON PAE BHAN DHA NAM**

*To the north is Padma Gyalpo who is red in colour.
On his body is a red gown and on his head is a very large turban.
In his right hand he has an iron hook and with his left he holds a skull.*

འར་ཕྱོ་ཉི་མ་འོད་ཟེར་སྐུ་མདོག་སེརཿ
སྐུ་ལ་ཨང་རག་སྲུག་འམ་རྣམ་རྒྱན་སྤྲསཿ
ཕྱག་གཉིས་ཉི་ཟེར་ཕྱི་གས་མཛུབ་ཁྲོ་བསྣམསཿ

## E. SADHANA: Main Part

**SHAR LHO NYI MA OD ZER KU DOG SER
KU LA ANG RAG TAG SHAM RUE GYEN TRAE
CHAG NYI NYI ZER DIG DZUB KHA TAM NAM**

*To the south-east is Nyima Odzer who is yellow in colour. On his body he wears angrag shorts and a tiger skirt and is adorned with bone ornaments. He has two hands and makes the subduing gesture with the sun's rays and holds a tantric trident.*

**LHO NUB SHA KYA SENG GE KU DOG SER
CHOE GOE NAM SUM TRUL KUI CHAE KYI GYAN
CHAG YAE SA NON YON PA LHUNG ZE NAM**

*To the south-west is Shakya Senge who is yellow in colour. He is adorned with the nirmanakaya dress of the three dharma robes. His right hand touches the earth and his left holds a bhikshu's begging bowl.*

**NUB JANG SENG GE DRA DROG KU DOG THING
THRO TUM CHAE DZOG KU TOD SENG PAG TRI
CHAG YAE DOR JE YON PAE DIG DZUB DZE**

*To the north-west is Senge Dradog who is blue in colour.
He wears the complete dress of a heruka and the upper part of his body
is draped with a lion skin. His right hand holds a vajra and
his left shows the subduing gesture.*

བྱང་ཤར་རྡོ་རྗེ་གྲོ་ལོད་སྐུ་མདོག་སྨུག༔
སྨ་ར་ཨག་ཚོམ་སྨིན་མ་མེ་ལྟར་འབར༔
ཆོས་གོས་གཡོན་དཀྱིས་མི་མགོའི་ཕྲེང་བས་བརྒྱན༔
ཕྱག་གཉིས་རྡོ་རྗེ་ཕུར་འཛིན་སྟག་མོའི་ཁྲིར༔
འགྱིང་ཞིང་འཚོལ་གཏུམ་དྲག་པོའི་སྐུ་རུ་གསལ༔

JANG SHAR DOR JE DRO LO KU DOG MUG
MA RA AG TSOM MIN MA ME TAR BAR
CHOE GOE YON TRI MI GOI TRENG WAI GYEN
CHAG NYI DOR JE PHUR DZIN TAG MOI TRIR
GYING ZHING CHOL TUM DRAG POI KU RU SAL

*To the north-east is Dorje Drolo who is reddish-brown in colour.
His whiskers, beard and eyebrows blaze out like fire. He wears dharma robes
draped over his left shoulder and is adorned with a necklace of human skulls.
His two hands hold vajra and kila and his throne is a tigress. His wild and
very fierce body is in the champion's posture. Meditate clearly like that.*

དེ་ཡི་ཕྱི་རོལ་ཀཱི་རིགས་བཞི་དང་༔
དཔའ་བོ་གིང་དང་རིག་འཛིན་རྣམ་པ་བཞི༔
ད་གྱུད་སྒྲོ་སྦྱོང་ཆོས་སྲུང་དམ་ཅན་ཚོགས༔
སྟོང་གསལ་མདངས་ལྡན་མ་འགགས་རིག་པའི་རྩལ༔
ཨེ་ཤེས་སྙིང་པོ་འོད་ཀྱི་སྐུ་རུ་གསལ༔

**DE YI CHI ROL DAK KI RIG ZHI DANG
PA WO KING DANG RIG DZIN NAM PA ZHI
TA KRID GO KYONG CHOE SUNG DAM CHAN TSOG
TONG SAL DANG DEN MA GAG RIG PAI TSAL
YE SHE NYING PO OD KYI KU RU SAL**

*Further out from them are the dakinis of the four kulas, and the heroes, the agents and the four classes of vidyadharas, the Takrid door protectors, with the hosts of dharma guardians and vow-keepers. With the radiance of voidness and clarity they are the unceasing flow of natural awareness. Meditate on them clearly as the light bodies of the pristine cognition essence.*

One of the things I think our culture is becoming more aware of now is the fact that identity is pluralistic. That is to say that all of us have sub-personalities, or self-states, or divergent tendencies which manifest in different situations. In the area of psychiatry and psychotherapy there is more and more a sense that many people manifest in what's called a borderline state. 'Borderline' means somebody who is finding it difficult to maintain a unitary kind of presentation in the world. Generally speaking, we can say of ourselves, "Oh, sometimes I'm very sad. Sometimes I'm very angry. Sometimes I'm very sweet," whatever it is. But if our central sense of self, our core self, is not very strong, we become less able to manage these different tendencies and they tend to split off. Then we jump from one position to another, often in response to an external trigger of stress or aggression. One of the demands from the culture is that we should be consistent, because, as we've seen earlier, to be consistent means that other people can predict how we're going to be and that then allows them to feel safe and relaxed near us. But nonetheless, we are complex, we are not just one thing.

These eight forms of Padmasambhava offer a method of showing how we can respond to different situations in different ways, and at the same time maintain a sense of integrity. We have to see this in terms of its historical context. What you usually have, in the original structure, are monks and nuns and lay people. Then, as tantra starts to develop, you have monks, nuns, lay people and yogis. Generally speaking, if you're a monk, you can't be a lay person. Monks live in monasteries so you can't really be a yogi either. I don't mean somebody who practises yoga but somebody who lives like a yogi. So we can say that these categories then become different and you have to make a choice which one you are going to be in. In order to take up a position in the world which is understandable to other people you have to close down on some other options of your existence. But what Padmasambhava demonstrates here is that he can show the form of a monk, he can show the form of a yogi, he can show the form of a very terrifying figure, and of a very, very sweet king. Different ways of being in the world are brought together through one central identity which doesn't self-limit. That's very important. One of the things it's opening out is the possibility that we can have not just different internal moods but that we can really manifest in different ways in the world.

Remember there was a song, "I'm a woman, w-o-m-a-n," you remember that song? It was very popular. No? Anyway, it's a very nice, strong, feminist song about this woman saying, "I can get up early in the morning, I clean the house, I take the children to school, I come back, I do this, I do that," describing a whole day. What she's describing is that to be a woman you have to turn your face in many directions and become different kinds of people; you could be a mother, a lover, you maybe have a job. Clearly, that's difficult. It's difficult for men as well. If you're working outside or in an office and you're full of work problems, when you come home and open the door, and there's a little child saying, "Oh, play, play!" you think, "Oh, please! I've just got back! Go away!"

So one of the things that we try to do when we move through these different identities is to go fully into an identity and then out of it and into the next identity. What we often experience is: we get into one mode, one mood, when we're at work and then we leave work but that mood goes with us. We're still caught up in our head about things that other people said, or things they didn't do, and we come home in the state of work. We arrive at home, and we are still at work. Or you go to bed and your friend wants to have sex, and you think, "I'm not even here! I'm not in my body, so how am I going to have sex with you?" This is a way in which attachment operates. Attachment is not just a conscious going out and attaching ourselves to something. More than that, it means that we get caught up in situations, conditioned by them, and then we can't leave them, so we are always off-balance, going from one situation to another without really arriving in a simplicity.

We could say that the central figure in the mandala is the core identity, Padmasambhava. All the other figures are extentions of him. In thangkas, Tibetan icons, the central figure is often depicted as larger in size than the rest, to indicate his/her special importance. Padmasambhava is the chief, the boss, yes, but its important to see that this is an organising function, a way of allowing the orderly structure of manifestation, which is often hidden in the chaotic hurly-burly of our daily lives. Each deity holds implements, which indicate particular activities, for example, a hook to control, a bell to subdue with wisdom, and so forth. The range of figures indicates that the four activities are fully attended to. They are: *pacifying* hunger, war, calamity, sickness and so on, *increasing* health, wealth, happiness and so forth, *overawing* enemies, troublemakers, political hot-spots etc., and *destroying* aggressive acts, upswellings of malicious intent, the deep hostility of the paranoid ego and so forth. The patterning of the mandala indicates that complex activity can be carried out, without contradictions, with the central figure of Padmasambhava as the source and reference point.

In the same way, we often have a core sense of self, our familiar sense of who we are, and when we behave in other ways, we make excursions from that core, and then return to it. To lose that core reference point, as in a profound depression, is very frightening. A central point, a core site/sense of identity is important. However, our ordinary identity is reified, essentialised and reinforced with personal narratives, in other words, we maintain this construct by the ways we think, talk, and act. Whereas, in this mandala the central figure and all the other figures have the same nature; Padmasambhava has no greater reality than the rest. As the last two lines of the description indicate, all the figures are the radiance of emptiness and clarity, a ceaseless flow of the energy of awareness. All the figures are form and emptiness, displaying the luminosity of the natural condition, your own nature. Thus the mandala shows an absolute equality, a one-taste, in the relation of manifestation to its ground, while simultaneously showing differentiation of function. This is vital to understand, especially for us living in such competitive times. The key point is the relation with the ground, with dharmadhatu: *this* is liberation. The forms that we take, our manifest functions in the world, are less important, for they do not define our value. That is given, it just is, pure from the very beginning.

If you have the time, you could try to spend a whole day doing this *Big Rigdzin* puja, and when you come to this part, you read the description of each of these deities, and then you try to live just in that part for maybe half an hour. So if you take the form, as it has here, of Padmasambhava in this form of a monk, and you have a cup of tea, you might like to drink it very sweetly, in a very nice way and then, if you become Senge Dradrog, or Dorje Drolo, you might like to fill a big bucket with beer and maybe have some red meat and eat it raw, and have the blood run — raw liver! In that way you really try to get the flavour of what the expression in this form is because it's not an abstract conceptual idea, it's a permission to open up and express a particular kind of energy. So, if you do Dorje Drolo, you can stand up and "Haaargh, huuuh!" and you really feel this in your body. You really feel, you can feel these flames coming up. Then, later, when you do the puja with other people, when you come to this part, it arises in your body as sensation and not just as a cognition. We are not becoming somebody else. What we are doing is having an energetic display which is arising in this form and then the energy dissolves back again. Then we go out in another form. Then we come back again.

### c. The Invocation

Then we have the invocation, which is the Seven Line Prayer plus three additional lines:

ཧཱུྃ༔ ཨོ་རྒྱན་ཡུལ་གྱི་ནུབ་བྱང་མཚམས༔
པདྨ་གེ་སར་སྡོང་པོ་ལ༔
ཡ་མཚན་མཆོག་གི་དངོས་གྲུབ་བརྙེས༔
པདྨ་འབྱུང་གནས་ཞེས་སུ་གྲགས༔
འཁོར་དུ་མཁའ་འགྲོ་མང་པོས་བསྐོར༔
ཁྱེད་ཀྱི་རྗེས་སུ་བདག་བསྒྲུབ་ཀྱིས༔
བྱིན་གྱིས་བརླབ་ཕྱིར་གཤེགས་སུ་གསོལ༔
གུ་རུ་པདྨ་སིདྡྷི་ཧཱུྃ༔

# E. SADHANA: Main Part

ༀ་ཨཱཿཧཱུྃ་བཛྲ་གུ་རུ་པདྨ་ས་མ་ཡ་ཛཿཛཿ

HUNG NGON GYI KAL PAI DANG PO LA
UR GYEN YUL GYI NUB JANG TSHAM
DHA NA KO SHAI TSO LING DU
PE MA GE SAR DONG PO LA
YAM TSHAN CHOG GI NGO DRUB NYE
PE MA JUNG NAE ZHE SU DRAG
KHOR DU KHAN DRO MANG PO DANG
RIG DZIN DRUB THOB GYAM TSOE KOR
KHYE KYI JE SU DAG DRUB KYI
JIN GYI LAB CHIR SHEG SU SOL
GU RU PADMA SID DHI HUNG
OM AH HUNG BENDZA GURU PADMA SA MA YA DZA DZA

*Hung. In the first of the previous aeons, in the north-west corner of the land of Urgyen, on an island in the lake of Dhanakosha, upon the stem and stamen of a lotus, are you who have the marvellous and supreme real attainments, Padmasambhava of great renown. As retinue many dakinis and vidyadharas and siddhas surround you. Following and relying on you I do your practice, therefore, in order to grant your blessings, please come here! Guru Padmasambhava, give me the real attainment of buddhahood. Indestructible Guru Padmasambhava having the three kayas, keep your vows. Come! Come!*

In the time before time, at the very, very, very beginning of the world, which has no beginning, in the north-west land of Urgyen, on an island in the Dhanakosha lake, which is where Padmasambhava was born, is Padmasambhava surrounded by many dakinis and by the great yogis and saints. This verse is frequently used at the time of invocation, and you will find it in many nyingmapa texts. It is very helpful to support your practice by reading the biographies of Padmasambhava. More of these are being translated, and they help to give us a sense of both the symbolic and emotional significance of this prayer. Then we recite the Seven Line Prayer three times:

ཧཱུྃ༔ ཨུ་རྒྱན་ཡུལ་གྱི་ནུབ་བྱང་མཚམས༔
པདྨ་གེ་སར་སྡོང་པོ་ལ༔
ཡ་མཚན་མཆོག་གི་དངོས་གྲུབ་བརྙེས༔
པདྨ་འབྱུང་གནས་ཞེས་སུ་གྲགས༔
འཁོར་དུ་མཁའ་འགྲོ་མང་པོས་བསྐོར༔
ཁྱེད་ཀྱི་རྗེས་སུ་བདག་བསྒྲུབ་ཀྱིས༔
བྱིན་གྱིས་བརླབ་ཕྱིར་གཤེགས་སུ་གསོལ༔
གུ་རུ་པདྨ་སིདྡྷི་ཧཱུྃ༔

**HUNG UR GYEN YUL GYI NUB JANG TSHAM**
**PE MA GE SAR DONG PO LA**
**YAM TSHEN CHOG GI NGOE DRUB NYE**
**PE MA JUNG NAE ZHE SU DRAG**
**KHOR DU KHAN DRO MANG POE KOR**
**KHYE KYI JE SU DAG DRUB KYI**
**JIN GYI LAB CHIR SHEG SU SOL**
**GU RU PAD MA SID DHI HUNG**

*Hung. In the north-west corner of the land of Urgyen, upon the stem and stamen of a lotus, are you who have the marvellous and supreme attainments, Padmasambhava of great renown, with a retinue of many dakinis around you. Following and relying on you I do your practice, therefore, in order to grant your blessings, please come here! Guru Padmasambhava, give me the real attainment of buddhahood.*

After that we invite the pure, spontaneous forms of the deities to come into the mandala that we have visualised:

## E. SADHANA: Main Part

HUNG HRI
UR GYEN YUL GYI GYAM TSOI NUB JANG TSAM
PAD MA TONG DEN GE SAR ZHAD PAI WUE
DE SHEG GYAL KUN THUG JE TRUL PAI KU
GU RU PAD MA JUNG NAE ZHE SU DRAG
DE TONG GYE DE DAK KI DAM CHEN CHE
DAE GUE MOE DUNG LO YI CHEN DREN NA
CHOG CHU GAR ZHUG DAG PA SANG CHEN ZHING
NGA YAB ZANG DOG PAL RI PHO DRANG NAE
UR GYEN THOD THRENG YAB YUM SHEG SU SOL

*Hung. Hri. In the north-west of the ocean in the land of Urgyen, in the centre of the fully open stamen of a lotus with a thousand petals, is the emanation of the compassion of all the sugata jinas, Guru Padmasambhava of great renown. Together with those who have the joys of happiness and sunyata, the dakinis and vow-keepers. When we invite you with yearning minds full of faith and devotion, from wherever you stay in the ten directions, from the very secret realm of the palace of Ngayab Zangdopalri, Urgyen Thod Threng and your consort, please come here!*

༄༅། །ཌཱ་ན་ཀོ་ཤའི་ཡུལ་གྱི་མཚོ་གླིང་ནས༔
གུ་རུ་མཚོ་སྐྱེས་རྡོ་རྗེ་གཤེགས་སུ་གསོལ༔
རྨོངས་པའི་མུན་པ་མ་ལུས་སེལ་མཛད་པའི༔
གུ་རུ་བློ་ལྡན་མཆོག་སྲེད་གཤེགས་སུ་གསོལ༔

**DHA NA KO SHAI YUL GYI TSO LING NAE**
**GU RU TSO KYE DOR JE SHEG SU SOL**
**MONG PAI MUN PA MA LUE SEL DZAD PAI**
**GU RU LO DEN CHOG SE SHEG SU SOL**

*From the lake in the land of Dhanakosha, Guru Tsokye Dorje,*
*please come here! You who clear away all the darkness of stupidity,*
*Guru Loden Chogsae, please come here!*

ཤེས་བྱའི་ཆོས་ལ་བློ་གྲོས་མ་རྨོངས་པའི༔
གུ་རུ་པདྨ་སམྦྷ་གཤེགས་སུ་གསོལ༔
ཁམས་གསུམ་སྲིད་གསུམ་དབང་དུ་སྡུད་མཛད་པའི༔
གུ་རུ་པདྨ་རྒྱལ་པོ་གཤེགས་སུ་གསོལ༔

**SHE JAI CHOE LA LO DROE MA MONG PAI**
**GU RU PAD MA SAM BHA SHEG SU SOL**
**KHAM SUM SID SUM WANG DU DUD DZAD PAI**
**GU RU PAD MA GYAL PO SHEG SU SOL**

*You whose intellect is not dulled regarding the phenomena*
*that can be known, Guru Padmasambhava, please come here!*
*You who put the three spheres and the three worlds under your power,*
*Guru Padma Gyalpo, please come here!*

# E. SADHANA: Main Part

སྐྱེ་མེད་རང་བྱུང་ཡེ་ཤེས་དོན་སྟོན་པའི༔
གུ་རུ་ཉི་མ་འོད་ཟེར་གཤེགས་སུ་གསོལ༔
བདུད་བཞི་ཟིལ་གནོན་ལམ་རྣམས་མཐར་ཕྱིན་མཛད༔
གུ་རུ་ཤཱཀྱ་སེང་གེ་གཤེགས་སུ་གསོལ༔

**KYE MED RANG JUNG YE SHE DON TON PAI**
**GU RU NYI MA OD ZER SHEG SU SOL**
**DUD ZHI ZIL NON LAM NAM THAR CHIN DZAD**
**GU RU SHAK YA SENG GE SHEG SU SOL**

*You who teach the original nature of the unborn,*
*self-occurring pristine cognition, Guru Nyima Odzer, please come here!*
*You who overawed the four maras and completed the stages and ways,*
*Guru Shakya Senge, please come here!*

མུ་སྟེགས་བདུད་དཔུང་ཕྱེ་མར་བཅག་མཛད་པའི༔
གུ་རུ་སེང་གེ་སྒྲ་སྒྲོགས་གཤེགས་སུ་གསོལ༔
དགྲ་བགེགས་དམ་སྲི་མ་ལུས་འདུལ་མཛད་པའི༔
གུ་རུ་རྡོ་རྗེ་གྲོ་ལོད་གཤེགས་སུ་གསོལ༔

**MU TEG DUD PUNG CHE MAR LAG DZAD PAI**
**GU RU SENG GE DRA DOG SHEG SU SOL**
**DRA GEG DAM SI MA LUE DUL DZAD PAI**
**GU RU DOR JE DRO LOD SHEG SU SOL**

*You who grind the throngs of tirthikas and maras down to dust,*
*Guru Senge Dradog, please come here! You who subdue all the enemies,*
*obstructors and vow-troublers, Guru Dorje Drolo, please come here!*

བདེ་སྟོང་དགའ་བཞིའི་འོད་ཕུང་འབར་བའི་ཀློང་ཾ
རིག་འཛིན་དཔའ་བོ་མཁའ་འགྲོ་གཤེགས་སུ་གསོལ་ཾ
ཕྲིན་ལས་བཞི་བསྒྲུབ་ཆོས་སྲུང་དམ་ཚིག་བདག་ཾ
བཀའ་སྲུང་ལས་བྱེད་དམ་ཅན་གཤེགས་སུ་གསོལ་ཾ

**DE TONG GA ZHI OD PHUNG BAR WAI LONG**
**RIG DZIN PA WO DAK KI SHEG SU SOL**
**THRIN LAE ZHI DRUB CHOE SUNG DAM TSIG DAG**
**KA SUNG LAE JED DAM CHEN SHEG SU SOL**

*You who are in the vastness of the rising mass of lights of the four joys of happiness and emptiness, vidyadharas, viras and dakinis please come here! You the dharma guardians with pure vows who practice the four activities, order guardians, workers and vow-keepers, please come here!*

རྣལ་འབྱོར་ཕྱི་ནང་བར་ཆད་བསལ་བ་དང་ཾ
མཆོག་དང་ཐུན་མོང་དངོས་གྲུབ་སྩོལ་བའི་ཕྱིར་ཾ
སྤྱན་འདྲེན་གནས་འདིར་བསྒྲུབ་པའི་རྟགས་མཚན་སྟོན་ཾ
བཛྲ་ས་མ་ཡ་ཛ་ཛཿ

**NAL JOR CHI NANG BAR CHE SAL WA DANG**
**CHOG DANG THUN MONG NGOE DRUB TSOL WAI CHIR**
**CHEN DREN NAE DIR DRUB PAI TAG TSEN TON**
**BENDZA SA MA YA DZA DZA**

*In order to clear the outer and inner obstacles of yogis, and to grant the supreme and general real attainments, show the signs and symbols of practice at this place to which you are invited. Keep your vajra vows! Come! Come!*

In tantra there are two aspects to the deities we visualise. The first form is called the *samayasattva*, or the *damtsigpa*, and the second form is called the *jnana-sattva* in Sanskrit or, in Tibetan, *yeshepa*. When you receive the initiation, you are given permission to do the visualisation. Which means you have to do the visualisation regularly and you are allowed, or more directly, you are empowered through your body, speech, and mind to enter into this state of connection with the deity. On the basis of this you do your best to visualize clearly, you attempt to be Padmasambhava. But then, we also believe that in Zangdopalri Padmasambhava is there, and on the basis of our faith and practice, he sends forth his pure form, which is called the *yeshepa*, that is to say his effortless natural form, as a spontaneous manifestation of wisdom.

So, first of all, when we did the visualisation of the mandala we were working with the *damtsigpa*, because we are trying to create the images described in the text, according to the vows that we have taken in the initiation but then, when we recite this invocation, we are inviting the *yeshepa* to come and merge into the *damtsigpa*. When you practice on your own, you can recite the Seven-Line Prayer many, many times, sing it with deep faith and try to feel the energy of the deities as they vitalise your visualisation.

This is not a dress rehearsal, this is the real thing. Keep praying until you have a vivid experience of the presence of Padmasambhava, till you feel it in your body, and your mind becomes relaxed and open. We read the description, and we try to experience this visualisation of ourselves as Padmasambhava, with the whole mandala becoming inseparable from Padmasambhava himself. You can imagine the pure forms melting in as rays of light, or like gentle snow dissolving in water. In that moment, the duality of the effortful creation and the spontaneous manifestation is dissolved in their union.

This has some resemblances to what happens in the christian mass, in which the priest, by his vows and ordination, is entitled to prepare the host and then, through the mystery of the mass, the transformation, the transfiguration, the mutation comes about so that the actual presence of Christ is there, in the host. And, of course, in the history of christianity there has often been a question of whether this is a metaphor or is a living reality. Is this really the blood of Christ or is it a symbol of the blood of Christ? We have the same issue here and we will get more benefit out of this if we can really believe that this is what has occurred. You can see it as a metaphor or symbol of something, but much better to be right in it — *this* is now actuality, this is it.

## Invitation to Sit

ཧྲཱིཿ བདེ་སྟོང་རཏྣ་འབར་བའི་དཀྱིལ་འཁོར་དུཿ
ཆགས་མེད་པདྨ་ཐབས་ཤེས་ཉི་ཟླའི་སྟེང་ཿ
དགྱེས་པར་བཞུགས་ལ་བར་ཆད་བསལ་བ་དངཿ
མཆོག་ཐུན་དངོས་གྲུབ་སྩོལ་ཕྱིར་བརྟན་པར་བཞུགསཿ
བཛྲ་ས་མ་ཡ་ཏི་ཥྚ་ལྷནཿ

**HRI DE TONG RAT NA BAR WAI KYIL KHOR DU**
**CHAG MED PAD MA THAB SHE NYI DAI TENG**
**GYE PAR ZHUG LA BAR CHE SAL WA DANG**
**CHOG THUN NGOE DRUB TSOL CHIR TEN PAR ZHUG**
**BEN DZA SA MA YA TISHTA LHEN**

*Hri. In the shining jewel mandala of happiness and emptiness, upon the lotus of freedom from desire and the sun and moon of supreme knowledge and compassion sit happily, and then in order to clear the obstacles, and to grant supreme and general real attainments, please stay here steadily. Keep your vajra vows. You must really stay here.*

We are already the god, so we are inviting ourselves to sit: "Padmasambhava, please be seated." "Oh, thank you." When we say, *sa ma ya tishta len*, this means the real fusion of the *damtsigpa* and *yeshepa*. They have completely merged. Firstly, we invited them to come, now we make them welcome. In order to welcome the other, we have to make space, we put ourselves out for the sake of the other, putting them first, focusing on them. Then we offer salutation:

ཧྲཱིཿ དུས་གསུམ་རྒྱལ་བའི་ཕྲིན་ལས་གཅིག་བསྡུས་ཤིངཿ
འགྲོ་རྣམས་རིག་འཛིན་སར་བགོད་རིགས་ཀྱི་ལྷཿ

# E. SADHANA: Main Part

HRI DUE SUM GYAL WAI THRIN LAE CHIG DUE SHING
DRO NAM RIG DZIN SAR KOD RIG KYI LHA
NA TSOG THRIN LAE DRUB PAI RANG ZHIN LA
DAG CHAG RAB GUE DUNG WAE CHAG TSAL LO
A TI PU HO PRA TI TSA HO

*Hri. The activities of all the buddhas of the three times assembled in one, the god of the lotus family who puts all beings on the vidyadhara's stage — to you, who have the nature of accomplishing many different activities, we make salutation with intense faith and devotion. Salutation to you. The very greatest salutation to you.*

Then we make this prostration, or homage to ourselves, in the form of Padmasambhava. You may know the writings of Walt Whitman. In one of his famous poems he says, "I sing the song of myself." We, of course, live in a culture which is very sensitive to pride, to narcissism and so forth, and we tend to be encouraged as children to think of the good qualities of others and not to show off, or not to take too much pride in ourselves. But in tantra they talk of *lha'i nga gyal*, which means pride in the deity. This means that we should take pride in being this divine form. This acts as an antidote to all the familiar samsaric things we pay homage to. This is safe, as pride, because the nature of the deity is wisdom and compassion, and this wisdom is the understanding of emptiness, of no inherent self-nature, so the pride is not going to puff up in some way. It just unfolds, and then dissolves.

## d. Offerings

HRI TSA SUM DAG NYID RIG DZIN KYIL KHOR DU
LHA DZAE NA TSOG CHI YI CHOD PA BUL
RANG JUNG NAM DAG NANG GI CHOD PA BUL
THUG DAM GYE KANG NGOE DRUB DENG DIR TSOL

*Hri. To the mandala of the vidyadhara with the nature of the three roots, we present the outer offering of the many different articles of the gods. We present the self-occurring very pure inner offerings. May your mind and vows be fully satisfied and happy and grant us real attainments here today!*

The outer offerings are described in the next verse, the inner offerings in the verse that follows it.

GURU PADMA SAPARI WARA BENDZA ARGHAM PHADYAM PUPE DUPE
ALOKE GANDHE NEWIDYE SHABDA AA HUNG

*Padmasambhava, to you and your circle we offer vajra drinking water, feet bathing water, flowers, incense, lamps, perfumed water, food, sound. Please accept these offerings which are pure in sunyata.*

## E. SADHANA: Main Part

མ་ཧཱ་སརྦ་པཉྩ་ཨ་མྲྀ་ཏ་ཁ་རཾ་ཁ་ཧི༔
མ་ཧཱ་བྷ་ལིང་ཏ་ཁ་ཧི༔
མ་ཧཱ་རཀྟ་ཁ་ཧི༔
མ་ཧཱ་སརྦ་པཱུཛ་ཁ་ཧི༔

**MA HA SAR VA PAN TSA AM RI TA KHA RAM KHA HI**
**MA HA BHA LING TA KHA HI**
**MA HA RAKTA KHA HI**
**MA HA SAR VA PU TSA KHA HI**

*Eat all the five great liberating elixirs! Eat the great sacrifice. Eat the great rakta! Eat all these great ceremonial offerings!*

And then we have these more secret offerings of union and liberation:

ཧྲཱིཿ སྣང་སྟོང་སྦྱོར་བའི་བདེ་ཆེན་བྱང་ཆུབ་སེམས༔
དགའ་བཞི་ཡེ་ཤེས་མཉམ་སྦྱོར་རོ་གཅིག་རྫས༔
ང་བདག་མཚན་མ་བསྒྲལ་བའི་རུ་དྲའི་རྫས༔
དབྱིངས་སུ་འབུལ་ལོ་རོ་གཅིག་ངང་དུ་བཞེས༔

**HRI NANG TONG JOR WAI DE CHEN JANG CHUB SEM**
**GA ZHI YE SHE NYAM JOR RO CHIG DZAE**
**NGA DAG TSEN MA DRAL WAI RU DRAI DZAE**
**YING SU BU LO RO CHIG NGANG DU ZHE**

*Hri. The union of appearance and emptiness is great happiness bodhicitta, the offering article having the one taste of the union of the pristine cognition of the four joys, and the offering article of the demon's corpse of the liberation/destruction of grasping thoughts — we offer these in the dharmadhatu, please accept them in the state of one taste.*

Emptiness and appearance are joined together, they are inseparable. This union, like sexual union, gives rise to pleasure, but here it is not the brief pleasure of sex but the unchanging happiness of enlightenment. The four joys are the movement of the united male and female energy up the central channel and then down again. Through this all energy becomes balanced, everything is balanced, calm and open, and this union is the basis for the understanding of one-taste.

On an ordinary level I think we can know that if you have good sex you feel better, because when you have sex, and you go fully into the process and you have an orgasm, and it's held in a space of warmth and respect, there's a dissolving and an opening. This process allows all the small nerves in the body to unwind a little bit so we feel much more relaxed afterwards, and that mood stays with us. The more one can give a focused attention to being with another person, and can work with form and emptiness, sensation and emptiness, you can build up more energy, and more openness at the same time, and that gives a better feeling. You can see this in metaphorical terms or you can see it as actual sexual union. We are offering the happiness of the dissolving of the barriers between self and other, the dissolving of entities, of duality, and with that the experience of an integrated field of arising.

The third line deals with liberation, with the killing-off of the constraints, the obscurations to the natural state. *Nga dag* means 'I myself', the strong sense of self, and *tsen ma* is a kind of sign or signification. *Tsen ma* can be used to mean a kind of magical dummy, a simulcrum, a representation. The notions of me, I, mine are just that — notions. Through the process of conceptualisation, we create objects, by the power of our own definition. It's the method by which we impute inherent self-nature to things which don't have it. That is, the energy of the mind creates the illusion of real separate entities, including the reification of the felt sense of self. This is the demon which we want to kill. This is a quality in ourselves, that we are the demons who create samsara. Our own attachment, our own investment of inherent self-nature, creates samsara.

Because this is our demon, other people can also be our demons. If you like, the root demon or the causal demon is our own attachment, our own over-investment. But given that I have a tendency to categorise, if Robert, for example, does something which hooks my category, in that moment he is like a demon to me, because my demonising tendency is wakened-up by his activity. It's not either/or, it's not that either that I am the demon or you are the demon. The real demon is duality, and duality brings two things into connection. It makes an entity in you, an entity in me. When these two bang together we get the friction, which is the suffering of samsara and that's why we call this *demon*, because it troubles us.

Sometimes we just have to cut whatever we're doing. Somebody says, "Oh, I can't get my life together," and you say "Why?" and he says, "Well, I'm quite lazy." All you can say is, "Just stop it!" There's nothing else to say. You can spend a lot of time, particularly a therapist like me, and get paid to do this, investigating why somebody is lazy, and why they don't manage to get their dreams fulfilled and do what they want to do with their life. But as the Buddha said, if a man suddenly finds that an arrow has stuck into his arm, he doesn't think, "Oh, where did this arrow come from? Who made it? What kind of wood is it made of?" He tries to pull it out. That's why buddhism and psychotherapy don't go very well together. Buddhism says that the causes of all our suffering are due to attitudes that we have in our own mind, they're not due to what our parents did. The main thing we have to do is to wake up, and take responsibility for the situation we find ourselves in, to stop wasting time blaming other people, and do something different in order to change the situation we're in. That's why it says that we should kill this demon. We're not going to try to educate the demon, or convert it to buddhism. We just want it to dissolve so that it doesn't trouble us any more. We waste a lot of time in our lives thinking, "Why?" and "How?" and "What?" It is much more effective to step back and think, "What do I need to do? What's stopping me doing it? Now I'm going to stop the thing that's stopping me." And then you go on and do what you have to do.

When I lived in C R Lama's house, he and his wife had a not-so-easy relationship. She would often come in and say, "Ah, this is going on, and that is going on," and he would listen and say, "Oh, leave it there, (*yuk sha*). Leave it there. Let's have some tea." Just cut it, because if you keep this in your mind cooking, cooking — they said that, and we said that, and what are we doing, and *blahblahblah* — you go mad. There is no end to that.

If you indulge your emotions, and they often feel very important to indulge, you feel something, and you really want to share it and tell someone, "You know, when you said that I really felt hurt," you want to really say that because it's important but, if you do that, it's like drinking salt water. You get some relief from thirst, because of the water, but then the salt makes you more thirsty. There's more to say, and more to do, and it never ends. Lasting happiness requires choosing to cut the chains, the tendrils of attachments, involvement, identification.

### Offering of the View

ཧྲཱིཿ གཞི་དབྱིངས་སྤྲོས་བྲལ་མཉམ་པའི་ཡེ་ཤེས་ལཿ
དགག་སྒྲུབ་འཛིན་པ་ཀུན་བྲལ་དེ་བཞིན་ཉིད༔
འཁོར་འདས་ཆོས་ཅན་ཆོས་ཉིད་རིག་འཛིན་ཀློང༔
མཐའ་བྲལ་ཆོས་ཟད་ལྟ་བའི་མཆོད་པ་བཞེས༔
བོ་དྷི་ཙིཏྟ་སརྦ་པུཛྪོ་ཧོཿ

**HRI ZHI YING TROE DRAL NYAM PAI YE SHE LA
GAG DRUB DZIN PA KUN DRAL DE ZHIN NYID
KHOR DAE CHOE CHEN CHOE NYID RIG DZIN LONG
THA DRAL CHOE ZAD TA WAI CHOD PA ZHE
BO DHI TSIT TA SAR VA PU TSA HO**

*Hri. The simplicity of the ground dimension, the even, original experience; the actuality free of all grasping, inhibiting and encouraging — please enjoy their offering of the view of the limitless liberation of phenomena in which samsara and nirvana, appropriation and actuality, are both the dimension of presence.*

This is very, very important, because this is really what we should be trying to awaken into. The ground of everything, of all of samsara and nirvana, is the infinite dimension, without beginning or end, free of any kind of constraints. When you find yourself in that state there manifests the original experience of the equalness of everything that arises. If you go to buy milk, you can buy homogenised milk, and it's standardised, so every bottle is the same. The maker can say, "We can guarantee equal quality across all our products." This verse does not mean that at all. It's not a homogenised equality. It means each thing is exactly as it is, manifesting all its difference, but its inherent self-nature is the same because its inherent self-nature is emptiness. That's why they say of the yogi, that he or she should be the same, whether good things come or bad things come. If you're happy, be happy, but happy in emptiness. If bad things come, and you become sad, be sad, but sad in emptiness. And the way you do this is by not identifying with the event, or conceptual experience, which manifests.

For example, when you are happy the reality is that happiness is a mood, or a colour which is passing through the space of experience. And the same when we're unhappy. It's not that we are unhappy but unhappiness is an impermanent mood, or colour, which is passing through this space of experience. Just as we sit in this room and now it's warm because the sun is shining in. After a while, the sun goes down, and the room gets cold. We can say, "Oh, the room is so hot, God, its hot!" and we open the window. But then we say, "Oh God, it's so cold. Can we put the heating on?" When this level of experience catches us, it means we are far from equalness. It is to be caught up in reactivity in which you identify with the moment, as if it were a total, true reality. When we are present in the state of evenness, we can be sad when we're unhappy, when we're happy, we can be happy. It looks the same as before but it's actually different and the more you do practice, the more you get some sense of this.

The second line states that actuality is free from all the grasping of possibilities of trying to stop the things you don't like, and encouraging the things you do like. Bad things come. In ordinary life sometimes we need to intervene and at other times we need to let things be. We need to know when it's worthwhile to try to fight and change situations. That depends also on our habitual nature. Some people are very much in the family of anger, of fire, and so they are used to pushing, manipulating the world, to try to get what they want and they quickly feel pushed by others. These people need to learn to accept more. Other people, who accept all the time and give in, are very much the water element. They flow around to fit in with other people. These people need to take a file and sharpen their teeth and practise biting.

We have to really understand what this text means. When it says be free of any pushing away or pulling in, it is not that that activity should not occur at all. I mean, you couldn't live on that level. If you took this literally, it says you can't say no, you can't say yes. Then a simple question like, "Would you like some tea?" would have you paralysed. What it means is that if your attitude is strongly real, if you are pushing it away because you really don't like it, that's no good. If you're pulling it towards you, because you think, "I really, really need this," that's not good, because it's too intense, it's too full of solidity. In the heart of everything is emptiness. Again and again, you should study emptiness, examine emptiness through impermanence in daily life, and really try to understand this.

In the dimension of understanding of the vidyadharas, which is to say in the nature of actuality itself, there is no separation between samsara and nirvana or subject and object. In this situation there are no limits at all. That is to say, we never come to something we need to jump back from. We can eat the world. We can go through any kind of experience, not as a superhero but as a spacious awareness. And in this view, all phenomena, (phenomena here means all things appearing to have inherent self-nature, things which seem to exist in themselves), all are exhausted. You no longer encounter any phenomena. This is the view that we offer.

For example, if you go to the cinema, first of all there is a white screen, then the film comes on, and you find yourself in the film. You can know in your head that this is only a film but if the film is a good film it's very difficult because it pulls you into it. What we're trying to do in this practice of tantra here is to experience the film of samsara but to know that it is a film as we experience it. Of course, it's more complicated, because we're not sitting in a cinema watching the film, we are in the film, as actors. And this is why, in the meditation practice sometimes we practise being in the audience, stepping back and just observing what is going on, and sometimes we become more the performer and step into it.

We offer this non-dual state, and seal it with the offering mantra.

### e. Praise of the Three Kayas

**HRI MA CHOE TROE DRAL LA MA CHOE KYI KU
DE CHEN LONG CHOD DZOG KU PAD MA JUNG
NA TSOG NAM ROL THAB GYI DRO WA DUL
KU SUM DAG NYID PAD JUNG JE LA TOD**

*Hri. The uncontrived guru free of all relative positions is the dharmakaya. The sambhogakaya of great joy is Padmasambhava. With the method of showing many different emanations you educate beings, we praise the noble Padmasambhava who has the nature of the three kayas.*

Once we have the presence of the deities we should praise them, because we want to say, "Oh, we are so glad you are here. We really honour you." One of the things that struck me when I was young and travelling in Africa and Asia was how very respectful people are in traditional cultures. We live in a culture nowadays where people want to be cool, they want to chill out, they don't want to take anything too seriously, and they find it very difficult to respect the great achievement that many people have made. These verses are a way of underlining to oneself just how important this kind of practice is. It's not just nothing, it's not just blahblah, this is a real transformation.

Praising is a very important and ancient tradition in buddhism. The very earliest worship of the Buddha consisted primarily of praise. For example, in the theravadin tradition today, although they don't have visualisation practices of the Buddha or any kind of tantric practice, they do recite verses of praise to the Buddha, which are not so different. Traditionally, we praise the king, and in doing so we are acknowledging the separation in status and powers between the king and the ordinary people. Nowadays, people may have democratic rights and be considered equal, yet there is still a huge variation in qualities. It is very important to be able to hold two levels at once. On the one hand, we need to merge with Padmasambhava and feel that experience and get used to it, and on the other, we need to be aware of how limited we are and, through praising the guru, come to emulate him and develop these qualities.

*Hri* is the seed syllable from the lotus family. Then *ma choe troe dral la ma choe kyi ku*, we know this line from before. Dharmakaya is the guru who is completely free of fabrication, of falseness and elaboration. Then, *de chen long chod dzog ku pad ma jung*, this is, of course, a variation on the standard form of this prayer, and here Padmasambhava is being seen as the samboghakaya form, rather than as in the previous rendition where he appears in the nirmanakaya form. One of the things that makes learning about Tibetan buddhism difficult is the way deities and words have different meanings and functions in different texts and contexts. So although we would normally say, dharmakaya is Amitabha, samboghakaya is Chenresi, nirmanakaya is Padmasambhava, Padmasambhava can be all three, dharmakaya, samboghakaya, nirmanakaya, or as here, his samboghakaya form can be highlighted. It's not that he is one thing or another, but that he manifests in different ways, and is ungraspable as an entity.

Buddhism is anti-fundamentalist, because the fundament or the basis in buddhism is emptiness, and you can't have a dogma of emptiness — although many scholars have been dogmatic about their interpretation of emptiness. The real nature is beyond expression, and so whatever we are saying or talking about is itself some kind of symbolic representation, some kind of 'gesture towards', but is never quite the thing itself.

The second line reads *de chen long chod dzog ku pad ma jung*, the samboghakaya whose quality is great happiness. This is Padmasambhava. Why is the samboghakaya described as *dechen*, as very happy, or full of joy? It's because, in the nature of ignorance, not knowing really who we are, our ordinary basis is not emptiness but is a sense of self. And this sense of self, because it is itself not true, carries anxiety with it. So when we go out from ourselves towards interaction in the world, that interaction, before we even encounter the situation, is full of hopes and fears. That root stupidity maintains the ground anxiety, and then desire and aversion carry the push-pull tension, and this dynamic triangle is operating before we come into activity. In the samboghakaya, the ground is not our anxious sense of self but the openness of the dharmakaya and so, as energy starts to be mobilised towards manifestation, it comes in a very relaxed mode. This is the basis of saying *dechen* here.

The third line reads, *na tsog nam rol thab gyi dro wa dul*, meaning that for the sake of helping other beings many different manifestations occur in an easy manner. The effortlessly arising samboghakaya energy displays many different forms in order to help beings. The word at the end, *dul*, is linked with *dulwa*, the *vinaya*, the set of rules followed by monks and nuns, and it implies a kind of constraint, or a kind of direction. In English you might say 'disciplined'. It carries with it the sense that all beings, whether human beings or cats and dogs, or gods or demons, are out of control. It means that these farmers around here, who lead very controlled, regular, and disciplined lives, milking their cows, cutting the grass and so forth, from this point of view are totally out of control. Even a general in the army is out of control, somebody whose life is completely held by rules and regulations. 'Discipline' here means that all the energy of karma must be turned in the direction of emptiness, and integrated into emptiness.

Because you cannot squeeze people into the right direction, the disciplining of beings is very difficult. Just as with some children, if you want to control them you have to shout at them, and with other children, if you want to control them you have to be very sweet with them. But shouting at a child to make it quiet in a state of fear is not helpful. They may be sitting without moving but inside there is a lot of movement going on. So *dulwa* here, is about reducing the vibration of dualistic energy so that it can relax back into ground emptiness, and then the three kayas can manifest. We can of course, learn to control our behaviour using rules and regulations, but the structure of that is that I am telling myself, or I am forcing myself, to be calm and quiet, so it remains inside a dualistic structure, and as long as that structure is being reinforced, the basis for the generation of more karma is in place.

This is why compassion is very difficult in buddhism, because compassion is about helping people to recognise the nature of their own disturbance and then to work, in relation with the dharma and the teachers and so forth, to calm that disturbance. When life is very easy it's often difficult to know that there is any work to be done. Renunciation, not just in the sense of taking on monks' vows, but of giving up the usual forms of comfort, is really the beginning of discipline. Renunciation is very important because by putting oneself into a state of vulnerability, through giving up layers of protection, one recognises for oneself that one's life is out of control.

Then, in the fourth line, we praise Padmasambhava, who is the integration or the manifestation of the three kayas. In the text, in terms of the visualisation, there are eight forms of Padmasambhava but there are also hundreds of thousands — millions — of forms of Padmasambhava. We can never really know who is Padmasambhava, for he is not an object of knowledge. He slips away. It's not that Padmasambhava has one real form, and then puts on some kind of fancy dress to help in different situations. Rather, these different forms arise according to different situations, and in each of these situations, it is the real Padmasambhava. Just as in our lives, in different situations we present ourselves differently. We show different forms. These forms that we show tend to be manifestations of our own karma. That is to say, how we manifest is determined by the interaction of internal and of external factors. We are showing a particular form because it's the best we can do under this circumstance. But Padmasambhava is here showing these different forms because of the need of the others. Often, the forms that he would show are not so different from the forms that we show, but the key difference lies in the ground, or basis, for the manifestation, whether it's self-referential attachment, or altruistic generosity and responsiveness.

I think one of the things that's interesting in the forms of Padmasambhava is that you don't have Padmasambhava as a toilet cleaner. You don't have Padmasambhava as a nurse, and you don't have Padmasambhava in a supermarket. But of course you *do*, though not in the puja. We need to remember that the forms in the puja are the praise forms, the elevated forms, and that they are not the only ones. The actual forms of manifestation of compassion of Padmasambhava are beyond imagining, and are encountered everyday, if we are open. It's very easy to get confused, to imagine that compassion is always a top-down phenomenon with a splendid being helping an inferior being. In fact, the compassion of the buddhas and of bodhisattva activity is displayed in countless ordinary ways by great beings who look, on the outside, like everyone else. It is important not to confuse the sambhogakaya forms of the practice, where forms are fixed and radiant, with the infinite variability of the nirmanakaya.[8]

སྐུ་ནི་མི་འགྱུར་ཀུན་ཏུ་བཟང་པོའི་སྐུ༔
གསུང་ནི་མི་འགགས་དྲུག་ཅུའི་གདངས་སྒྲ་ཅན༔
ཐུགས་ནི་མི་གཡོ་སྨྲ་བསམ་བརྗོད་པ་བྲལ༔
སྐུ་གསུང་ཐུགས་ལྡན་མཚོ་སྐྱེས་རྗེ་ལ་བསྟོད༔

**KU NI MI GYUR KUN TU ZANG POI KU**
**SUNG NI MI GAG DRUG CHUI DANG DRA CHEN**
**THUG NI MI YO MA SAM JOD PA DRAL**
**KU SUNG THUG DEN TSO KYE JE LA TOD**

*Your speech is the unchanging body of Kuntu Zangpo.*
*Your speech is never ceasing with the sixty melodies of Brahma.*
*Your mind is unwavering, beyond speech, thoughts and expression.*
*We offer praise to Tsokye Dorje who has such a body, speech and mind.*

The body of Samantabhadra is the body of emptiness. Samantabhadra has never changed from the very beginning. This body is the basis of all manifestation. It is the dharmadhatu, the infinite expanse of manifestation, with no beginning or end. When we relax our habitual fixations, we see that eve-

---

[8] See Chapter 5 of *Simply Being*

rything is manifesting at once in an integrated form from the ground, and see that there is no difference between ground and manifestation.

This integration is the body which never changes. Manifestation is always occurring. Its content, or the waves of form, are always changing. All the forms which are manifest in the world in terms of nirmanakaya, all the things that we see, all levels of manifestation, don't make any change to their own ground. It's because of this that the verse says the body is unchanging. Bodies themselves, of course, change all the time. From the very beginning of time, the unborn body of Samantabhadra has been sitting without moving.

The speech is this ceaseless flow of the sixty different melodies and sounds. Sixty melodies is an old hindu notion that Brahma, the god who is the creator of the world, used sixty different sounds to bring about manifestation. It means that all the sounds that we hear, no matter what kind they are, whether it's an aeroplane going by, a glass being broken, somebody screaming in pain or horror, someone crying in despair, all of these sounds are the ceaseless play of the samboghakaya level.

Then, mind is unmoving and beyond all speech, thought, and expression. Just as many animals, when they are hunted by other animals, if they sense any danger, they stand very, very still because they know if they move they'll be easier to see, so the nature of the mind, because it doesn't move at all, is very difficult to find. This mind can never be described. That is to say, it does not exist as an object. We, as human beings, reveal ourselves through our activity. Usually, when we describe someone in terms of their qualities, we describe things that they do. The description is a verbal manifestation, and has some parallels with activity manifestation. But the mind itself, our true nature, is not a manifestation. It cannot be seen, described, measured. One can only find oneself present in it, and then one has no words.

Then the next verse:

འགྲོ་བའི་དོན་དུ་ཡིད་བཞིན་ནོར་བུའི་སྐུ༔

མཚན་ཚམ་ཐོས་པའི་སྒྲག་བསྒྲལ་སེ་ལ་མཛད་ཅིང༔

སྨིན་ལས་མཐར་ཕྱིན་གྲུབ་བརྙེས་མཚན་མཆོག་བརྒྱུད༔

ཨོན་དན་རྟོགས་པའི་རྗེ་ལ་ཕྱག་འཚལ་བསྟོད༔

**DRO WAI DON DU YID ZHIN NOR BUI KU**

**TSEN TSAM THOE PAI DUG NGAL SEL DZAD CHING
THRIN LAE THAR CHIN DRUB NYE TSEN CHOG GYAD
YON TEN DZOG PAI JE LA CHAG TSAL TOD**

*Yours are the wish fulfilling bodies which bring benefit to beings.
Just to hear your name removes all sorrows. You have eight excellent
forms who completed your activities and gained siddhis. We offer
salutations and praise to the noble one who has all good qualities.*

For the sake of benefiting beings you show this wonderful jewel-like body. Just to hear your name liberates the suffering of beings. And, through these eight modes, you have the fulfilment of all the activities. This means that, through these eight forms of Padmasambhava, every single kind of activity, particularly the four basic activities of pacifying, increasing, overpowering and destroying, are performed. We praise you who have these complete, or perfect, qualities.

Many of the ways of conceptualising people, or describing them in terms of lists and categories, are determined by pre-existing structures. So in buddhism you have a lot of threes, a lot of fours, a lot of fives, sevens, eights, and so forth. Here in this verse, although it's not fully there, we have body, speech, mind, activities and qualities, which is a very standard five-fold category. In these kind of praise verses you'll get many, many things pushed into these standard forms. These are modes of rhetoric.

The next verse:

མདོར་ན་སྣ་ཚོགས་རིག་པའི་གཞི་རྩལ་ལྷ༔
གང་འདུལ་སྤྲུལ་པའི་བྱེད་པོ་པདྨ་འབྱུང་༔
གསང་གསུམ་བཀོད་པ་རྒྱལ་བའི་དཀྱིལ་འཁོར་རྫོགས༔
ཕྱིན་ལས་རྫོགས་པའི་རྗེ་ལ་ཕྱག་འཚལ་བསྟོད༔

**DOR NA NA TSOG RIG PAI ZHI TSAL LHA
GANG DUL TRUL PAI JED PO PAD MA JUNG
SANG SUM KOD PA GYAL WAI KYIL KHOR DZOG**

## THRIN LAE DZOG PAI JE LA CHAG TSAL TOD

*In brief, the many different gods of the energy flow of the ground of natural awareness are the emanations produced by Padmasambhava according to the needs of beings. You who have the complete Buddha's mandala of the three kayas, we salute and praise the noble one who has all activities complete.*

This is the concluding praise. You are the deity, who is the basic energy of this multifarious quality of awareness. That is to say, all these forms of the deity which manifest are not self-existing, they are all simply modes of the energy of awareness, and awareness or rigpa is always integrated with the ground, which is emptiness. This is important because, as we discussed previously, in christianity human beings' relationship with God is a very uncertain one. In general, we believe that God is friendly towards us, but when we ask God to do something, he may do it or he may not do it. This is a part of the anxiety of duality — you act, but you've no idea how the other person will respond to what you do.

But in buddhism the idea is that things manifest according to the principles of dependent co-origination. That is to say that we live in a world of mutual interaction. If somebody is nice to us we feel happy, if somebody is not nice to us we feel sad. If you put wood in water, it will float and if you put wood in the fire, it will burn. In the same way, if you do the practice, you get the result. It's not that Padmasambhava has moods, or desires, or likes or dislikes. It is an automatic process. The limitation on the process arises out of our limitation, our inability to go fully into the process, but from the side of the deity there is no limitation. Now, because I'm quite fat, if I have to get up, I have to wheeze and push a little bit, but Padmasambhava has a light body, so — snap! It's just like that. No calories at all in Zangdopalri, it's a great miracle!

Recognising this, we can avoid using devotion in the wrong way. The devotion is not, "Oh please, give me this," as if we are a small child asking for a present. The devotion is a method of settling the anxiety in the mind, which otherwise goes into distraction. We rest in the confidence that the meaning of the text will be manifest through its practice.

This view helps the next part, the mantra practice, to be effective. A mantra is not a magical function, it's not creating its result because it has some special power. There are some people who translate mantra as 'spell' as if it was something that would put a kind of enchantment on someone, like Sleeping Beauty. Actually the mantra is operating much more like the cog in a wheel, it drives activity. When you put on an electric kettle, you press in the button and the button joins the current, and then the energy flows and the water heats up. Similarly, the mantra is a means of establishing an energetic connection which continues as long as one is reciting the mantra. That's why Tibetans tend to do long periods of recitation and that's why it's helpful to give yourself enough time to do a lot of mantras, for they perform the essential activity. Otherwise, you go into town, you go to the shop, you buy some tea, you buy some milk, you buy some sugar, you come home, you're very tired, you put water in the kettle, you sit down and you're waiting, but the kettle never boils — because you didn't press the button.

These practices are very long, and you can spend a lot of time not doing the key things which make a difference. In that sense it's much better to do the *Small Rigdzin* and spend a lot of time doing mantra than to do the *Big Rigdzin* and have no time to do the mantra and the meditation thoroughly, because when you read autobiographies of lamas, they don't tell you how many times they did the whole puja, they tell you how many million mantras they did.

### f. Mantra Recitation

### The stages of Mantra Recitation

བདག་ཉིད་ལྷར་གསལ་ཐུགས་དབུས་ཉི་མའི་སྟེང༔

ཧྲཱིཿཡིག་རྩ་སྔགས་ཕྲེང་བས་རྒྱལ་ཀུན་བསྐུལ༔

བྱིན་བརླབས་བདག་ཐིམ་དབང་ཐོབ་ཡེ་ཤེས་རྒྱས༔

ཕར་འཕྲོས་འགྲོ་བའི་ལས་དང་བག་ཆགས་སྦྱངས༔

སྣང་སྲིད་རྒྱལ་བའི་སྐུ་གསུང་ཐུགས་སུ་གྱུར༔

ཨོཾ་ཨཱཿཧཱུྃ་བཛྲ་གུ་རུ་པདྨ་སིདྡྷི་ཧཱུྃ༔

**DAG NYID LHAR SAL THUG WUE NYI MAI TENG
HRI YIG TSA NGAG THRENG WAI GYAL KUN KUL
JIN LAB DAG THIM WANG THOB YE SHE GYAE
PHAR THROE DRO WAI LAE NGAN BAG CHAG JANG
NANG SID GYAL WAI KU SUNG THUG SU GYUR
OM AA HUNG BENDZA GU RU PAD MA SIDDHI HUNG**

*With myself clearly as the god, on top of a sun disc in the centre of my heart is the letter Hri with the mantra chain around it from which rays of light radiate upwards invoking all the buddhas. Their blessings are absorbed into me and I gain initiation and the pristine cognitions develop. Then the light radiates outward, purifying all the bad karma and subtle traces in all beings. All possible appearances become the body, speech and mind of Padmasambhava. Indestructible guru Padmasambhava possessing the three kayas, please bestow real attainments.*

On the sun disk there is the letter *Hri*, and around this the mantra is turning clockwise. You imagine it as a complete circle. As it turns, rays of light come out from it, from the *Hri* and from the mantra, as an offering and evocation to all the buddhas, all the bodhisattvas, all the gods and goddesses. In response to this offering, they send the light back to us in an amplified form, so that all their blessing comes and merges into us. We get the initiation, and our wisdom and compassion develop. Then the light radiates out from us again, this time going down to all the beings suffering in samsara, particularly those in the lower realms, in the hells, the hungry ghosts and to the animals. This purifies all their karma and all the subtle traces of karma. In this way, all manifestation becomes as the body, speech and mind of the Buddha. So in this way, nirvana, or the dimension of the buddhas, and samsara, the dimension of suffering, are brought together into one point. Reciting the mantra is very, very important, because the mantra really gives us the full sense that there is no stain left anywhere. If we really apply this mantra and the visualisation with faith and identification we are actually transforming the existence in which we live.

Now you might wonder, how can it be that rays of light can transform something very unpleasant and horrible into something perfect? After all, light bounces off objects. We would think that in relation to a wall, light is not very powerful. This view arises because we believe that there is an inherent self-nature, a self-substance in things, which keeps the light out. This light that is shining here is not ordinary light, it's wisdom light. That is to say, it is the light of wisdom, which recognises the inherent emptiness of all phenomena, and by doing the mantra for a longer period of time one can have the experience that everything is touched by this light, everything is incorporated in the dimension of wisdom. That is to say, it arises from emptiness, and has no self-separating essence to it.

If hell realms really were terrible places which were truly hellish, a piece of light would not transform them. From the very beginning everything has been empty. Emptiness manifests in many different forms. Although it shows many different forms, these forms are all empty. You can't find one form which is a true or self-existing form. In that way, we can see that samsara has the same structure as nirvana, because Padmasambhava, as was being described in the previous pages, is a manifestation who shows further manifestations, but none of these forms of Padmasambhava is the true Padmasambhava. Due to the interaction of forces, different forms arise. When the karmic operation is occurring intensively due to the absence of wisdom, we have the conditions for the manifesting of states of terror, isolation, desolation, all the qualities of hell. When into that matrix, which gives rise to this pattern, the light of wisdom is introduced, the structure of that matrix is altered. Then the matrix is transformed by this light of wisdom.

For example, yesterday, before I left my house, I was creating a matrix of cooking. I was frying something in a pan, and into this kitchen matrix came *dring-dring*, the telephone. The telephone hooked me. I talked on the telephone, and in doing this transformed my lunch from nirvana to deep, hellish, samsara. This is exactly what samsara is. Samsara is a pattern of relatedness, a particular kind of resonance which maintains itself due to causes and conditions. When we go into an energetic vibration similar to that dimension, we enter into that dimension. When we cease to be in that dimension, we leave it. If something else takes you out of a state you are in, then you're not in it any more. For example, if somebody is depressed and they take Prozac, they will be benefited by that in most cases. However, Prozac has some side-effects as well. This psychotropic medication, working on the brain and the nervous system, is never very precise, because what it's doing is taking a matrix and pushing it with something else, so you have the sense of one particular form being met by another form and transformed. But here this is different, because the light which is coming down into these realms is showing the real nature of these realms. It's not introducing something new but it is showing the actual quality out of which these are forming and so, by making the link through the light of the sambhoghakaya radiance, the form manifestation is turned from its samsaric nature into nirmanakaya form.

The light comes and shows that the level of manifestation is a form of light, and so the samboghakaya reaches out to the forms of the six realms and integrates them back into the ground, bringing liberation. That's why it says at the end *ku sung thug su gyur*, everything is integrated in the nature of the Buddha. Of course the power of obscuration is great, and the moment of integration is soon replaced, in most beings' experience, by the return of their habitual patterns, because they take their patterns to be real. This is why the practice has to be repeated again and again.

We are now really at the absolute heart of tantra. The function of tantra is to transform the world by revealing the continuity of samsara and nirvana. From the very beginning, everything has been pure, but we don't realise that. Because we don't realise it, it seems to be quite a difficult situation we find ourselves in but actually, it is not a really serious situation. So we have a difficulty: if we trust our senses we think there is a lot of work to be done, and if we trust the teaching then it would appear that there is almost nothing to be done, since everything's been perfect from the beginning. The purpose of tantra is to bring together these two positions, our felt sense that things are difficult, and the dharma teaching sense that everything is pure. Between the naturally existing pure nature — or we can say, the side of nirvana — and the side of confusion, covered by illusion, there is the figure of the deity, and the deity crosses this boundary and unites the two.

### The Seven-Line Prayer

ཧཱུྂ༔ ཨོ་རྒྱན་ཡུལ་གྱི་ནུབ་བྱང་མཚམས༔

པདྨ་གེ་སར་སྡོང་པོ་ལ༔

ཡ་མཚན་མཆོག་གི་དངོས་གྲུབ་བརྙེས༔

པདྨ་འབྱུང་གནས་ཞེས་སུ་གྲགས༔

འཁོར་དུ་མཁའ་འགྲོ་མང་པོས་བསྐོར༔

ཁྱེད་ཀྱི་རྗེས་སུ་བདག་བསྒྲུབ་ཀྱིས༔

ཧྲིན་གྱིས་བརླབ་ཕྱིར་གཤེགས་སུ་གསོལ༈
གུ་རུ་པདྨ་སིདྡྷི་ཧཱུྃ༈

**HUNG UR GYEN YUL GYI NUB JANG TSHAM**
**PE MA GE SAR DONG PO LA**
**YAM TSEN CHOG GI NGOE DRUB NYE**
**PE MA JUNG NAE ZHE SU DRAG**
**KHOR DU KHAN DRO MANG POE KOR**
**KHYE KYI JE SU DAG DRUB KYI**
**JIN GYI LAB CHIR SHEG SU SOL**
**GU RU PE MA SID DHI HUNG**

*Hung. In the north-west corner of the land of Urgyen, upon the stem and stamen of a lotus, are you who have the marvellous and supreme attainments, Padmasambhava of great renown, with a retinue of many dakinis around you. Following and relying on you I do your practice, therefore, in order to grant your blessings, please come here! Guru Padmasambhava, give me the real attainment of buddhahood.*

Nuden Dorje then gives some instructions on practice. He says that if you recite this mantra, which includes the buddhas of all the different families, then you will see the original face of Padmasambhava and have all obstacles cleared. The original face of Padmasambhava is emptiness. If you recite the mantra for a long period of time, with real concentration, thoughts fall away, and there is the undistracted movement of the practice. The visualisation and recitation help to stabilise the mind, allowing the experience of the whole as a play of emptiness. Its all going on, yet nothing is happening.

The text then says that feelings, understanding and merit will be gained. 'Feelings' means feelings of happiness in the body, feelings of lightness, feelings of absence of fear in relation to others, and so forth, and that also can refer to experiences in dreams. Later, you can have images of purification, flying in the sky and so forth. It also refers to the three *nyams*, or meditation experiences, of happiness, clarity, and the absence of thought.

Then, it also says you can find treasures, if you wish — if you wish! Your own ideas will be pacified, and you'll be able to control the thoughts and experiences of others. Much more interesting! That's something to think about. Do you want to control the thoughts of others? It means being able to influence people, and this of course is where tantra becomes potentially dangerous, because real meditation will develop power, and then you have to think what you want to use that power for. It's exactly the same issue in martial arts: the more you develop the ability to control your own body, and you control the bodies of others, you have to have a very clear motivation. One has to be careful with that.

Then the text says that you will be able to gain the stage of the vidyadhara guru, enlightenment. Having done the practice (this gets repeated later), at the end of this recitation you should take all appearance to be the form of the guru, all sound to be the sound of mantra, and whatever thoughts arise in the mind to be the thoughts of Padmasambhava. It's really important to try to investigate and understand what this means, and we'll look at it in more detail further on in the text *(See Section E:l)*. You've done the transformation, now that transformation has to be sustained in all aspects of life.

Nuden Dorje concludes saying that you should practise this with unwavering single-pointedness of mind. When the mind wavers, the force of the practice is cut. It's a bit like a bicycle, if you keep turning the pedals, the bicycle will move and you won't fall over. If you stop pedalling, the bicycle will stop and you will fall over. So if you are not applying the view, nothing is being transformed. You can do the puja every day for fifty days, or fifty years, and if you don't maintain this view nothing will be changed. Without the view, you are like a very bad actor who reads the script again and again, but never enters into the role, so that the part never comes to life.

This part of the text now concludes with the seals, indicating that it is a terma. This text, from Padmasambhava, is sealed by him in the dharmadhatu.

The text now takes one of its shifts. We've been doing the mantra, and in the mantra we are in the form of Padmasambhava, and we have got the buddhas up above and the different realms down below, and now we are going to come back to making offerings to Padmasambhava. Within the calm state of the three kayas, the activity of presenting offerings and linking the various realms and beings continues.

## g. Offerings and Praise

### Presenting Offerings

ཧྲཱིཿ རྩ་གསུམ་བདག་ཉིད་རིག་འཛིན་དཀྱིལ་འཁོར་དུཿ
ལྷ་རྫས་སྣ་ཚོགས་ཕྱི་ཡི་མཆོད་པ་འབུལཿ
རང་བྱུང་རྣམ་དག་ནང་གི་མཆོད་པ་འབུལཿ
ཐུགས་དམ་དགྱེས་བསྐང་དངོས་གྲུབ་དེང་འདིར་སྩོལཿ

**HRI TSA SUM DAG NYID RIG DZIN KYIL KHOR DU
LHA DZAE NA TSOG CHI YI CHOD PA BUL
RANG JUNG NAM DAG NANG GI CHOD PA BUL
THUG DAM GYE KANG NGOE DRUB DENG DIR TSOL**

*Hri. To the mandala of the vidyadhara with the nature of the three roots, we present the outer offerings of the many different articles of the gods. We present the self-occurring very pure inner offerings, may your mind and vows be fully satisfied and happy and grant us real attainments here today!*

Whenever we make vows of any kind, or any kind of intention, especially one which we set up to last for a very long time, there is always going to be the problem that we might break that vow, so one of the very important dimensions of tantric practice is the reparation of broken vows. When the vow is broken then the line of energetic connection between samsara and nirvana breaks, and then you can feel cut off and disconnected from the mandala which you were introduced to at the time of initiation. So it's very important to believe that these pathways can be repaired.

The last line of the verse refers to the *thug dam*, which is the sign of our connection with these gods, that we have this *dam* from the *damtsig*, from the samaya at the time of initiation. This is not like someone in a relationship who does something wrong and then goes along with a bunch of flowers to their partner and says, "Oh please, forgive me." The connection here is automatic: if you make the offerings, the re-connection is there in an automatic manner. Therefore, of course, you should do it with respect. You shouldn't do it just like switching some light on or something, but one has to have the confidence that by doing this everything returns back, and so the practice can continue. The gods are not fickle. We are.

Samaya is a bond, and a bond is a contract. We make bonds in tantric practice with people who are very happy to make bonds, that's their job, to make connections. The buddhas and the bodhisattvas, they always have their hands out ready to shake and make a connection. But once you make this bond, then it ties you into certain attitudes. It is customary now in the west for Tibetan lamas not to go into very much detail about tantric vows. However, there are now translations of the vows, with commentaries on what they mean. It is helpful to study them because they support the practice of the vajra nature, the indestructible nature of body, speech and mind as the actual living presence of the three kayas. This is the real nature of everyone we meet, every insect we meet on the road, every form of manifestation. This means that the real heart of this tantric way, the vajrayana, the way of the vajra, the indestructible way, is to enter through the initiation, and through the mantra practice, into the direct recognition that this world itself is the mandala.

Clearly, we all break that vow a lot of the time. We get distracted, we get confused, we get locked in our habitual karmic thoughts, and we don't stay present, living and existing with respect for all beings as enlightened forms. The tantric vow system is much more radical and difficult than the understanding of *prajnaparamita*, because generally speaking, from the prajnaparamita, although we have an understanding that form is emptiness and emptiness is form and so on, it links in with the *madyamika* system of the two truths, of relative truth and absolute truth.

These two truths offer the possibility of saying that in our ordinary interactions with things, of course we need to understand the economic dimension, sociological dimension, political dimension of complication, and make certain kinds of adjustments and understandings and, in terms of the relative truth, one has to enter into judgement. But then, in the ultimate truth, or this absolute nature, everything has absolute purity of emptiness. On that level, no discrimination at all is possible. But on the level of tantric samaya, when we say, "Now we look on all forms as the form of the guru's body, as the absolute enlightened form," we therefore say all forms have the same nature.

Now clearly, when we open our eyes and we look into the world, there are many strange things going on. There are many forms of cruelty, exploitation, and so forth. Does that mean that these forms, the experiences in a torture chamber, for example, are a manifestation of Padmasambhava? Can we have no discrimination of value and function?

We have to remember that the practice is not designed to provide evidence in a court of law. We're not saying that this is some kind of evangelical position to go out and convert people into. What it is, it's a meditation practice, it is a particular kind of view, and to hold to that view helps the mind to unlock from the intensity of its habitual discrimination of good and bad. This does not mean that the capacity to make discriminations, the capacity for clarity, to see how things are, is not vital, but it does need to function inseparably from emptiness. This is where the understanding of non-duality is very important. We, through the practice, may come to the realisation that all beings we meet are forms of enlightenment and in terms of the view, this is absolutely correct. From the very beginning there has only been enlightenment. But the people don't recognise their own nature, and this is also true. However, if the bad behaviour of others is enough to destroy our view, then our understanding was not deep. Do not be seduced by the strong emotions generated by extreme examples. Rather, recognise the empty nature of both the example and your reaction, and continue in the practice.

Within non-duality, we have dualistic movement. All beings are inseparable from the natural condition, yet they live as if it were absent. Through the practice of openness and connection, we offer them awakening to presence. We should never abandon the enlightened nature of others, but at the same time, we should also be aware of the fact that they are not in touch with their enlightened nature. This is the middle way. If you think, "These people are truly awful, they are the very opposite of enlightened," this is not the teaching of the Buddha. On the other hand, if you say, "Everything is perfect, all beings have been enlightened from the very beginning, it doesn't matter how people behave or what they do," this is also not the teaching of the Buddha. It doesn't matter whether you're talking about a business man, or a butcher, or a guru, how they manifest carries with it an energetic charge, which shows clarity or lack of clarity. Although there is not a hair's breadth of difference between a Buddha and an ordinary person, there is a huge difference between a Buddha and an ordinary person. It is vital to remember that we do the practice to shift our experience. To use the view as if it were a dogmatic truth claim is to lose the point. The view is a practice of awareness, not a representational statement of faith.

You must always remember, enlightenment is not a title. When we name things, the actual presence of what is there and the name may meet briefly, but then they slip apart, so the name can be appropriate for some time and then it vanishes. It's very, very important always to stay close to your own experience, because the vow is kept only on the basis of your experience. Yet many, many things are done in the dharma on the basis of names and titles.

In an English paper that had a report recently on the two Karmapas there was an interview with a chief of police in West Bengal. He said, "I just wish these Karmapas, both of them, had never come to India. They bring only violence and trouble. We have buddhist monks running around with guns. We've already had poisonings and murders." This is what happens when people attach themselves to a title, no matter how high the title, and lose the sense of what the reality is.

We really have to remember that the samaya vow is a method for awakening, it is not a method for going into slavery, so be careful about who you make a power relationship with. The first basis for anyone who takes on any title is to have humility and self-observation and to know their own state. But we know that this is very hard. One of my patients was telling me that his father was a psychiatrist, and when he was getting quite old, his hand was shaking, and he would be trying to give people an injection and the patient would have to hold his hand so he could put the needle in their arm. Because doctors were seen as wonderful, we had a system in Britain that they never needed to retire, you could go on being a doctor just as long as you were alive! The person and the title had become fused, so that in seeing the title, the frailties of the person would be hidden.

Hopefully, in the future, at least some of you will go on to teach dharma to other people, so it's important to remember that the first rule is to be honest about your own limitations. Encouraging students to have faith is very important but it can become a way of disguising the limitations of the teacher. This is not necessarily done with any bad intention for the tradition says if you pray to your guru as if he is a buddha, you get a buddha's blessing; if you pray to your guru as if he is an ordinary person, you get an ordinary person's blessing. According to that structure, it's very helpful if the guru allows the students to see him or her as enlightened.

But gurus may not be enlightened. And they also may have bad patches in their lives, where they become confused. If that can't be talked about, or be understood, or at least be stated by the teacher, "I'm afraid, I've lost it a bit," so that the students can hear, and then see for themselves, "Oh, he *has* lost it a bit," then you have a confusion. We have to very carefully separate projection from actuality and at the same time maintain the view of nonduality. Although our view is to see all manifestation as forms of Padmasambhava, we also have to relate to the actual energy and qualities of manifestations, as they present themselves. But the ones who help us to be enlightened, to recognise our own enlightenment, who we have to believe are enlightened, may not be enlightened — although from the very beginning, of course, they are inseparable from enlightenment. Therefore, one should think carefully before taking initiations. After the initiation, it is vital to rest in the view and not deviate from it. That is why this verse points to the need to repair slippages in samaya. If the student breaks samaya, that causes trouble for themselves and their teacher. Likewise, if the teacher acts in ways that are beyond the capacity of students to integrate in the practice, then they are responsible for breaches in samaya.

We begin in the dharma in the hope of gaining enlightenment, and then we develop the bodhisattva vow in order to help all sentient beings. This is a true basis of the practice, to make all beings happy, this is what the tantric initiations are for. They are a powerful method of fulfilling that intention and that is why we keep the samaya. The samaya is there to maintain this connection. It may well be that western people need to talk about their experience in the way that Tibetan people didn't do, as a means of trying to clarify for themselves the nature of some of their experiences. We know in the west, from our experience of sects — especially sects where people end up by killing themselves, or being murdered — these are groups in which discussion of the process is impossible. There's a big difference however, between gossiping, and struggling to make sense of one's experience.

We want, by these offerings, to make a connection with the deities to strengthen our samaya vow.

### Offerings to Padmasambhava and all his Circle

**GURU PADMA SAPARI WARA BENDZA ARGHAM PHADYAM PUPE DUPE ALOKE GANDHE NEWIDYE SHABDA AA HUNG**

*Padmasambhava, to you and your circle we offer vajra drinking water, feet bathing water, flowers, incense, lamps, perfumed water, food, sound — please accept these offerings which are pure in sunyata.*

**MA HA SAR VA PAN TSA AM RI TA KHA RAM KHA HI**
**MA HA BHA LING TA KHA HI**
**MA HA RAKTA KHA HI**
**MA HA SAR VA PU TSA KHA HI**

*Eat all the five great liberating elixirs! Eat the great sacrifice. Eat the great rakta! Eat all these great ceremonial offerings!*

*Maha amrita*, great nectar, here is a transformation of what is repulsive into liberating elixir. By moving substances from one category to another, the dualistic tension of the binary opposition of pure/impure is deconstructed. This releases a lot of energy. The greater the prior tension, the greater the release.

For example, there is the Tibetan practice of *chod*, where you go into the cemetery and offer your body to ghosts and demons. If you don't believe in ghosts it is not so very scary and so the practice becomes less intense and less effective. Things which don't disgust you are not going to be very useful. Disgust is very deep in us. We know that many animals experience disgust with respect to certain substances; chimpanzees, for example, about the smell of their own shit, cats have a similar repugnance.

This doesn't mean that one has continuously to consume things which one would find disgusting. Rather, it is an opportunity to affirm the view that everything is pure should not be limited by anything. Therefore, hold that view when you encounter things which you would normally react against, and experience for yourself how the bad object is transformed into a basis for freeing yourself from conceptual limitation. What we are actually offering to the gods is the transformation of all that is limiting and problematic, through the view.

*Maha bhalingta* means great sacrifice, it means killing. What is being offered here is this transformation through killing. According to our vows we will kill any sentient being we see. And how will we kill them? With emptiness, that's how we do it. We don't use guns or poison, we just say *phat* and they pop because we have already done the mantra. The result of the mantra is that the whole universe, the whole of creation, is inseparable from the vajra nature. Because of that, everything has the nature of the god: there are no suffering sentient beings in samsara. To believe in sentient beings is to continue in ignorance and to reaffirm their existence in ignorance, and that's what we cut.

*Maha rakta* means great blood, two kinds of blood: menstrual blood and killing blood, the blood of birth and the blood of death. Blood has this shiny quality. We see it when we cut ourselves. It comes out, and this shininess is the quality of life. The blood stands for life, like the quality of the life force. Blood as entity keeps us alive as people. The great blood of emptiness keeps us alive as buddhas. Ordinary blood is generated from food, while great blood is a quality of awareness.

In Tibet, people had many reminders embedded in the culture of the dharma. They had stupas, they had mantras carved in stone. They had, when they walked on the street, the sight of monks and yogis. Every house had a shrine in it, and so forth. It was normal to say prayers a lot, to have a rosary in one's hand, and to have a prayer wheel also. So it's important to remember that our situation has less cultural support and so we're likely to have to apply much more effort. Because there are far fewer reminders coming from outside, support for our practice will have to reside in our own intention and wish.

The danger is that we become like the Albanian immigrant who comes to Germany, and then lives in a little grouping of Albanians, and actually speaks Albanian and cooks Albanian food and is really an Albanian living in Germany, and doesn't integrate. In that situation, the Albanian doesn't want to be German; the Albanian wants to be Albanian in a better kind of Albania, called Germany.

We can easily do the same with dharma. We can want to have our samsaric existence but have it in a slightly more comfortable situation, with some dharma ideas around to provide some social support, social security. This is why it's very important to understand the basic principles in dharma, that although we have faith and we believe that Padmasambhava is looking towards us, if we don't look at him the connection won't be made. We have to be committed to finding a new identity in/through him, and to make this more important than any of our existing identities. This is more the old American notion of immigrants letting go of their roots and being reborn through the melting pot. Although it is frequently said that we should look on the teacher as a doctor and the dharma as the medicine and ourselves as a patient, and then take the medicine according to the instruction from the teacher, it's a big mistake to imagine that the guru is a surgeon, that the initiation is an operating theatre, and that the blessing is an anaesthetic. You can't just do it in a passive way and expect the teacher to do it for you, or to you. If you do that, then very little will happen. It's actually much more like a psychotherapy, that the patient gets the benefit through participation. The therapist and the patient have to engage together. Padmasambhava is willing to engage but *we* have to engage, and the whole puja structure is about that engagement. Without the relationship, nothing happens.

The same problems that arise in psychotherapy arise in dharma. Patients can be too far away, they miss appointments, they don't turn up, they fall asleep, they arrive drunk, and so on. Or the patient can be too involved. They can be very attacking towards the therapist. They can attack them physically, they can insult them, they can fall on the ground and cry, they can turn on the fire alarms. They do many things, and we say that these modes of withdrawal or invasion attack or undermine the working alliance. That's really what the samaya is, it's the working alliance. It's the commitment from the guru, from Padmasambhava, from the buddhas, to compassionately make a connection with us, and from our side to respectfully and gratefully receive that connection and to maintain it. Nowadays, most psychotherapists would say that the work is done in the relationship, the relationship itself *is* the work.

It's the same in tantra. The transformation of tantra occurs through the relationship. The classic example of this is Milarepa, where in the early days of his relationship with Marpa, the relationship largely turned around the purification of his sins, limitations and obscurations and then later, through the development of the relationship, he began to be able to integrate himself with the state of Marpa. So Milarepa said, "When I understood my guru, I understood my mind." The relationship in tantra is absolutely central and that's why the practices of praising are very important.

## Praise and Integration with the Guru

ཧྲཱིཿ གདོད་མའི་རང་མདངས་སྐུ་གསུམ་བླ་མ་རྗེཿ
སྐྱབས་ཀུན་འདུས་པ་རང་རིག་པདྨ་འབྱུངཿ
རིག་རྩལ་སྤྲུལ་པ་དཀྱིལ་འཁོར་ཡོངས་རྫོགས་ལཿ
བདག་ཅག་རབ་གུས་གདུང་བས་ཕྱག་འཚལ་བསྟོདཿ

**HRI DOD MAI RANG DANG KU SUM LA MA JE
KYAB KUN DUE PA RANG RIG PADMA JUNG
RIG TSAL TRUL PA KYIL KHOR YONG DZOG LA
DAG CHAG RAB GUE DUNG WAE CHAG TSAL TOD**

*Hri. The primordial radiance, the reverend three-kaya guru,
the encompasser of all the refuges, my own awareness, Padmasambhava
— to the complete mandala, the emanation of the energy wave of
awareness, we make salutation with intense faith and devotion.*

From the very beginning of time there has been the unchanging nature of the three kaya guru. Not dependent on anything, it manifests according to causes and conditions. For us, it manifests as Padmasambhava, our own awareness, the unification, or assembly, of all the different refuges. My awareness, *rangrig*, needs to be understood correctly. It is closer to me than my heart beat yet infinitely foreign to my ordinary sense of self. If the ego grasps at it, it will only get a concept and become foolishly inflated. We are not who we think we are. Our awareness, our nature, is revealed when we drop reliance on concepts.

We are used to being ourselves, being Robert, being James, being whoever it is, but we have only been in this identity for a very short time, and in all our previous lives we've had different identities. Our enduring identity is as Padmasambhava, as the three-kaya guru. But if this is not clear then, as with this story of the immigrant, if you think, "Well, Albanian James is going to wrap himself in German Padmasambhava in order to have a nice life," you will get completely confused, the false self will become inflated, you will think you've got something and then this misunderstood dharma will become a poison.

This is why the preparatory practices in dharma are very important. They establish you in the correct frame of reference regarding time and space. I meet many buddhists, who say, "Well, I don't believe in past lives. I don't believe in future lives. Dharma for me is a way of understanding my present existence." But it seems, to me anyway, impossible to really practise tantra from that point of view. The reason we need to move out of being Robert or James or whoever, is because this is not a good basis for life, because death will come and the mind will whirl off and go somewhere else, and unless you have an identity which can contain and direct this anxious self at the moment of death, it will be terrified. The identification with Padmasambhava is something which moves across the three times. Padmasambhava is master of the three times: in the beginning was Padmasambhava, at the end of the world will be Padmasambhava.

It is not that I am James pretending to be Padmasambhava; I am Padmasambhava forgetting myself, and then pretending or imagining that I am James. That is the real thing, that is what we get in the moment of the initiation, it's the introduction to who we are in terms of the samboghakaya identification. And then from the experience of being Padmasambhava, that being you can see, Robert, is an aspect of this, it's integrated. So when people say, "Hey Robert," you say, "Yes, hello," without collapsing into that identification, but keeping being Robert as an aspect of your three kaya nature.

To you, Padmasambhava, I offer salutation, but I'm also Padmasambhava at the same time. Padmasambhava is located everywhere, nobody can have a monopoly of him. Without losing my own maintenance of the three-kaya view I can praise Padmasambhava with deep love and devotion. There is no contradiction in the drama of non-dual manifestation.

### Praying to the Lama as the Unity of the Three Jewels

དེ་ལྟ་མ་མཆིན་ནོ༔

གང་གཉིས་གཙོ་མཆོག་གི་སངས་རྒྱས༔

ཞི་བ་ཆགས་བྲལ་གྱི་དམ་ཆོས༔

ཚོགས་མཆོག་འཕགས་པ་ཡི་དགེ་འདུན༔

མཆོག་གསུམ་ཀུན་འདུས་ཀྱི་དོ་བོ༔
དྲིན་ཆེན་རྩ་བའི་བླ་མ་རིན་པོ་ཆེ་མཁྱེན་ནོ༔

**AE LA MA KHYEN NO
KANG NYI TSO CHOG GI SANG GYAE
ZHI WA CHAG DRAL GYI DAM CHOE
TSOG CHOG PHAG PA YI GEN DUN
CHOG SUM KUN DUE KYI NGO WO
DRIN CHEN TSA WAI LA MA RIN PO CHE KHYEN NO**

*Oh! Master hear me! Buddha, the chief and supreme of all humans, the holy dharma, peaceful and free of desire, the noble sangha, the most excellent assembly, the epitome of these three excellents who include them all — most kind, precious, root guru — please hear me!*

One of the very big questions for our time is, what is love? Traditionally, according to buddhism, love is the wish *may all beings be happy*, so love is a positive thought for the well-being of others. But of course, we're aware in our own lives that feelings of love towards someone carry a lot of dependence with them, a lot of longing, a lot of neediness. We often go towards other people with a sense of some kind of inner emptiness, or loneliness, and then we meet someone that we really like, and we hope that that person is going to take this away from us. Sometimes, of course, mutual dependency can be a good basis for relationships to continue through time but, often, extreme dependence from one person destroys relationship. In this practice we take all the sadness and loneliness and fear and anxiety of our life, and we bring it into an appeal to the guru to not cut off from us. When we say *lama khyenno*, we mean, "Be with me, stay with me, pay attention to me." Just as when a small child says, "Papa," it's very strong, because it feels irresistible.

In this prayer, we have the three jewels of refuge: the Buddha who is the best of all two-legged creatures, the dharma which is peaceful and free from desire, and the sangha which is the best assembly. When C R Lama explained this to me, he said that the best refuge of all is the dharma, because dharma doesn't want anything from you. Every other refuge wants something.

Then the prayer identifies the precious lama as the essence, or the real nature of the integration, the meeting of these three jewels. In most cultures, children call their parents 'mother' and 'father'. In some families, in the sixties, children were encouraged to call their parents by their personal names, John, Mary and so forth. This emphasised that we interact as people but it disguised role obligation. In this prayer we can put the person's name in, but primarily we're talking about the person in a role, performing a function. We say 'lama' because the person is there as a lama, in their function of lama to us. We say 'Rinpoche', not just because that lama is precious for us, but because they take up the position of a Rinpoche, a position which carries very clear patterns of behaviour, a very clear identity.

If somebody calls out, "Oh, James," then I have to think, "What is my relationship with this person?" But if my son says to me, "Dad," then "Oh, I'm already in that relation with him. I don't have a choice about that," and it's exactly like this here. When we say 'Lama Rinpoche' you lock onto a particular structure of relating, so there should be no doubt or hesitancy about what will happen.

### Praying to the Lama as the Unity of the Three Roots

ཨེ་བླ་མ་མཁྱེན་ནོ༔
བྱིན་རླབས་གཏེར་མཛོད་ཀྱི་བླ་མ༔
དངོས་གྲུབ་ཀུན་འབྱུང་གི་ཡི་དམ༔
བར་ཆད་ཀུན་སེལ་གྱི་མཁའ་འགྲོ༔
རྩ་གསུམ་ཀུན་འདུས་ཀྱི་ངོ་བོ༔
དྲིན་ཆེན་རྩ་བའི་བླ་མ་རིན་པོ་ཆེ་མཁྱེན་ནོ༔

**AE LA MA KHYEN NO JIN LAB TER DZOD KYI LA MA
NGOE DRUB KUN JUNG GI YI DAM
BAR CHAD KUN SEL GYI KHAN DRO
TSA SUM KUN DUE KYI NGO WO
DRIN CHEN TSA WAI LA MA RIN PO CHE KHYEN NO**

*Oh! Master hear me! Guru, the treasure house of blessings, wishing god, inexhaustible source of real attainments, dakini who clears away all obstacles, the epitome of these three roots who includes them all, most kind, precious root guru, please hear me!*

The guru is able to bless because he, or she, is not distracted, is not caught up in reacting to events, is not dispersing her energy in identification with objects of attachment. Blessing is not just a concept but a living, communicable quality of the lama. Just as a *chi kung* master can use *chi*, or energy, for healing or defence, so a lama, through their practice, is able to store and release energy. This release can come in the form of a warm reassuring feeling, or as a more robust shaking of our energetic balance, often bringing visions.

The yidam is the source of attainment, of both supreme and ordinary siddhis. The supreme siddhi is the realisation of one's own nature, and the ordinary siddhis are the energetic powers that flow out from that: being able to tell the future, being able to read other people's minds, and so forth. Siddhis are one of the fruits of the practice. To spend one's life developing an apple tree that gives no fruit would be silly. We practice the dharma in order to get something, even if it is not a thing which can be got. Ambition is mobilised towards actualising the desireless state.

The dakini is the one who clears away all obstacles. There are many kinds of obstacle, but in general an obstacle is something which sabotages our intention towards enlightenment. We can experience it either as the world blocking us, or a particular way in which we get lost. The dakinis move freely in space, nothing blocks them or gets in their way; they are a bit like Mercury, performing communicative and connective functions. In the word *barchad*, obstacle, *bar* means middle, and *chad* means to cut, in other words, an interruption. For example, we have some intention in our life: we're going on a journey, but then there is a landslide or we get a puncture or we don't have the visa to cross the border, in that way our journey gets interrupted. The connective quality of the dakini makes links, puts bridges across these interruptions. If a link is not made, if the flow of energy is blocked, we tend to get stuck, to feel blocked, heavy, angry, hopeless, and so on. All these feelings intensify dualistic thinking and the felt sense of being an isolated, limited being, so having the help of the dakinis to get out of them quickly is a great help.

## Praying to the Lama as the Unity of the Three Kayas

ཨེ་བླ་མ་མཁྱེན་ནོ༔
ངོ་བོ་ཀ་དག་གི་ཆོས་སྐུ༔
རང་བཞིན་ལྷུན་གྲུབ་ཀྱི་ལོངས་སྐུ༔
ཐུགས་རྗེ་ཀུན་ཁྱབ་ཀྱི་སྤྲུལ་སྐུ༔
སྐུ་གསུམ་ཀུན་འདུས་ཀྱི་ངོ་བོ༔
དྲིན་ཅེན་རྩ་བའི་བླ་མ་རིན་པོ་ཆེ་མཁྱེན་ནོ༔

**AE LA MA KHYEN NO NGO WO KA DAG GI CHOE KU**
**RANG ZHIN LHUN DRUB KYI LONG KU**
**THUG JE KUN KHYAB KYI TRUL KU**
**KU SUM KUN DUE KYI NGO WO**
**DRIN CHEN TSA WAI LA MA RIN PO CHE KHYEN NO**

*Oh! Master hear me! Dharmakaya, the real nature, pure from the very beginning, sambhogakaya, the natural quality effortlessly arising, nirmanakaya, the all-pervading compassion, the epitome of these three kayas who includes them all, most kind, precious root guru — please hear me!*

In tantra, we talk of dharmakaya, samboghakaya, nirmanakaya. In dzogchen, we talk more of *ngo wo*, *rang zhin* and *thug je*. Sometimes they are treated as being identical and sometimes as different. It is important not to be complacent when we read dharma texts. The meaning of a word lies in its contextual usage, not in a fixed dictionary definition. We have to see how different writers use technical terms and how they vary their own usage. Relying on fixed meanings is just another form of attachment. We have to be open to change, contingency, emergence. After all, there are no fixed entities; language is not referring to things 'out there' but is part of the process of our experience. In this verse, they're brought together and treated as being pretty much the same. The first line says that the dharmakaya is the natural condition, which is pure from the very beginning. Dharmakaya is not the result of any process. Pure from the very beginning, it is self-existing, requiring no props, no purification, no developments.

In the dharma texts of Tibetan buddhism it is common to find lines like "Please bless us with the understanding of the dharmakaya, may I realise the dharmakaya, may I gain the dharmakaya", yet the dharmakaya is not an object to be gained. We have to remember that puja texts use different aspects of ourselves to mobilise the energy inherent in these self-states, these sub-personalities, in the direction of the dharma. Therefore, although dharmakaya is never created, sometimes we have to pray for it, as if somebody was going to give it to us like a Christmas present.

If you go back to European philosophy and Kant's discussion of the relation between means and ends then, although the end of dharmakaya has been there from the very beginning and so is a paradoxical end, it is also an end which is not determined by the means by which we get to it. It's not that the means determines the end, but that the means are determined by the obstacles to the end. This is crucial, because it is the essence of why we have so many methods in buddhism: the method is there to help you deal with your own particular limitations, and because we have many different kinds of limitations, knowing many different methods is useful. However, none of these methods determine or create the end result because it has been there from the very beginning.

In the next line the samboghakaya is described as the effortless display of the radiance, or the natural quality, of the ground nature. *Rang zhin*, my face, is that which is revealed without any effort out of the ground nature. A traditional example for that is, if a person is healthy then their face will shine, the skin will be good, and they look alive and vital. It's not that the health in the body has to somehow push itself out, it's not putting on a show, it's not intentional, it just radiates out. At the moment we have the Cannes film festival, and there will be a lot of artificial radiance on display there. This is different.

Then we have the nirmanakaya, which is the presence everywhere of compassion. Now, *kun khyab* is not spreading out from one point, not from here to there. It is omnipresent. Compassion is not something that I have and then give to others. It is a quality of connection, of non-interruption, of the free flow of energy in the dharmadhatu. In terms of the bodhisattva idea, there are two main kinds of compassion, with an object, and without an object. Compassion without an object doesn't mean that you just kind of get a cup of compassion and throw it someplace because it doesn't matter where it goes. In Tibetan it's called *mig me nying je*. *Mig pa* means to have a precise identification of the other. It's like a kind of assessment of the other, like a psychiatric assessment. *Mig me* is the negation of that, it is an openness, a non-appropriation, a non-totalising welcome to whatever manifests. It does not reduce the phenomenological field to a finite number of entities. Rather, because of its spaciousness, it tolerates not knowing, the revelation of becoming and, free of strategy and tactics, responds freshly into the moment.

What this is describing is actually compassion which has a subject. That is to say, I enter into a relation with you, but I don't know who you are because I'm appreciating you as a subject who reveals themselves — indeed, it is not something apart from the revelation. My compassion can't be based on an assessment of you, as I know you to be, because that will be already a violence against you, so I await your presentation and, of course, each presentation is unique and specific because of impermanence, because our energy is changing all the time. Therefore, I need to attend to you in this moment, as you are in your presentation of being, and then respond to that from my state in *this* moment. Now, if I have been doing the practice, my state will be the integration of *ngo wo* and *rang zhin*, of the real nature and its natural radiance and then, from that, the response will arise, uncontaminated by karma, habit, conditioning, obscuration, and so forth.

Now, today is Saturday, and on Saturday afternoon people will be playing football, and whenever a professional football match takes place there are people there watching it with video cameras, and these video cameras are taken back and the recordings watched, because all the time teams want to work out what is the standard game plan of the opposition team they're going to play. That is also how we behave in life. We check people out, we act on the basis of assumptions, and if we have accurate assumptions about other people we can act in ways that fit in with (if we want to), or are against (if we want to), their game plan, and in that way we can get close to them or control them, or mess them up, depending on what we want to do. We say 'knowledge is power', and on the basis of this we have industrial espionage, or the *Stasi*, or spies of various kinds.

As we've discussed before, this arises out of anxiety. Every company nowadays, in this time of intense capitalist competition, has to make good alliances. Motorcar companies are always trying to work out who to make alliances with. I.T. companies, technology companies, they're very anxious about the future, who will be the enemy, who is the ally, so they want to have information to stay ahead of the game.

The ego is structured in exactly the same way. The ego is always anxious about its own identity, feels under threat from others, wants to expand and have a universal empire, and so it tries to rely on information of the field, of the environment, in order to develop its best chance. Our root question is always, "What's in it for me?" and a lot of compassion is also structured around this question. For example, America under Clinton has been championing free-trade status, best trading-partner status, for China but this is not compassion for the starving people in China, compassion for the Tibetans, it's based on the economic interests of America.

A lot of my work in hospital is with quite violent men, and I have an interest that they should be less violent. Hopefully it will make their lives nicer, but it also makes one less dangerous person walking down the street at night. That is a key motivation, to make my world safer for me, so it's very, very important for us always to examine ourselves, our relation with our own ego attachment, our relation with our own five poisons, before we think about compassion, because it's very easy to get lost in compassion, to get to think one's acting from a pure basis but then find one was really just trying to take care of oneself.

The pervasive nature of responsive energy arises with the sense that self and other arise together in an integrated field of manifestation. Movements anywhere in that field will bring about shifts and changes, and the whole field has to be privileged, because the whole field is the natural expression of dharmakaya, dharmadhatu.

If you get an itch in your neck and you scratch it, you don't then thank your finger. It's the same in the world. When we see that the world is integrated and that we are part of the world and the world is part of us and that we are inseparable, then there is no need to make any profit out of compassion, because why would you not act for the benefit of others, when others are not separate from you?

The profit motive was, of course, very much criticised by Karl Marx as a barrier to developing a collaborative, communal society, and profit is also a sign for us that our practice is going in the wrong direction. If we want to get recognised as a great meditator or a very nice person, if we are concerned with name and fame and reputation, this is a sign that we are not really practising dharma.

Just as, according to the general mahayana principles, at the end of a piece of dharma practice we dedicate the merit, so in this more finely attuned movement, each gesture, each breath, is dedicated in the moment of its arising, so that it leaves no trace, there is nothing for us to take away with us.

This is self-liberating compassion. Then we say, "You are the root, or the essence, of these three kayas. Precious guru, please listen to us".

These are prayers we can say again and again and again, many, many times. You can change your tone of voice, go through all kinds of emotions. It's a very powerful way of making connection. Then you can also recite the following line, putting your guru's name into the verse:

ཊིན་ཆེན་རྩ་བའི་བླ་མ་..............རིན་པོ་ཆེ་མཁྱེན་ནོ༔

**DRIN CHEN TSA WAI LA MA (NAME) RIN PO CHE KHYEN NO**

*Very kind root guru, precious (his or her name), please hear me!*

What is the meaning of root guru? 'Root' means the guru who helps you recognise your own nature. Usually we are leading our life *here*, we are walking on a surface which is the surface of our own ignorance, our karma, our assumptions, and we are interacting with the world. Below this surface is the real nature, the ground of the dharmakaya, dharmadhatu, but we don't see that, and when we interact with other people, they all tell us, "Oh yeah, you're doing fine, this is life", and so we keep going on that level. The root guru is the one who removes this veil of illusion and plants you back in your own real nature. He is the root of your enlightenment because he roots you in your own nature. That doesn't mean that this teacher is the most glamorous teacher in the world or the most wonderful teacher in the world, but he or she is the one who performs this function. And just because somebody has a special name and a special title, it doesn't mean that they will be able to provide that function for you.

## h. Encouragement on Impermanence

ཨོཾ་ཨཿཧཱུྃ་མ་ཧཱ་གུ་རུ་སརྦ་སིདྡྷི་ཧཱུྃ༔
འཇིག་རྟེན་སྣང་བ་སྒྱུ་མར་གོ་ལགས་ཀྱང་༔
འཁྲུལ་སྣང་འདི་ལ་དྲང་བདག་འཛིན་སྐྱེས༔
བདག་གི་ཉོན་མོངས་བག་ཆགས་མ་སྟོངས་པར༔
ཆགས་ཞེན་རྩད་ནས་ཆོད་པར་བྱིན་གྱིས་རློབས༔

**OM AH HUNG MA HA GU RU SARVA SIDDHI HUNG
JIG TEN NANG WA GYU MAR GO LAG KYANG
THRUL NANG DI LA DA DUNG DAG DZIN KYE
DAG GI NYON MONG BAG CHAG MA TONG WAR
CHAG ZHEN TSAD NAE CHOD PAR JIN GYI LOB**

*Body, speech, mind. Great teacher, grant me all real attainments. Although I know worldly appearances/ideas to be illusory, there still arises grasping at these bewildering appearances as being something inherently real. My afflictions and their subtle traces are not yet finished. Please bless me by cutting the root of attachments and longing.*

This prayer comes from the great terton Rigdzin Godem. It was an important part of his own practice, as it was for C R Lama.

*Om Ah Hung Maha Guru Sarva Siddhi Hung* is said to be the inner mantra for Padmasambhava. We can use it to evoke his presence in front of us, in order to call on his help in a dualistic way. We can also use it to instantly bring us into the three kaya state of Padmasambhava, to integrate with him and use the prayer as a means of re-integrating our energy. You choose the approach according to your capacity and condition. The prayer reminds us of mistakes, of things that go wrong, so we can use it for an honest appraisal of how we are doing. However, it is important not to get caught up in guilt, shame, worry, self-recrimination and attack. These will not help. Relax, trust the guru and the practice, and trust the view. No matter what you have done or not done, your own nature is always there, pure, perfect and open.

So according to one's mood, (and again, there is no right or wrong way to say this), when you feel out of control, then you pray to big Padmasambhava, when you feel a bit more in control and you want to settle in yourself, you use this as a way of just settling.

It begins: 'Although I know all worldly phenomena are illusory.' In the tradition of mahayana buddhism there are twelve famous examples given to show the illusory nature of the world: the reflection of the moon on water, a mirage in the desert, the child of a barren woman, the horns on the head of a hare, and so forth. And there are many explanations of emptiness, showing that the world is like a dream. 'Yet although I may have a clear intellectual understanding, and know all the theory, grasping, powerful grasping, emotional grasping, still arises towards these confusing appearances.'

This arises because of *dag dzin*, our tendency to impute inherent self-nature to self and other. We don't have any sweet term in English for this. It doesn't really mean the same as attachment to something. For example, I can be attached to my pen or my watch because it's mine, so I have an emotional attachment to something which is important to me. This emotional attachment is impossible without the sense that there is something here which has a separate existence, which is autonomous and self-existing, in other words, the sense of the watch as a separate entity is prior to my attachment to it. Its own seemingly inherent self-nature becomes the support for all the emotional reactions. In English there's a word 'reification' which speaks to this, the sense of the 'thingness' of the phenomena. The things we see appear to be just themselves, existing by, and out of, themselves. They appear to be entities, to be both separate and self-confirming, having their own independent existence complete with functions, qualities and value.

It's not that we just have some wrong thoughts that we can analyse and correct. It's something prior to that, rooted in fundamental ignorance itself. That's why it is so difficult to get rid of this because, in our karmic dimension, this is our automatic response to things. In fact it's one of the reasons why the tantric method was developed, for it was clear that intellectual analysis coupled with mindfulness practice were not enough to cut the root of entitative experience. Real life is fast and complex, we can't just step out of it and calmly analyse things, for we live in the thick of it. We need to be able to be with phenomena without being trapped.

Thus, in tantra we spend a lot of time developing the mandala out of emptiness, to experience directly that when we visualise Padmasambhava or the mandala, it is there, it looks there, it seems real. But we know, experientially rather than analytically or intellectually, that it is the fruit of emptiness, it is itself emptiness. And that's also one reason why, in the nyingma traditions, they often don't privilege logic and debate. A good grounding in the mahayana texts is very helpful, but the key tool for awakening is practice, and the maintenance of the experience of the world as the deity in all situations.

It's also interesting that the text says *dag dzin kye*. *Kye* means to be born or to arise, and I think that speaks to our experience, we find ourselves caught up in something. You try to do the practice, at the end of it you come out and suddenly you're gone, you're just caught, suddenly merged in a flow of ideas. That's how it happens, it just arises and it seems right because it's so very familiar. In that sense it's a bit like the Freudian unconscious, things arise from our unconscious and we find ourselves caught up in them. In English we say, "It took me over," (the 'it' of the unconscious), and so it's very difficult to resist. However it is clear that we are not *doing* it, this is not an ego function, this is something which is prior to ego. Without *dag dzin*, reification, you don't have ego in the sense of me, *as me*, separated out.

Although it feels as if it is the king, the agent, the self-existing one who makes things happen, the sense of self is actually a product, a dynamic product that continues as long as its constitutive process flows on. We behave like small children who think that they are the centre of the world and that they make everything happen. Like them, we don't stay in touch with the fact that we're very small, it would be too annihilating to face the truth, and so the ego lives in fantasy like an anxious child.

When we do *shiné/shamatha* practice to calm the mind, one of the key benefits is to realise how wild our mind is. Recognising our chaos can help expose the ego's pretensions.

The ego cannot manage the complexity of the mind. When life gets difficult and the waves of emotion and so forth run through us, what do we do? We repress, we dissociate, we regress, we make use of objects in the world to change our mood. We get drunk, we get stoned, we have a fight, we have a fuck, we do all sorts of things, we watch television till four o'clock in the morning, some stupid American film, anything to take you out of yourself. And then in the morning you think, "*How* many bags of popcorn? Who drank all these bottles!" This is very, very important, because it's not then to say, "Oh the ego is bad," it's simply that the ego is a function of our existence which is very useful for certain tasks, but not for all tasks, and if you try to do very, very complicated tasks with a very, very simple tool, you will always fail.

In Britain, we have a general ruling that doctors shouldn't prescribe for their own family because they're too involved with these people and it's better to have someone with a bit more professional distance. That's very much the same with this ego. The ego is too involved. The ego is the aspect of ourselves that's very busy, very attached, self-protective and so forth, so it's always spiralling every possibility round about itself, "What about me? What about me?" Only awareness, only this quality of dharmakaya, is vast enough, open enough, to be able to hold the complexity without distorting it around a point of self. So what's really important here is not to beat yourself up and say, "Oh I must try harder," because if it's the guilty ego part of yourself that's going to try harder to control something which is outside its control then you have the basis for very bad meditation practice.

The third line says, "My afflictions and the subtle traces are not finished, they haven't gone". The afflictions are the more gross form of energetic interaction with the environment. The five main afflictions are stupidity, aversion, desire, jealousy and pride. When Buddha Shakyamuni got enlightened under the Bodhi tree, he stopped all his afflictions, but for the rest of his life, until his final and complete enlightenment, he was still having to deal with the residual subtle traces, they hadn't finished at that time. The traditional example for this is, if you have a pot and you put a musk pod in the pot, and leave it for some time, and then take it out, there will still be the smell of the musk. The subtle traces are important because they can, if we are drawn into them, easily spiral us back into the afflictions.

Having taken the bodhisattva vow, and committed ourselves to the welfare of all beings and that their enlightenment and our enlightenment are inseparable, we have to accept that their afflictions and subtle traces are also ours. Its not just a case of becoming very calm and undisturbed but of being in the world with others without being conditioned by the many afflictions, vexations, hooks to attachment, and so on, that arise. This is where we need the powerful methods of tantra. When we merge with the guru we practice that all experience is inseparable from his nature. The guru is not fenced off from samsara but neither is he caught up in it or contaminated by it. So, in the practice, we relax and all experience manifests as the pure form of the guru, all outer and inner experience, shapes, sounds, thoughts, feelings. The form of the arising is not changed. It may be an affliction, a rough and troublesome thought, but by giving it space it goes by itself, revealing its empty nature.

In this way, without trying to change or alter all the many troublesome objects in the world, including the arising of those aspects we call 'self', the open nature of awareness remains undefiled. When we forget this we are again trapped in the flow of afflictions and subtle traces that have no end, so rather than try to finish (*tong wa*) the afflictions, we want to cut the root by cutting reification.

ༀ་ཨཱཿཧཱུྃ་མ་ཧཱ་གུ་རུ་སརྦ་སིདྡྷི་ཧཱུྃ༔
སྙིགས་མའི་ལས་ངན་མི་རྟག་རང་གཟུགས་ལ༔
ངེས་འབྱུང་སྐྱེས་ནས་ཆགས་ཞེན་ཡུལ་བོར་ཡང་༔
ཕྱིས་ནས་རང་བདེའི་ཡུལ་འདོད་དུ་ཁས་མནར༔
འདོད་སྲེད་རྩད་ནས་ཆོད་པར་བྱིན་གྱིས་རློབས༔

**OM AH HUNG MA HA GU RU SARVA SIDDHI HUNG
NYIG MAI LAE NGEN MI TAG RANG ZUG LA
NGE JUNG KYE NAE CHAG ZHEN YUL BOR YANG
CHI NAE RANG DEI YUL DOD DU KHAE NAR
DOD SED TSAD NAE CHOD PAR JIN GYI LOB**

*Body, speech, mind. Great teacher, grant me all real attainments. Towards the impermanent manifestations of the bad actions of this debased period renunciation arises and I discard the objects of my attachment and longing. Yet later on I am troubled by the sufferings of desire for the objects of my daily use. Please bless me by cutting the roots of desire and craving.*

There is a traditional belief that the world is in a state of decline and that the decline will continue until either the world is destroyed and renewed or until the next buddha, Maitreya, appears. Although our material wealth, at least in western countries, is increasing, perhaps we are in decline. Paradoxically, the more we feel we are in control, setting the agenda, making things happen, we deepen our already serious problems. When we feel that we human beings, through science and through our own efforts, have made the world a better place, this reinstalls our belief that the ego is the king, and so the more we seem to be powerful, the more we go under the power of ignorance and the afflictions. There is little evidence that our money makes us better people, let alone develops a desire to question what it means to be human.

From a buddhist point of view this really is a bad time because the possibility of practising dharma becomes more and more faint, and even when people do practice dharma, they often become confused. Also lineages get lost, and as the dharma community weakens people get involved in their own private games. In this time bad karma ripens and our negative tendencies increase. This manifests in the ever increasing rate of change, as impermanence undermines the fragile sense of familiarity and security that most people rely on to maintain their sense of self. We can see this in terms of technological change. It's just galloping and galloping, each day brings some new discovery. The form of the world is changing so quickly, people are rushing to get back in control. Living in Britain is like being in a car with a drunken driver, it's accelerator/brake, accelerator/brake, as we lurch between order and disorder. And clearly for some people, fundamentalist ideologies, both religious and secular, provide a false security. It is this pervasive anxiety which is really the quality that takes people further into samsara, as they seek mastery rather than relaxation.

As the second line of the verse states, towards this situation renunciation arises, and I cut or get rid of the objects of my attachment and longing. But then later, the objects of my own happiness come and hook me back again, which brings suffering. Most people who have done meditation retreats will have experienced this kind of situation, where you live in a little room and you have no contact outside for a long time and you have nothing much to do, other than the puja. Except, every now and then you have *tsog*, an offering ceremony, and so you have your bag of nice things that you're going to offer for the *tsog*, and you look at that bag every time, and you take out the little sweets and put them in a row and count them up and down and think, "Well, today I'll have two," and then the whole world becomes these very small objects.

The prayer is stating very clearly that we have a real problem. If you try to purify an object, you may succeed with that object, but because the tendency to get involved, the tendency to invest objects with meaning, is so powerful in the mind, in samsara, it cannot be simply discarded like a chocolate cake. Rather, the most stupid little object can easily be invested with great meaning, and then it hooks us. Cutting attachment and longing is very difficult for it is woven into the structure of the world we live in. If we stop buying, the economy falters and unemployment starts to increase.

Although desire and craving have infinite objects to be interested in, they only have one root, ignorance, which is not knowing our own nature, emptiness. It's always the same root. That's what makes it easy, if you get that one root, the whole of samsara is gone. If you cut the root of the subject connection with object, all objects go free. It doesn't mean you have to annihilate the object, or kill it off, but it is no longer disturbing. In order to do this you have to cut the root of identification with the subject. As long as we reify the subject we reinforce duality, and blind ourselves to the fact that the self or subject is manifestation devoid of inherent self nature. In that way the reified radiance of the dharmata blocks the integration of the energy into its own ground, creating misery and chaos.

ༀ་ཨཿཧཱུྃ་མ་ཧཱ་གུ་རུ་སརྦ་སིདྡྷི་ཧཱུྃ༔
དུག་གསུམ་ཉོན་མོངས་སེལ་བའི་ཐབས་ཆེན་པོ༔
རྒྱལ་བས་ལུང་བསྟན་མང་པོ་གསུང་ལགས་ཀྱང༔
ཕྲ་བའི་བག་ཆགས་དབང་དུ་ཤས་ཆེར་ཤོར༔
ལས་ངན་རྩད་ནས་གཅོད་པར་བྱིན་གྱིས་རློབས༔

**OM AH HUNG MA HA GU RU SARVA SIDDHI HUNG**
**DUG SUM NYON MONG SEL WAI THAB CHEN PO**
**GYAL WAE LUNG TEN MANG PO SUNG LAG KYANG**
**PONG KAI BAG CHAG WANG DU SHAE CHER SHOR**
**LAE NGEN TSAD NAE CHOD PAR JIN GYI LOB**

*Body, speech, mind. Great teacher, grant me all real attainments.*
*Great methods for clearing away the afflictions of the three poisons have*
*been spoken by the jinas in many teachings, yet I very strongly go under*
*the power of the subtle karmic traces that are so difficult to abandon.*
*Please bless me by cutting the root of all bad actions.*

All the buddhas have in their teachings described many different methods for removing the affliction of the three poisons, from the basic hinayana methods of renunciation, through the paths of the accumulation of merits and the accumulation of wisdom, all the prajnaparamita teachings, logic and so forth, right up to the highest teaching of tantra and dzogchen. Yet, although all these teachings exist, and although we may, in fact, know many aspects of them, yet we are still very strongly under the power of the subtle traces that are so difficult to remove.

Because our ego, our conscious sense of self, is so fragmented, so functionally incoherent, it is easy for us to compartmentalise our knowledge of our experience. Just because we know something and can act in a certain way when we are calm does not ensure that one can, and will, behave the same way under pressure. For example, in war time, we know that people do terrible things that they wouldn't do in other circumstances. The civilising influences that keep people a little bit calm, a little bit clear, are removed, and although it's the same people, very educated and civilised, when they encounter provocation they start to behave from a much more primitive aspect of themselves, and afterwards they wonder what came over them. This is a very common experience.

That's why it's very important to really observe yourself under all circumstances and to keep trying to apply the dharma during the most difficult times of your life, really applying it into life. As Shantideva says in the *Bodhicaryavatara*[9], your best friend is your enemy, because your enemy shows you your anger and your limitation. If you have nice friends, and your nice friends let you have nice times with them, you come into the illusory notion that you're a nice person. That's fine if we simply want to pass an easy life, but at other times things happen and we realise that we really are selfish and we really are cruel. Often these things arise when we are not so powerful, so that we collapse and learn nothing but the practice of self-pity. It's important not to be seduced by fantasies about yourself, while at the same time maintaining the view of the three kaya guru.

One of the functions of thinking about past lives and karma is that it helps us to see that in our previous lives we have probably done very horrible things. The five poisons are not just a passing mistake, they are a mode of functioning which is at the core of our ordinary sense of self, so it's very helpful to have teachers like Chhimed Rigdzin who can be very provocative and make you more aware of your own limitations, because, if you realise your own limitations early, then you have more time to work on them. But you know, one of our big tendencies in life is to brush things under the carpet. Often we manage a situation in our life, and we don't know how we managed it, but anyway we think, "Oh God, happy that's over," and we go on to the next thing. We don't learn anything about what we were caught up in.

---

[9] Santideva: *The Bodhicaryavatara* (*Oxford World's Classics*) Translated by Kate Crosby, Andrew Skilton. (Oxford University Press, 1998)

Through this avoidance we are condemned, by ourselves, to repeat the same mistakes. Therefore it's vital to recognise the deep cause of our behaviour, and that's why the text says, "Please bless me by cutting the root of bad activity".

What is the root of bad activity? It is wrong thinking and heedless impulses. Both arise from ignorance and the consequent force of attachment which rests on seeing things — situations, memories, thoughts, perceptions — as being inherently real. Usually we have a great resistance to seeing this. If it is well structured, group therapy can be much more effective than individual therapy. As the group forms, members come to realise that everybody else is messed-up too, and that's a great relief, because then you don't have to pretend so much. You don't have to pretend because you look around and you can see, "Oh, everybody here is limited, therefore my limitations are not special, so I don't need to take them so seriously". To be human is to be very concerned with other people's opinions about us. We want to make sure that other people don't see the things that we are ashamed of.

We want approval. We go to anyone for feedback, and if you go to people who are unclear mirrors, they will tell you bullshit about yourself, which you will believe because you want to please them, because you don't want to be rejected. This is a very powerful spiral into samsara. It's bad enough to be a puppet of your own karma, but to be the puppet that hands the strings to anyone you meet, that's very silly.

ༀ་ཨཱཿཧཱུྃ་མ་ཧཱ་གུ་རུ་སརྦ་སིདྡྷི་ཧཱུྃཿ
ཕྱི་རྐྱེན་ནང་རྐྱེན་དེ་མ་ཐག་པའི་རྐྱེན༔
ཐམས་ཅད་བསྐྱེད་པའི་རྩ་བ་གཉིས་འཛིན་དུ༔
ད་གཟོད་གོ་ཡང་མདུད་པའི་རྩལ་མ་གྲོལ༔
རང་སེམས་གཅེར་བུར་འཆར་བར་བྱིན་གྱིས་རློབས༔

**OM AH HUNG MA HA GU RU SARVA SIDDHI HUNG**
**CHI KYEN NANG KYEN DE MA THAG PAI KYEN**
**THAM CHE KYED PAI TSA WA NYI DZIN TU**
**DA ZOD GO YANG DUD PAI TSAL MA DROL**
**RANG SEM CHER BUR CHAR BAR JIN GYI LOB**

*Body, speech, mind. Great teacher, grant me all real attainments.*
*Outer causal situations, inner causal situation, and suddenly occurring*
*causal situations all arise from the root of belief in duality.*
*I now know this, but am still not free from the power of mara.*
*Please bless me that my mind may arise nakedly.*

The three kinds of conditions, outer, inner and suddenly occurring, arise from the root of dualistic experience. Once we start identifying with the subject, we find, because subject and object are arising together, that our sense of self is at the mercy of the object field. Ignorance of our nature, and its consequent experience of duality, are the root causes which create a vulnerability to the secondary conditions. When they arise, they impact us very strongly because of our identification with our body and our self-narrative. For example, to illustrate sudden, contingent circumstances: you're working in the kitchen and you're chopping up the vegetables and someone says, "Hey!", you turn around, you cut your finger. Things happen very easily because we are easily distracted, because the balance between inside and outside is not fixed, and these suddenly occurring circumstances catch us off-guard. Outer conditions come from object towards subject, in other words, inflation making prices go up so you have less money to spend. Inner conditions arise in the subject and impact the relational field, for example, getting sick and then being off work.

Then the next line says, "I know this intellectually, but I'm not free from the energy of the demons, the troublesome quality of ignorance". This will always be the case until we let go of the sense that 'I am living in the world that is separate from me'. The Buddha said in many teachings, not just in the high tantric and dzogchen teachings, but in many teachings, "Life is like a dream, everything is an illusion. Living in your own body is an illusion, walking along the road is an illusion, everything you see is an illusion, it's there, but it has no inherent self-nature". When we don't recognise this we believe what is outside is real, what is inside is real, we relax into our assumptions, stop paying attention, and then get hit by circumstances. That's what this is referring to. The main *mara*, or demon, is self-pre-occupation, self-referencing, a tendency which stops us being present in the moment as an aspect of the energy field.

Then it says, "Please bless me that my mind may arise nakedly". 'Naked' is a quality of the dharmakaya, indicating that it is not covered by anything, not obscured, not conditioned, not resting on anything. It indicates direct, fresh, raw — just *there*. The naked mind is the mind which is in emptiness. Out of emptiness all kinds of thoughts and feelings arise; these are the ornaments of the mind, like the necklaces and bangles on the naked, dancing dakini. This is very different from thoughts and feelings being used as a kind of embarrassed, shamed, clothing for the ego that's not sure whether it exists or not. Shameless nakedness allows the ornamentation to be worn as play, as pleasure, whereas fearful, anxious nakedness means that we wrap ourselves defensively in all kinds of clothing, whatever we can grab quickly, and the nearest thing is always the five poisons.

Now, what is the connection with the practice? Later on *(See Section E:l)*, we receive the four initiations and then Padmasambhava dissolves into our body, and we go into the ball of light and vanish down into one tiny point, and then...nothing. In this process we start with a sense of buddhas and lights and the whole universe full of good qualities. Gradually it becomes more and more and more simple, more and more clothing is going off, ornaments are going off, the other vanishes, self vanishes, until finally there's only a simple ball of light, and then that ball of light itself vanishes. There is no clothing at all, nothing to cling to or be distracted by. This is the point where you can realise the naked nature of your mind. That's why it's important to do that bit of the meditation very carefully, because if you recognise the naked mind, then all obscurations are recognised for what they are, all attachment drops and non-duality is revealed. You recognise: "Oh, that's just an ornament, that's not the real basis of my existence," and that is liberation. If only, in the story of the Emperor's new clothes, when the little boy pointed out that the Emperor was naked, everyone had taken their kit off!

ཨོཾ་ཨཱཿཧཱུྃ་མ་ཧཱ་གུ་རུ་ས་རྦ་སི་དྡྷི་ཧཱུྃ༔

གཉིས་འཛིན་བློ་གས་ལས་གྲོལ་བར་བྱིན་གྱིས་རློབས༔

ཞེས་པ་གཟོ་མེད་རང་ལུགས་སུ་ག་པ་ལ༔

མཁས་གྲུབ་ལི་གས་པའི་རང་བཟོ་མ་བྱས་ཤིང༔

བྱིང་འཕྲོ་བས་ག་ཡེང་བའི་བཙོན་རར་མ་བཅིངས་པར༔

བཀག་མེད་རང་ངོ་ཉིད་འཚེར་བའི་རིག་པ་འདི༔

ཆོས་ཉིད་ཡངས་པའི་མ་དང་བུ་འཕྲད་ནས༔

## E. SADHANA: Main Part

ཨེ་ལོ་ཀྱེན་གྱི་གྲོགས་ཕྱིར་མ་འཐོམས་པར༔
ལེགས་པའི་ཁང་བུར་གཅེས་པའི་གཉེར་བྱས་ཏེ༔
མྱུར་དུ་ཆོས་ཉིད་མ་དང་བུ་འཕྲད་ནས༔
ཕྱིར་ཆད་འགྲོ་དོན་སྟོབས་ཆེན་བྱེད་པར་ཤོག༔
བྱང་ཆུབ་སེམས་དཔའི་སྤྱོད་པ་བྱེད་པར་ཤོག༔
གཞན་དོན་དགེ་བ་རླབས་ཆེན་བསྒྲུབ་པར་ཤོག༔
འཁོར་བ་དོང་ནས་སྤྲུག་པའི་མཐུ་ཐོབ་ཤོག༔

OM AH HUNG MA HA GU RU SARVA SIDDHI HUNG
NYI DZIN DROG LAE DROL WAR JIN GYI LOB
SHE PA ZO MED RANG LUG LHUG PA LA
KHAE KYANG LEG PAI RANG ZO MA JAE SHING
JING THIB YENG WAI TSON RAR MA CHING PAR
TRAG DANG RANG OD TSER WAI RIG PA DI
CHOE NYID YANG PAI MA DANG BU THRAD NAE
LE LO KYEN GYI DROG CHIR MA THOM PAR
LEG PAI KHANG BUR CHE PAI NYER JAE TE
NYUR DU CHOE NYID MA DANG BU THRAD NAE
CHIN CHAD DRO DON TOB CHEN JED PAR SHOG
JANG CHUB SEM PAI CHOD PA JED PAR SHOG
ZHEN DON GE WA LAB CHEN DRUB PAR SHOG
KHOR WA DONG NAE TRUG PAI THU THOB SHOG

*Body, speech, mind. Great teacher, grant me all real attainments. Please bless me with freedom from the fetter of belief in duality. Mind itself is unmade, coming easily in its own mode. It is not made by the good deeds and qualities of the Buddha, and it is not bound by the prison of sinking, fogginess and wavering. With this, primordial wisdom's brilliant, radiant, natural, shining light, dharmata's vast mother and son will meet.*

*So not being made stupid by the bad friends of lazy, relaxed situations, I will strongly and lovingly protect the good house of sunyata, and by that dharmata mother and son will quickly meet.*

> *Then, from that time, I must strongly act for the benefit of those moving in samsara. I must perform the deeds of a bodhisattva. I must accomplish a great wave of virtue for the benefit of others. I must gain the effective power to upturn and empty samsara.*

Isn't it about time I stopped being trapped in the fetter of belief in duality? I, myself, can let go; and indeed only I, myself, *can* let go. It's like the Chinese story of the monkey that puts its hand in the jar to get the peanuts, tries to pull its hand out and it can't, because it's stuck, because it's bunched in a fist. And it pulls and pulls, and pulls and pulls, and only when it lets go of the peanut its hand comes out.

We are wired-up for activity. Energetically, in our bodies, we are a bit out of balance and so we twitch and we move, and activity is what we're about. It is very difficult for human beings to relax. This is why, certainly in Britain, you now have thousands of magazines out every week on every possible activity, you know, hang-gliding and yachting and catamaranning, every kind of sport has its own magazine now, because people are obsessed by sport, and they spend a whole weekend doing things. Even if we don't do sport, it affects us because we are also always implicated in the karma of the time we live in, it's not just an individual thing. Activity pulls us, people need to do more and more, and this fetter, this locking, this shackle of duality, only vanishes when we relax enough to let go of it. No activity can remove it but, because we are addicted to activity, the buddhas in their kindness taught the tantras, and tantra is a deconstructive activity.

In the next line we have more instruction on our own real nature. *She pa*, mind itself, means *your* own mind, not just the Buddha's mind, *your* mind is not made or contrived. *Rang lug* means 'how it is', relaxed and spontaneous. The mind itself has no desire to make anything or construct anything. It, itself, is not made or constructed, it just hangs easy.

Then, the next line: the mind is not created by the good works of good people, of the buddhas. The activities that we do in and around monasteries, burning butter lamps, polishing the floor, painting thangkas and so on, all of these are methods of helping to develop concentration, compassion, thoughtfulness for others, and so forth, but they don't create the buddha nature. For example, most of us here are reasonably healthy. Every now and then we get sick. When we get sick we go to the doctor and we get some medicine. We take our medicine, and the medicine helps to remove either the cause or the symptoms of the illness, and then we feel better. The medicine doesn't make us healthy, but the medicine deals with the imbalance that was stopping us being healthy. Dharma activities have a similar function.

Similarly, our bad qualities, our various meditation faults, sinking, fogginess, getting distracted, bind the ego, not the mind itself. 'Sinking' is when you're very tired and you can't quite hold the focus of the meditation; 'foggy' is when you're just caught up in the thoughts and the feelings, there is no perspective at all; and 'distraction' is when you are caught up in the many different kinds of thoughts, feelings, sensations. Although these experiences are powerful and seen to imprison us so that we feel trapped, when we relax they pass. The mind itself is not an entity, it cannot be held anywhere.

That's why the dzogchen teachings say, if your mind is a mess, if you realise you can never meditate, if you're always distracted, don't worry, don't try harder — just relax. If you relax, and sit calmly and simply, everything will pass by. But when things don't go well we have, generally speaking, two responses: either we try harder or we give up in despair. Both of these help to bind us into the level of mixing with the arising, rather then separating out.

Then the text says: 'This awareness is shining and brilliant, radiant with its own luminosity.' Even today, when we can't see the sun clearly because of many, many clouds, if you wanted to look for the sun, you wouldn't think of using a torch because the sun provides its own light. But this is what we often try to do when we look for the mind. We go out with our little lamp, ego's little lamp, trying to find this mind, as if the mind was some little dark pocket, instead of being the site of complete radiance and illumination.

It's important, especially after merging with the guru, not to make effort but to relax and to trust that what is there will reveal itself to you by its own light. The dharmakaya is not an object which can be seen or grasped. Rather, it is an experience, our nature revealed by relaxing into it.

With the presence of this nature there is the integration of our experience with what has always been. What *is* — the mother, the ground, actuality — meets us without reserve. The mother and son meet. There is no gap, no hesitation nor artificiality; it is as if they had never been apart. Dharmata is the facticity of non-duality, the uncontrived actuality.

But then the text reminds us not to get lost in just hanging-out in happy situations, with easy situations, don't just have fun and chill-out, this is not going to take you anywhere. In dzogchen, the idea of relaxation is to be relaxed under all circumstances. It's not just that you are relaxed at the weekend or when you're stoned or whatever, but to be relaxed even in the face of very difficult circumstances. So don't confuse easy social company with dzogchen realisation, but rather maintain a permanent connection, a real friendship or relationship with this good house of shunyata. That is to say, live in that house.

With shunyata as your frame of reference there will be no danger of getting lost, and then the text says, 'The mother and son dharmata will quickly meet.' When that happens you become stabilised in your own nature and so your activity can move in the world with complete freedom.

The last four lines are about the nature of non-dual activity. In order to act very powerfully for the benefit of others and perform the activity of the bodhisattva one has to be free of self-concern as one's organising principle. The activity arises effortlessly out of the non-dual nature, it is not something that we do. Infinite generosity arises with our freedom. It's not a matter of duty, it is just how it is. Naturally virtuous, without effort, always good, Kuntu Zangpo.

Then the text says, 'I will upturn and empty samsara.' This means that there will be no sentient beings left living in samsara. In the view, there never have been any sentient beings. Living that view, we confirm their liberation by not confirming their karmic expectations and assumptions. That is to say, when we're with people, we shouldn't strongly believe in their identity or in what they say, but neither should we abandon them by saying, "Oh, it's all emptiness, anyway, just an illusion", but we should hold them lightly, by giving them space to present themselves, so that their energy manifests and they have a chance to recognise themselves as manifesting energy. By not confirming their karmic agenda, and having none ourselves, the solidity of the situation is loosened and there is room to move, to experience something fresh.

According to this view, people don't get enlightened by having the correct conduct. Enlightenment is revealed through being oneself. Therefore, compassion is not about changing other people's external behaviour or doing something for them or to them. It's not about helping them to be more polite, or more able to get a job, or any socially useful function, it's about helping them to stop being so obsessed with externals and to gain a moment where they might relax into their own process of existence.

## i. Praying for What We Want

ཕྱི་ལྟར་བདེ་དོན་རྟགས་རྫོགས་རྔ་ཡབ་གླིང་༈
ནང་ལྟར་རང་ལུས་ཕུང་ཁམས་མཁའ་འགྲོའི་གྲོང་༈
གསང་བ་བདེ་སྟོང་དབྱེར་མེད་ཐིག་ལེའི་ཀློང་༈
ཡང་གསང་བྱ་རྩོལ་བྲལ་བ་གཉུག་མའི་གཤིས༈
རང་བྱུང་རང་ཤར་རང་གྲོལ་བདེ་བ་ཆེ༈
གཉིས་མེད་རྒྱལ་པོ་དོན་གྱི་ཧེ་རུ་ཀ༈
གནས་གསུམ་མཁའ་འགྲོའི་གཙོ་བོ་པདྨ་འབྱུང་༈
སྐུ་གསུམ་དབྱེར་མེད་ཞབས་ལ་གསོལ་བ་འདེབས༈

CHI TAR DA DON TAG DZOG NGA YAB LING
NANG TAR RANG LUE PHUNG KHAM KHA DROI DRONG
SANG WA DE TONG YER MED THIG LEI LONG
YANG SANG JA TSOL DRAL WA NYUG MAI SHI
RANG JUNG RANG SHAR RANG DROL DE WA CHE
NYI MED GYAL PO DON GYI HE RU KA
NAE SUM KHA DROI TSO WO PAD MA JUNG
KU SUM YER MED ZHAB LA SOL WA DEB

*Generally, in Ngayabling with the perfect signs, where everything has deep meaning, in particular, in the dakinis' city of the skandhas and dhatus of one's own body, deeply in the vastness within the ball of the inseparability of happiness and sunyata, and most secretly, in and as the original, unchanging, nature free of deeds and effort, self-existing, self-arising, self-liberating, and of great happiness — the king of non-duality, free of both samsara and nirvana, the genuine, original heruka, the chief of the dakinis of the three places, Padmasambhava, we pray to you in whom the three kayas are inseparable.*

Many years ago in Shantiniketan, Rinpoche found this prayer in a dream. He wrote it down the next day, and we translated it immediately and used it in the practice called *A Rainfall of Blessings*.

On the outer level there is the island of Camaradvipa, home of Zangdopalri, and an environment where everything is meaningful. We actually live now in a world in which everything is meaningfully meaningless. Children and adults fall prey to advertising and invest great value in empty commodities. The supply of new, fascinating, objects is ceaseless and this disguises the futility of consumerism. Whereas, on this island, everything is meaningful for it turns you towards the meaning of the dharma and, in particular, towards awakening to your own nature. If we go to Sikkim, or Ladakh, or Tibet, we come into environments full of images and meaning, and when you walk down the street, seeing the stupas and the people with prayer wheels, then suddenly everything is powerful. Now, think of Tibetans, living in such worlds and yet saying, "Hey, there's another place where everything is really meaningful!" It shows just how sad and difficult our situation here is.

On the more inner level, one's own body, composed of the five skandhas, (which it describes), the eighteen dhatus (the six senses, their objects, and their consciousnesses, and so on), that is to say, the whole dynamic interactive field of one's being, is a dakini's palace. We believe that in each little pore of the body, each little opening on the skin, there is a dakini. That means that this body itself, in its ordinary form, is a sacred place.

Then, on the secret level, happiness and emptiness are inseparable in the dimension of the *thigle*, or *bindu*, a ball or sphere of light. When we visualise a deity like Padmasambhava, he is always in a rainbow thigle. You don't really see it. In thangkas, it looks more like a kind of aureole around the back of the head but really it is a three-dimensional enclosure, the whole of the body is inside a shining ball of light. In meditation we use the spheres to focus our attention and to control energy. The sphere is round, it has no edges or corners to it so it doesn't catch on to anything else. In the state of calm relaxation there is a kind of completion, or rounding, in which the energetic disturbance that gets us into many events, is settled. This is achieved by keeping the energy in the central channel through focusing on the spheres.

The next line refers to something even more secret; that is, less elaborated, less manifest in the world. This is the original ground nature which is free of all activity and effort. A lot of the activity that we make is because of impulses arising inside us. These impulses we don't resist because really we can't resist them, they just catch us. We go along with them, and so our energy is moved here and there. But when our attention is grounded in the original nature, then the ego dissolves back into its own ground of open awareness and so there is effortless radiance.

In this state there is the great happiness of experiencing everything as self-arising, with there being no-one to have any need to make things happen. This state is self-existing because it has no cause, it is present of itself, like the sun rising in the morning. It is self-liberating because it is not an object, and it leaves all manifestations free to vanish by themselves. The ground nature is unborn, it has no origin, it doesn't rest on anything, and yet it's manifestation is ceaseless. But our existence is predicated on the fact that if we don't keep ourselves together we're going to fall apart. We believe that we are the responsible agents of our lives and it's up to us to hold it together, to make things happen.

Karl Marx, in his concept of mystification, said that one of the great things in this world is the way that the people who own the big factories can make the workers grateful to have a job. It is as if the owner of the factory is doing the worker a favour, a great compassionate gesture, to give them a badly-paid job. The worker never gets to feel that they're doing the boss a favour by coming to work. Though the boss is making the profit, the profit that the boss makes is always invisible to the worker, because it doesn't enter into the domain of the worker. In the old days, a company would never publish its financial report and put a copy in the workers' tea-room — impossible! Now to apply this structure here, ignorance is the factory owner, and the ego is the worker, and the ego thinks, "Oh, I need an identity, I need an identity", so it works very, very hard, but it doesn't realise that every action it performs generates a profit for ignorance, and ignorance becomes more and more strong. The ego is just grateful to have a job, an identity.

When trade unions first formed, the first power that they realised they had was the power of striking, going on strike, the withdrawal of labour, so in this text Lenin Lama says, "Stop work! No more production, no more samsara! Close the factory!" That's very anxiety-provoking for the workers. Going on strike is terrifying. You're made to feel bad because so much of your sense of identity comes through employment, and then you worry about money and so forth. We have to really think about this seriously, because one of the reasons we don't do very much dharma practice, and we do a lot of nonsense things, is because nonsense provides work for the ego. When you practise more in the style of dzogchen and really renounce busy activity, it doesn't mean that external activity will stop, but there is a particular relationship, a kind of pay-off of identification with work, and when that becomes renounced anxiety arises, then one has to work on relaxing the anxiety.

The next line points to the freedom that arises from integration. The king of non-duality is unobstructed in all directions, able to enjoy his domain without interruption. This is Padmasambhava, in whose spacious presence the dakinis of movement come and go as the unique specificity of embodied existence. 'We pray to the inseparability of the three kayas.' This is the harmonious integration of all the multiple, pluralistic modes of existence.

དེ་ལྟར་གསོལ་བ་བཏབ་པའི་བྱིན་རླབས་ཀྱིས༔
ཚེ་འདིར་མངོན་སུམ་ཁྱོད་ཞལ་མྱུར་མཇལ་ནས༔
ཉོན་མོངས་ཤེས་བྱའི་སྒྲིབ་པ་ཀུན་དག་ཅིང༔
གཞོན་ནུ་བུམ་སྐུའི་རང་ཞལ་མཇལ་བར་ཤོག༔

**DE TAR SOL WA TAB PAI JIN LAB KYI
TSE DIR NGON SUM KHYOD ZHAL NYUR JAL NAE
NYON MONG SHE JAI DRIB PA KUN DAG CHING
ZHON NU BUM KUI RANG ZHAL JAL WAR SHOG**

*By the blessing of having prayed in this way, in this life
may we quickly see your face directly. Then, with
all the obscurations of the afflictions and subtle traces being purified,
may we see our own true face of the ever young original nature!*

འདི་སྐྱོང་ནུབ་ཚེ་དཔའ་བོ་མཁའ་འགྲོའི་ཚོགས༔
རོལ་མོ་སྒྲ་སྙན་སྒྱུ་དབྱངས་དམ་ཆོས་སྒྲས༔
ཉི་མ་ཟླ་དང་མཆོད་རྫས་ཕྱོག་བྱས་ནས༔
མ་སྐྱོད་ཇ་ཡབ་དཔལ་རིར་འཁྲིད་པར་ཤོག༔

## E. SADHANA: Main Part

**DI NANG NUB TSE PA WO KHA DROI TSOG
ROL MO DRA NYEN LU YANG DAM CHOE DRAE
DA MA RU DANG CHOD DZAE THOG JAE NAE
SA CHOD NGA YAB PAL RIR THRID PAR SHOG**

*When this life is ending, may hosts of viras and dakinis make sweet sounding music and melodious songs, all with the sound of the holy dharma. With all of them holding damarus and offering things, may they guide us to the glorious mountain at Sachod Ngayab.*

དེ་མ་ཐག་པར་གུ་རུ་ཡབ་ཡུམ་གྱིཿ
ཞལ་མཇལ་གསུང་ཐོས་གདམས་ངག་ཀུན་ཐོབ་ནསཿ
ས་ལམ་མཐར་ཕྱིན་རིག་འཛིན་རྣམས་པ་བཞི་དིཿ
གོ་འཕང་མྱུར་ཐོབ་ཨུ་རྒྱན་པདྨ་དངཿ
དབྱེར་མེད་འགྲོ་བའི་དཔལ་དུ་བདག་གྱུར་ནསཿ
མཁའ་མཉམ་འགྲོ་བ་མ་ལུས་འདྲེན་པར་ཤོགཿ

**DE MA THAG PAR GU RU YAB YUM GYI
ZHAL JAL SUNG THOE DAM NGAG KUN THOB NAE
SA LAM THAR CHIN RIG DZIN NAM PA ZHI
GO PHANG NYUR THOB UR GYEN PAD MA DANG
YER MED DRO WAI PAL DU DAG GYUR NAE
KHA NYAM DRO WA MA LUE DREN PAR SHOG**

*Immediately on arriving there, may we see the face of Padmasambhava with his consort, hear his speech and all instructions from him. Then, completing the stages and paths, may we quickly get the rank of the four kinds of vidyadhara. Then becoming identical with Padmasambhava, may we be leaders for all beings without exception, as many as would equal the sky's extent.*

གལ་སྲིད་དེ་མ་ཐོབ་པར་གྱུར་ན་ཡང་༈
བདག་གཞན་འདི་ནས་ཚེ་འཕོས་གྱུར་མ་ཐག༈
འཆི་བ་འོད་གསལ་ཆོས་ཀྱི་སྐུར་སྨིན་ཅིང་༈
བར་དོ་ལོངས་སྤྱོད་རྫོགས་སྐུར་རབ་སྨིན་ནས༈
སྐྱེ་བ་སྤྲུལ་སྐུའི་འགྲོ་དོན་བྱེད་པར་ཤོག༈

**GAL SID DE MA THOB PAR GYUR NA YANG
DAG ZHEN DI NAE TSE PHOE GYUR MA THAG
CHI WA OD SAL CHOE KYI KUR MIN CHING
BAR DO LONG CHOD DZOG KUR RAB MIN NAE
KYE WA TRUL KUI DRO DON JED PAR SHOG**

*Even if it is not possible to gain that attainment in one life,
when I and all others are leaving this life, immediately may death develop
as the clear illumination dharmakaya, with the bardo developing
as the sambhogakaya, so that birth is as nirmanakaya,
making benefit for those who are moving in samsara!*

To see the face of Padmasambhava is to see your own face on it's many levels. It is to see your face as primordial nature, dharmakaya, infinite, open, relaxed. It is to see your face as radiance, sambhogakaya, light, sound, vitality, impressive translucent forms. It is to see your face as energy, as nirmanakaya, moving, changing ceaselessly for the other. When that happens, all the obscurations and subtle traces will be removed.

There are two kinds of obscurations, the obscuration of the five poisons and the obscuration of assumptions. It is on the basis of our cognitive assumptions that the five poisons get awakened. Clearly, some people are more mobilised through emotion and some people are mobilised more through thinking, and the same person will move between these two modes because of their luck.

When the ever-fresh, unobscured nature is realised, there is enlightenment. If this is not managed in this life then we pray for a safe passage to the pure land of Padmasambhava. When you get there, you immediately see Padmasambhava and his consort. You see their faces. You hear instructions from his voice, and because of this it becomes very easy to realise the ten stages and the five paths, the standard mahayana stages of progress, and also to pass through the four levels of the vidyadhara. Having achieved all of that, we quickly become inseparable from Padmasambhava and then become able to act for the benefit of all sentient beings, so we become a guide for infinite numbers of beings.

Generally, it is believed that to be reborn in one of the pure buddha lands is much better than to be born in the ordinary human dimension, because there is no disturbance there, everything is directed towards liberation. If we're not able to get that attainment in one life, then may we have liberation in the bardo, so that death develops as dharmakaya. At death, after the dissolving of the elements, we enter the bardo or phase of dharmata, actuality. At that point everything collapses, everything vanishes and you have a kind of blackout, and in that blackout you can recognise your own nature, if you've done a lot of dissolving practice. If you don't get liberation at that point then manifestation starts, as you can read in the *Bardo Thodrol*: first the peaceful deities, then the wrathful deities, and if you can identify with these deities, if you know their mantras and have a connection with them and are not afraid of them, then you get enlightened into the samboghakaya level. Then, flowing out from them, you are reborn in a nirmanakaya in order to perform benefit for beings. To be reborn in nirmanakaya in this way means that you bring into life with you a conscious intention of what you're going to do in dharma. I remember Rinpoche saying that even if a tulku is born in a country where there is no dharma, and nobody recognises him, or helps him or her, they will grow up with a clear notion of what they are going to do in this life and will start to practise and teach dharma.

Perhaps our lives are rather different, driven by worldly enthusiasms. As a child I collected different kinds of special things for my bicycle, and these things were very important. So I would come home from school and get on my bicycle, and that was the important thing in my life, it wasn't dharma, it wasn't Padmasambhava, it wasn't the bodhisattva vow. It was my bicycle. That's a sign I'm not a very enlightened person. And if we think about our lives, how many enthusiasms we've had, how many courses our lives could have taken, and in some ways it's just by, suddenly, a little bubble of good luck that we got a connection with dharma. We could easily have gone off and got into something else. This prayer is reminding us of the need to make plans for the future, not to rely on luck, but to develop a kind of compass inside us to keep us on track, so that we can continue to develop our dharma awakening for the sake of all beings. This is very precious.

## j. Short Phowa Practice

རང་གི་སྙིང་ཁ་ནས་རྔ་ཡབ་དཔལ་རིའི་བར་དུ་འོད་ལྔའི་ལམ་གསལ་ཞིང་འཚེར་བ་ཐལ་ལེ་ཟུགས་པའི་སྟེང་དུ་རང་སེམས་རང་གཟུགས་ཀྱི་རྣམ་པ་ཅན་གྱི་གཡས་གཡོན་མདུན་རྒྱབ་ཐམས་ཅད་དཔའ་བོ་རིག་འཛིན་མཁའ་འགྲོའི་ཚོགས་ཀྱི་གྲོགས་དང་བཅས་ཏེ་འོད་ཀྱི་ལམ་གྱི་སྟེང་ན་ཕར་ཉམས་དགའ་ཡལ། བྱིན་འཐིབ་འཐིབ། སྣང་བ་བདེ་ཆམ་ཆམ་བྱིན་ཏེ་འཛི་ག་རྟེན་མི་ཡུལ་གྱི་སྣང་བ་ཐིབ་ཐིབ་ནུབ་ཏེ་ཕྱིར་ཕྱིར་ལུས་མཁའ་སྤྱོད་ཟངས་མདོག་དཔལ་རི་བཀྲ་ལམ་ལམ་ཤར། ཨུ་རྒྱན་པདྨ་རིག་འཛིན་ཡི་དམ་མཁའ་འགྲོའི་དབུས་ན། བཞུགས་པ་དང་རྗེ་ཉེར་སོང་ཏེ་མཐར་རང་གཟུགས་གུ་རུའི་ཐུགས་ཀར་སིབ་ཀྱིས་ཐིམ་པར་བསམ།

**RANG GI NYING KHA NAE NGA YAB PAL RI BAR DU
OD NGAI LAM SAL ZHING TSER WA THAL LE ZUG PAI TENG DU
RANG SEM RANG ZUG KYI NAM PA CHEN GYI YAE GYON DUN GYAB THAM CHE
PA WO RIG DZIN KHAN DROI TSOG KYI DROG DANG CHE TE
OD KYI LAM GYI TENG NA PHAR NYAM GA YAL
JIN THIB THIB NANG WA DE CHAM CHAM JIN TE
JIG TEN MI YUL GYI NANG WA THIB THIB NUB TE CHIR CHIR LUE
KHA CHOD ZANG DOG PAL RI TRA LAM LAM SHAR
UR GYEN PAD MA RIG DZIN YIDAM KHAN DROI WUE NA ZHUG PA DANG
JE NYER SONG TE THAR RANG JUG GU RUI
THUG KAR SIB KYI THIM PAR SAM**

*From my heart centre until Zangdopalri there extends a path of five coloured light. It is clear, shining and direct and on top of it is my mind with the form of my present body together with hosts of viras, vidyadharas and dakinis all around, at front and at back and on either side, acting as helpers. Then, on top of this path of light, I go very happily, feeling light and happy on the wave of blessing. With this very good feeling I go there, and all the ideas of the human world fade away and vanish until all are left far behind. Then Kachod Zangdopalri arises very clearly for me. Padmasambhava is sitting in the centre of many vidyadharas, wishing gods, and dakinis and I approach closer and closer until finally my own body melts into his heart.*

This practice is a more literal description of the second verse of the previous prayer. You can do this just sitting very quietly. You can imagine Zangdopalri, with Padmasambhava in front of you, and develop a strong wish to go there. Again and again practice moving towards him. In this way, leaving this world becomes wonderful. Death is not the enemy, not something which is attacking us. Our death is already in our body, and our body will fall away, fall away forever. The body, our precious flesh body that we protect so well, is actually made of light, so we practice our own ordinary body dissolving into the body of Padmasambhava. This body is already pure. We should never hate it, turn it into an object, or become too attached to it. The practice is to experience its inseparability from Padmasambhava. With the view of the three kayas it's not that there is a pure mind trapped in an impure body. All aspects of our existence have been pure from the very beginning, but thinking will not establish this for us, we have to do the practice.

## k. Receiving the Four Initiations

**LA MAI NAE SUM LAE OD THROE
OM AH HUNG YI GEI NAM PA
RANG THIM WANG ZHI DZOG DRIB DAG
KU DANG YE SHE NGA NGON GYUR
LA MA RIN PO CHE KHYEN NO**

*From the guru's forehead, throat and heart, light radiates in the form of the letters Om, Ah, Hung. They are absorbed into me, and I fully receive the four initiations and my obscurations are purified, and the five kayas and five pristine and supreme knowledges become manifest in me. Precious guru, please hear me!*

Om Ah Hung represent the three vajras, the three indestructible aspects of our dimension of mind, voice and body, which is to say, dharmakaya, samboghakaya, nirmanakaya. This is our true nature. This is not some goal that we have to create or develop for ourselves. It is our real nature now as we are sitting here. It is the indestructible basis of our existence. In the system of tantra, it's as if the guru is giving this to us as some kind of gift. As the earlier prayer, *Encouragement on Impermanence* says, good deeds don't make for the development of dharmakaya, and bad deeds and meditation confusion don't cover it up. If your nature was not already gold, nothing could make it gold, but by the power of this initiation, and our faith, we focus on dropping our identification with the obscurations, so that our bodies fill with light and we relax into the state, free of attachments.

The following lineage explanation was first used in conjunction with the text, *Rainfall of Blessings*. It sets out the practice clearly and one should follow the steps slowly and carefully so that you enter fully into the experience.

ॐ

*From a white letter Om on the guru's forehead, rays of white light come out and melt into your own forehead, purifying the sins and obscurations of the body. The blessing of the body is obtained. You now have received the* bumpa *or pot initiation; a pot of purifying elixir is poured over you. Your body is empowered to do the meditations of the developing system of visualisation. Now your body is purified, so you can meditate on it as the pure form of the deity. You now have the opportunity to gain the fruition of nirmanakaya. You now have the chance of getting the fully developed vajrakaya, a very strong body, never changing or destroyed, like a diamond. The inside of your body becomes full of rays of white light. Meditate on this for some time.*

# E. SADHANA: Main Part

ཨཱཿ

*Then from a letter Ah at the guru's throat come rays of red light which melt into your own throat, purifying the impurities of speech. You receive the* sangwa *or secret initiation. Your speech is empowered to read mantras, do sadhanas and to do long recitations of mantras. You now have the opportunity to gain the fruition of sambhogakaya. You now have the chance of getting the vajravak. It is the strongest voice, to which all others submit, like the roar of the lion. Its words are never changed, once uttered. The inside of your body becomes full of rays of red light. Meditate on this for some time.*

ཧཱུྃ

*Then, from a blue letter Hung at the guru's heart, come rays of blue light which melt into your own heart, purifying the sins and obscurations of mind. The blessing of mind is obtained. You receive the* sherab yeshe, *or wisdom initiation, and your mind is empowered to meditate on the happiness/void mahamudra. You now have the opportunity to gain the fruition of dharmakaya. You now have the chance of getting the* vajracitta, *invulnerable mind that is totally triumphant, knowing the nature of all that appears to it. It is the strength of the dharmadhatu jnana. The inside of your body becomes filled with rays of blue light. Meditate on this for some time.*

ༀ ཨཱཿ ཧཱུྃ

*Again from the guru's three places of forehead, throat and heart, come rays of light, respectively white, red and blue, which melt into your own body, speech and mind, purifying the sins and obscurations which diversely effect them. You get the blessing of body, speech and mind, good qualities and spiritual activities and*

> *receive the fourth initiation, the precious* tshig, *or word, initiation. You are thus empowered to meditate on your own mind as voidness and clarity, effortlessly arising. You now have the opportunity of gaining the inseparability of the three kayas, the svabhavikakaya, and now have the chance of gaining the four kayas. The inside of your body becomes filled with white, red and blue light rays. Meditate on this for some time.*

In tantra, initiation or empowerment is very important. To practice is to be part of a lineage. You cannot just pick up a ritual text and do it, you have to have the initiation (*wangkur*), the transmission (*lung*), and the explanation. It is a whole package, and you need the lot. Then, due to our own errors, we weaken the connection with the lineage, and so need to restore it, for it is through the lineage that we are awakened to ourselves. Enlightenment is connectivity, not autonomy. Therefore take time to do this part of the practice, and recite the lama khyeno with great faith and devotion. Also do the seven-line prayer and open your heart to the transmission. Burst the bubble of self!

When we do the *Om Machig Ma* you have the same kind of thing, so if this practice is not very clear for you, you can really practise it by working with, reading the *Machig Ma* prayer[10] again and again. As you're doing the prayer with a lot of devotion to her, you imagine the light coming in and purifying your body and then, when you come to this part in the puja, you just use the same process.

The reality is that Rinpoche will die. He's not very well, and no one lives for ever. Often we can be a bit lazy, and when our practice gets a bit weak, we think, "Oh anyway I'll see Rinpoche, and then we'll do the practice every day, so I'll become stronger again". But some time he will not be there to do that[11]. Then the only re-energising power you will have is practising on your own or with some other people. So, it's very, very important that you gain confidence that the practice will work for you. Hold the blessing from the past, trust your connection to Rinpoche as Padmasambhava, and do not rely solely on the physical form of Rinpoche.

---

[10] See Appendix in *Being Right Here* (Snow Lion, 2004)

[11] This talk was given shortly before Rinpoche died, in 2002.

# E. SADHANA: Main Part

## 1. Dissolving into the Guru and Maintaining the View

ཁྱབ་བདག་སྐུ་བཞིའི་དབང་ཕྱུག་རྡོ་རྗེ་འཆང་༈
མཁྱེན་བརྩེ་ཐུགས་རྗེའི་གཏེར་ཆེན་རིགས་ལྔའི་ལྷ༈
དྲན་པས་ཡིད་ཀྱི་གདུང་སེལ་གུ་རུ་རྗེ༈
མཉམ་མེད་དཔལ་ལྡན་དྲིན་ཅན་བླ་མ་ལ༈
བདག་སོགས་སྙིང་ནས་གསོལ་བ་འདེབས་ལགས་ན༈
སྐད་ཅིག་ཙམ་ཡང་འབྲལ་མེད་རྗེས་བཟུང་ནས༈
བྱིན་གྱིས་རློབས་ཤིག་གུ་རུ་བཀའ་དྲིན་ཅན༈
ཉིད་དང་དབྱེར་མེད་མཛོད་ཅིག་བླ་མ་རྗེ༈

KHYAB DAG KU ZHII WANG CHUG DOR JE CHANG
KHYEN TSE THUG JEI TER CHEN RIG NGAI LHA
DREN PAE YID KYI DUNG SEL GU RU JE
NYAM MED PAL DEN DRIN CHEN LA MA LA
DAG SOG NYING NAE SOL WA DEB LAG NA
KE CHIG TSAM YANG DRAL MED JE ZUNG NAE
JIN GYI LOB SHIG GU RU KA DRIN CHEN
NYID DANG YER MED DZOG CHIG LA MA JE

*Dorje Chang — pervading lord with the power of the four kayas, the gods of the five families, the great treasures of compassion, having true knowledge and compassion, the reverend guru, remembrance of whom removes our mental troubles, unequalled, glorious, most kind guru — if we pray to you from the heart, you must hold us as disciples without separating from us for even an instant, and must grant us your blessings. Most kind master, please make us without difference from yourself, oh, reverend guru!*

Then imagine that Padmasambhava or your own guru is smiling radiantly at you. He comes to the top of your head, resting on a lotus cushion. Then from the feet up and the head down he dissolves gradually (or instantaneously, whichever is easier for you) into a ball of light which is absorbed through the crown of your head and descends into your heart. It melts into your own heart, so that your body, speech and mind become inseparably merged into the guru's body, speech and mind, like water poured into water. Remain in that state without doing anything at all, keeping calm and relaxed.

Our guru is in the form of Padmasambhava, inseparable from Dorje Chang, the primordial buddha. All the qualities of all the buddhas are in this one figure; there is nothing, and no one, higher or better, so we should open fully to him. Then, in the state of merging there is nothing to be done. Dropping all attachment, identification, and involvement, let whatever arises pass freely.

**Verses from the Le'u Dunma**

འདི་ལྟར་མིག་གི་ཡུལ་དུ་སྣང་བ་ཡི༔
ཕྱི་ནང་སྣོད་བཅུད་དངོས་པོ་ཐམས་ཅད་ཀུན༔
སྣང་ཡང་བདག་འཛིན་མེད་པའི་ངང་ལ་ཞོག༔
གཟུང་འཛིན་དག་པ་གསལ་སྟོང་ལྷ་ཡི་སྐུ༔
འདོད་ཆགས་རང་གྲོལ་གྱི་བླ་མ་ལ་གསོལ་བ་འདེབས༔
ཨུ་རྒྱན་པདྨ་འབྱུང་གནས་ལ་གསོལ་བ་འདེབས༔

**DI TAR MIG GI YUL DU NANG WA YI
CHI NANG NOD CHUD NGOE WO THAM CHE KUN
NANG YANG DAG DZIN MED PAI NGANG LA ZHOG
ZUNG DZIN DAG PA SAL TONG LHA YI KU
DOD CHAG RANG DROL GYI LA MA LA SOL WA DEB
UR GYEN PAD MA JUNG NAE LA SOL WA DEB**

*As regards the eye's objects which are the appearances/ideas of absolutely all the outer and inner entities of the universe and its inhabitants, maintain the state where there is appearance yet without grasping at it as being something real, neither cultivating nor discarding. The divine body of clarity and emptiness, pure and free from graspable objects and grasping mind, I pray to the guru of self-liberating desire. I pray to Urgyen Padma Jungnae.*

This is the first of four verses from the Le'u Dunma, the seven-chaptered prayer[12]. They are considered to be a direct heart teaching of Padmasambhava. As Rinpoche has explained in the past, this verse applies to all experience, to all that happens via the senses, including touch, smell, and so forth. This is a practice to be applied. It's the opposite of being asleep. Often, in buddhism, we talk of awakening, but the power of karma is very strong, the power of assumptions is very strong, so it's very easy to do a puja and come out of it and just fall asleep again, go completely back into ordinary karmic perception. These verses are designed to operate like a kind of wedge that you tap in between the karmic habit of sense experience and the possibility of staying more alert. It really requires us not to be caught up in the demands coming from the experiential field, and especially from other people. These verses help us to stay awake ourselves, but also give us a way of continuing to relate to people within the rules and regulations of the dimension that we live in. We always have to integrate wisdom and compassion, and not be confused by the invitations to confluence and collusion.

When we see something, say for example, a cup, it would be mad and unhelpful to try not to see a cup. If someone says, "Give me the cup", we know what to give them, to act otherwise would be stupid. Knowing that the sight of the shape and the sound of the word and the concept of cup are all empty, they can arise without hooking reification and attachment. This is the integration of experience into Padmasambhava. There are no separate entities, merely processes of arising and passing, but these processes are not chaotic, they are patterned, shaped by karmic cause and effect. The reliability of the form does not indicate an underlying essence. Padmasambhava has a clearly defined shape, while being inseparable from emptiness, and so it is with all other arisings.

---

[12] Terma by Rigdzin Godem, the great terton of Byangter (Northern Treasures, 14th century)

This cup, which I can hold in my hand and which we can all see, this cup has never been *born* as a cup, this cup is unborn, but it is also unceasing in its presentation in the form of a cup. If I were to drop the cup and the cup was broken, we could say, "Oh, he's killed the cup", but what would be killed? What is the cup-ness of the cup? This is the essential thing that you have to really investigate for yourselves and get clear, otherwise these kind of verses don't mean very much. We have to recognise that we, through our own set of assumptions, act as if this cup was something self-existing. But if I stop holding it and it drops, it will break, so it's not self-existing, it's held here because my hands are holding it. Our mind separates the cup from my hands, but if my hand is separated from the cup, it would drop, smash, and then there would be nothing for your concept of cup to be put on.

It's the same with people. We imagine that people really exist but, of course, we know from our own bodies that they're always changing; we eat and then we shit, we drink and we piss, we clean our teeth, our hair grows and our nails grow, and we also know, on a more subtle level, that physiological changes are going on all the time. The body is a process. There is no self-substance in it, though there is a general continuity of form. This means that the James-ness of James, or the Robert-ness of Robert, is a kind of illusion, that Robert has never been born as a thing, but Robert is Robert-ing continuously.

Of course, this process of being ourselves is influenced by many, many factors. People say something and suddenly we feel very sad. People say something, and we get angry. You know, we're not in control of how we are, yet we feel we are, or at least that we should be, because of this appropriation, this centralisation, this kind of organisation.

Why is it that we would want to impute inherent self-nature when there isn't something there? It lies in the condition of the imputer. Due to the power of ignorance there arises this sense of being a separate self, and this separate self needs somewhere to rest, it needs something to sit on, and it sits on its sense of embodied being. But this embodied being, because it's connected with other people, needs to have some stability in the environment as well, in order for it to feel safe.

Being close to others can be satisfying, but it is often also disturbing. Then we find ourselves saying things like, "Ah, I can't think about my work. Whenever my relationship gets disturbed, then I'm just full of these emotions all the time, and I spend all my time thinking, 'But why did he say that? What was it?'" This is because our sense of identity, our sense of ourselves, has become very interwoven in how we are with the other person. It's as if the other person has become the basis of our life and so, if the other person moves a bit, our whole life is moving, and then we don't know who we are. What we crave then is reassurance, to be told that its okay, that we are still important, still loved and wanted, and that therefore things will continue as before. The basic pattern, as we have seen before, is ignorance, absence, core anxiety, sense of separate self, maintenance anxiety, busyness controlling self and other, upswelling emotions, feeling out of control, struggling to reassert control, no rest, always on the job.

The verse says *dag dzin med pai ngang la zhog*, which means that we allow the whole field of perception to arise without any separation. So, for example, I'm looking out now and I see you all sitting there. I see the walls and some flowers on the table and so forth, and this is one seamless event with stable and moving aspects. The whole thing is a field, including myself, it is one process. It's not that there is one person here, then another and another, each a separate entity with its own history and ground. Everything is arising together, in the same moment.

The next line says *zung dzin dag pa sal tong lha yi ku*, 'by purifying the sense of real, self-existing, objects outside and a real, self-existing one inside, who needs to rely on objects? The divine body or form is revealed.' The object of grasping, and the mind that is doing the grasping, are made for each other because they are both operating on the level of imputed identity. When we purify them, in other words, drop the imputation, there are still objects outside and there is still a mind inside, but they are relaxed. Everything becomes more light, more free, and therefore more spontaneous. There is more possibility of direct interaction. When that's achieved, then we have the experience of clarity and emptiness, which is the nature of the body of the deity.

When we look at Padmasambhava's body, clearly, we can see something but there is no substance in that. Padmasambhava manifests out of emptiness, and then goes back into emptiness. When we see an image of Dorje Drolo we might think, "Oh, this is a very strong person, I wouldn't like to meet this person on a dark night." But what is it that makes Dorje Drolo strong? Is it the fact that inside him there is a real, very tough Dorje Drolo or the fact that it is a particular way of processing? He is a particular form of manifestation, an energetic movement.

Free of karmic impulses, this is the unborn energy of the dharmakaya. This is the key thing. It's a very simple point, but we have to go over it again and again in our own minds, day-by-day, moment-by-moment. When I experience myself as James, then the ground of my being is a mass of constructs held in the *alaya*, in the *kun ji nam pa she pa*, the deepest level of dualistic, organising self-consciousness, consciousness-as-me. In the absence of the presence of the natural condition, this feels to be the ground of my existence. Yet this seeming ground is actually a manifestation of emptiness. It is not in itself self-existing, but I *think* it is, I *feel* it is. This is what ignorance is. And then I think, "Oh, I come from me, I am just through and through me", rather than, "This is emptiness". This is the big confusion. This is all that ignorance really is, this is a mis-take.

It's like a child who's grown up in the city. If you ask them, "Where does food come from?" they say, "From the supermarket", because that's their real experience. The supermarket presents the food all wrapped in plastic, with each little cabbage or bit of broccoli having cellophane around it, so that it comes completely sealed-in as a separate piece of broccoli. Then you can't imagine that it comes from a field. If you see it in the field, you see it has roots and it goes into the earth, and it's connected with the sun and the rain and so on, but in the supermarket it seems a thing apart, entire unto itself. This is what it's like for us to be born, we feel separate and apart, fresh from Mummy's supermarket.

To support our re-grounding of ourselves and the re-grounding of the world in their true ground, which is emptiness, we pray to the guru who self-liberates attachment or desire. This guru is our own awareness. It is the state of meditation, where desires still arise but our relaxed and calm presence is like the surface of a mirror, so that these objects of desire arise, reveal themselves, but then pass on back into emptiness because we're no longer there as an anxious ego to invest them with special importance. It's not that thoughts or feelings or sensations are bad, they don't need to be given up *per se*. With the integration of clarity and emptiness, we experience directly that there is no danger of attachments, and so we can playfully enjoy the creativity of the imagination dancing in this empty, open, world.

Yesterday little Paul was running around with a big stick, a very dangerous man going to do very terrible things, and we can look at him and: "Yes, Paul, it's very dangerous," but we also know he's not so very dangerous. He knows he's not so powerful, but he also knows he wants to be very powerful, and he needs us to believe that he *is* powerful, otherwise his being powerless is too terrifying for him. This is one of the wonderful qualities of our mind, that fantasy, the life of creativity and the imagination, means we can construct all sorts of realities and believe in them, and then dissolve them. We know we do this: on the beach, you can make a sand castle, or you can be in a theatre company, you can make all sorts of things happen, and then at the end of it, the show is closed and you go home. The problem with samsara is that we start to live in the theatre and then we don't know where our home is any more. So dharma is really just about going home. It doesn't mean you then have to abandon the theatre. You can come back into the theatre because there are many people still trapped in the theatre, so you continue in the drama with others, but with the connection home. This is compassion.

འདི་ལྟར་སྣ་བའི་ཡུལ་དུ་གྲགས་པ་ཡི༔
སྙན་དང་མི་སྙན་འཛིན་པའི་སྒྲ་རྣམས་ཀུན༔
གྲགས་སྟོང་བསམ་མནོ་བྲལ་བའི་ངང་ལ་ཞོག༔
གྲགས་སྟོང་སྐྱེ་འགགས་མེད་པ་རྒྱལ་བའི་གསུང༔
གྲགས་སྟོང་རྒྱལ་བའི་གསུང་ལ་གསོལ་བ་འདེབས༔
ཨུ་རྒྱན་པད་མ་འབྱུང་གནས་ལ་གསོལ་བ་འདེབས༔

**DI TAR NA WAI YUL DU DRAG PA YI**
**NYEN DANG MI NYEN DZIN PAI DRA NAM KUN**
**DRAG TONG SAM NO DRAL WAI NGANG LA ZHOG**
**DRAG TONG KYE GAG MED PA GYAL WAI SUNG**
**DRAG TONG GYAL WAI SUNG LA SOL WA DEB**
**UR GYEN PAD MA JUNG NAE LA SOL WA DEB**

*As regards the ear's objects of the sounds which are held to as being pleasant and unpleasant: for all sounds, maintain the state of sound and emptiness, free of all involved thinking, quite unaffected. Sound and emptiness, the Jina's speech which never becomes limited, I pray to the Jina's speech of sound and emptiness, I pray to Urgyen Padma Jungnae.*

The sounds that we hear, sweet sounds and unpleasant sounds, all the sounds that we grasp at, are our own discriminations. Sound or hearing is the one sense that is very difficult to turn off. Emptiness doesn't mean that we can blank-off sounds. What we're concerned with here is how we take the sound's meaning to be really existing. This is why we do mantra, because mantra is sound and emptiness: "Om, om, om, om, om, om, wha, wha, wha, blah, blah, blah". That's what it's doing. It's all the time moving from meaning into meaninglessness, meaninglessness to emptiness, emptiness to meaninglessness to meaning, moving up and down, pulsing up and down. Then we see how we add semantic value to the open, empty, pure vibrating quality of sound.

Many meditation methods involve sound, because sound can hold our attention fully. Sound is simply energy. Unless you keep making sound there isn't sound. It is energetic movement, like the sound arising through the vibrations in the voice box in my throat — rrrrr. If you stop the vibration, there is no sound. This whole world also is vibration. When the vibration stops, the world ends. When we do the dissolving practice with light, the light also is vibration, as we know very well, and when the light vanishes, vibration goes down, there is nothing, just space, unborn. But this unborn nature is full of resonances, and these vibrations start, so then you have energy and light, thoughts, feelings and so on, and then we're in this world.

When you do the mantra practice, really allow yourself to be present in the sound, as the sound, and observe the different quality of experience as you focus in turn on the sensation of the mantra, its sound, and then its meaning. Sound helps us to see the link between emptiness and semantic form, that is why it is linked to the sambhogakaya.

འདི་ལྟར་ཡིད་ཀྱི་ཡུལ་དུ་འགྱུ་བ་ཡི༔
ཉོན་མོངས་དུག་ལྔའི་རྟོག་པ་ཅི་ཤར་ཡང་༔
སྔོན་བསུས་རྗེས་གཅོད་ལྟོ་ཡིས་བཅོས་མི་གཞུག༔
འགྱུ་བ་རང་སར་བཞག་པས་ཆོས་སྐུར་གྲོལ༔
རིག་པ་རང་གྲོལ་གྱི་བླ་མ་ལ་གསོལ་བ་འདེབས༔
ཨུ་རྒྱན་པད་མ་འབྱུང་གནས་ལ་གསོལ་བ་འདེབས༔

**DI TAR YID KYI YUL DU GYU WA YI**
**NYON MONG DUG NGAI TOG PA CHI SHAR YANG**
**NGON SUE JE CHOD LO YI CHOE MI ZHUG**
**GYU WA RANG SAR ZHAG PAE CHOE KUR DROL**
**RIG PA RANG DROL GYI LA MA LA SOL WA DEB**
**UR GYEN PAD MA JUNG NAE LA SOL WA DEB**

*As regards mentation's objects of the restless movement of whatever of the five afflicting poisons' thoughts arise: don't be involved in the intellect's unnatural activities of expectantly welcoming future thoughts and following after past thoughts. By keeping mind firm, and leaving the restless movement in its own place, it is liberated in the dharmakaya. I pray to the guru of self-liberating fundamental awareness, I pray to Urgyen Padma Jungnae.*

The mind is always moving, it is its nature to be restless, something is always happening. Don't worry about the movement of the mind; the thing we have to be careful with is the artificial activity of our intellect, of our intelligence. Just give space to whatever occurs, don't wait expectantly for the next thought, becoming interested in pursuing a line of thought, and don't rush after past thoughts, trying to work out what something meant. Now, clearly, if you live in the world with other people you will have a lot to think about. It's necessary to make plans. It's necessary in some ways to be preoccupied about things. If you have children, you find yourself thinking, "Oh God, why are they doing this?" and "I wonder…" It's not possible to be a parent and not have these thoughts, so it's really important to get the subtle quality of the instruction. It's not that you shouldn't do these things, but *stay present*, stay in awareness as this activity is going on, and then you are not fully fused into the activity. Don't get lost in it, but also don't try to block it from occurring altogether.

Generally speaking, social relationships are contractual. Parents make a kind of contract with society to take care of their children. People who decide to get married make a contract to stay together. Outside of contract, human relationship moves very quickly. Something arises due to energy and then, if it's not maintained by a contract, it will vanish again. Contingency, dependent co-origination, is the structure of the world we live in. It means, just like happenstance, a conjunction between events with a sense of randomness. We have to make effort if structures are to be maintained but this is not the same as being artificial. Effort can be the energy of openness or the anxious controlling function of the ego. Our own state determines how 'I' manifests.

Often we are chasing after our thoughts because we are looking for something permanent. We are building up structures which we think we can rely on. But the fact of impermanence puts pressure on all structures. Reliability, in the ordinary sense, has to be contractual, for it is a struggle against impermanence, for manifestation in the world is not reliable. It's very important, in relationship, to know what the difference is between comfort and openness. The ego seeks comfort. The ego seeks other people to be reliably there, and it also seeks, more intimately, thought patterns as comfort. Just as the baby sucks its thumb, we suck our thoughts. This is what this *ngon sue je chod* means. It means we get involved in thoughts, we wrap ourselves around them and construct our own identity through them.

Padmasambhava comes and goes. He comes and goes. He teaches impermanence, and you can only survive in a world of impermanence if you are not relying on solid things. This is the whole teaching of the dharma. It fits exactly together. There's no contradiction. The more you invest other people with a solid reality, and you try to rest on them, the more you set yourself up for betrayal. What is required is that we collaborate with how things are, rather than try to impose our fantasies, our artificial constructs. Working with what's there means being present in the moment, on the evolving cusp of actuality.

ཕྱི་ལྟར་གཟུང་བའི་ཡུལ་སྣང་དག་པ་དང་༔
ནང་ལྟར་འཛིན་པའི་སེམས་ཉིད་གྲོལ་བ་དང་༔
བར་དུ་འོད་གསལ་རང་ངོ་ཤེས་པ་རུ༔
དུས་གསུམ་བདེ་གཤེགས་རྣམས་ཀྱི་ཐུགས་རྗེ་ཡིས༔
བདག་འདྲའི་རང་རྒྱུད་གྲོལ་བར་བྱིན་གྱིས་རློབས༔

**CHI TAR ZUNG PAI YUL NANG DAG PA DANG**
**NANG TAR DZIN PAI SEM NYID DROL WA DANG**
**BAR DU OD SAL RANG NGO SHE PA RU**
**DUE SUM DE SHEG NAM KYI THUG JE YI**
**DAG DRAI RANG GYUD DROL WAR JIN GYI LOB**

*By holding to the actual purity of the appearances/ideas of the outer objects of grasping (in other words, don't go under their power), and maintaining the liberation of the grasping mind within (in other words, keep the mind free of mixing with the confusing afflictions), while doing these two things there is clear illumination in which one's own nature is known. In this manner, by the compassion of the buddhas of the past, present and future, may I and all beings gain the blessing of the liberation of our natures.*

Externally, the objects which we grasp are purified, they are no longer hooking us, and the mind that can grasp, or wants to depend, wants to rely on things, wants to build up on top of a substantial base, is liberated. The graspable object and the grasping mind are like velcro: as soon as they come in contact, they lock on very solidly, so, one is like a hook and one is like a ring. What we're trying to do here is just have two rings, so both are complete and they don't lock on to each other. When that happens, one has the possibility of recognising the natural clarity of one's own mind. The clarity is simply the quality of not being caught up in things. For sure, we have all had that kind of experience in its most ordinary form. On a nice summer's day when you're happy and you're just walking along and you feel very connected with everything, and as you look around, everything seems wonderful. That's the kind of feeling-tone of happiness. Inside that, one is not making discriminations. One becomes lighter, and you just recognise, "Oh, I'm part of this world, and this world is…Oh! Its rising as experience…" In that moment, if you know how to look, you see right down into the root: empty nature.

Then the text says, 'By the kindness of all the buddhas of the three times, may I and all beings like me have their stream of personal identity liberated'. *Rang gyud* means the stream of personal identity, the ongoing flow that makes me feel like me. In sanskrit it's *santana*, and if you know the music of Carlos Santana, it goes on and on and on, it's very similar. When liberating this train of continuity, it doesn't mean that we cease to exist, or we vanish. We remain the same kind of people. It's just that instead of being immersed in the horizontal movement of being woven into the ongoing construction of one's life, one has relaxed into the state of the mirror, and one's own life is then revealed as an experience rather than as an identity, so there is space and clarity rather than anxious investment.

དེ་ལྟར་གསོལ་བཏབ་ཆོས་ཉིད་རྗེན་པར་རྟོགཿ
སྣང་རིག་གསལ་སྟོང་འཛིན་འོད་ཕྱག་ལྡི་ཁམསཿ
ཕྱག་མཚན་སྐུ་དང་ཡེ་ཤེས་མཚོན་གྱུར་ནསཿ
ཀ་དག་ལྷུན་གྲུབ་གདོད་མའི་རྩལ་རྫོགས་ཤོགཿ

**DE TAR SOL TAB CHOE NYID JEN PAR TOG
NANG RIG SAL TONG JA OD THIG LEI KHAM
CHAG TSEN KU DANG YE SHE NGON GYUR NAE
KA DAG LHUN DRUB DOD MAI TSAL DZOG SHOG**

*In accordance with what I have prayed for, may the natural condition be realized just as it is, with appearances/ideas, fundamental awareness, lucidity and emptiness, the sphere of balls of wisdom's rainbow light. With god's symbol, kayas and pristine and supreme knowledges becoming clearly manifest in and for me, I must truly get the primordially pure, effortlessly arising, original and genuine flow of energy*

Resting in the natural state, all aspects arise in emptiness: appearance, clarity, awareness; unimpeded integration displayed in the manifestation, balls of rainbow-coloured light, balls called *thigle*, a bit like these little bubbles that children blow. In this dimension everything arises fully-formed, effortlessly, with all qualities complete. Through this we come to fully trust the process, to relax further and relinquish anxious activity.

Tibetan is a very beautiful and wonderful language to be able to put all these incredibly complex terms together in such a beautiful way. We can't do this in European languages, and so we have to make these very complicated constructions which always sound heavy, whereas in the Tibetan it's very light, it's like poetry. Whatever we experience is the energetic manifestation of natural purity. It doesn't matter what its quality is, whether it's nice or not nice, whether it's easy or difficult, it always has the same ground. The manifestation is defined by the nature of the ground, not by the relative qualities it displays.

# F. Dharma Protector Practice

RAM YAM KHAM OM AA HUNG
HUNG GU DEN LA MA SANG GYAE DAM PAI CHOE
PHAG PAI GE DUN KU SUM YONG DZOG LHA
YI DAM GYUD DE ZHI DRUG KHA DROI TSOG
PADMA JUNG NAE DRANG SONG MON LAM DRUB

*Hung. The guru having the nine lineages, the Buddha and the excellent dharma, the arya sangha and the gods having the perfect three kayas, the wishing gods of the four and six sections of tantra and the hosts of dakinis, Padmasambhava, the sages and those who accomplished their aspiration;*

ཕྱག་དྲུག་ཡབ་ཡུམ་བསྟན་སྲུང་ཡོངས་རྫོགས་ལྷ༔

CHAG DRUG YAB YUM TEN SUNG YONG DZOG LHA
GON CHEN MA NING DE NGA TSOG KYI DAG
E KA DZA TI DUR THRO MA MO SUM
RE TI MA DUN TAN MA CHU NYI PO
LHA CHEN SOG PUR DRAG SHUL NYI MA ZHON

*Mahakala with his consort, the god who encompasses all the dharma-protectors; Mahanath, the Maning Denga and Tsog-Kyi-Dag; Ekajati and the three Durtro Mamo; Remati; the Wongi Madun and the Tanma Chunyi; Lhachen, Sogpur, Dragshul and Nyima Zhonu;*

གཟའ་བདུད་སྤུ་གྲི་རྡོར་ལེགས་གཉན་ཐང་ལྷ༔
སྟོང་དཔོན་ཡབ་ཡུམ་སྐུ་ལྔ་སྐྱ་བཙུན་བདུན༔
མཐུ་ཆེན་སྡེ་བཞི་བཀྲ་བཟང་གཞི་བདག༔
དུར་ཁྲོད་བདག་པོ་དམ་ཅན་ནོར་ལྷའི་ཚོགས༔

ZA DUD PU TRI DOR LEG NYEN THANG LHA
TONG PON YAB YUM KU NGA KYA TSEN DUN
THU CHEN DE ZHI TRAB ZANG ZHI TER DAG
DUR THROD DAG PO DAM CHAN NOR LHAI TSOG

*Zadud Putri, Dorleg and Nyan Thanglha; Tongpon with his consort, the Kunga and the Kyabtsandun, the Thuchen Dezhi, treasure lords, the lords of the cemetery, the hosts of vow-keepers and wealth gods;*

མདོ་སྔགས་བསྟན་བསྲུང་ཆོས་སྐྱོང་སྲུང་མའི་རིགས༔
ཕྱི་ནང་གསང་བའི་ལྷ་སྲིན་སྡེ་བརྒྱད་དམག༔

## F. Dharma Protector Practice

ཟབས་རི་བཙན་རྒོད་སྤུན་བདུན་ལ་སོགས་པའི༔
འཛམ་གླིང་གཞི་བདག་གཏེར་བདག་ཀླུ་གཉན་སོགས༔

**DO NGAG TEN SUNG CHOE KYONG SUNG MAI RIG
CHI NANG SANG WAI LHA SIN DE GYE MAG
ZANG RI TSEN GOD PUN DUN LA SOG PAI
DZAM LING ZHI DAG TER DAG LU NYEN SOG**

*All the guardian groups of doctrine guardians and dharma protectors of sutra and tantra, the armies of the outer, inner and secret eight groups of Lhasin; the Zangri Tsangod Pundun and so on, all the land lords, treasure lords and snake gods in the world.*

མ་ལུས་འདིར་གཤེགས་གདན་བཞུགས་གུས་ཕྱག་འཚལ༔
ཕྱི་ནང་གསང་གསུམ་མཆོད་པའི་སྤྲིན་གྱི་དཔུང་༔
མཆོད་ཡོན་ཞབས་བསིལ་མེ་ཏོག་བདུག་སྤོས་དྲི༔
སྣང་གསལ་དྲི་ཆབ་ཞལ་ཟས་རོལ་མོའི་སྒྲ༔
གཟུགས་སྒྲ་དྲི་རོ་རེག་བྱ་ཆོས་ལ་སོགས༔
རྒྱལ་སྲིད་སྣ་བདུན་བཀྲ་ཤིས་རྫས་བརྒྱད་ཀྱིས༔

**MA LUE DIR SHEG DEN ZHUG GUE CHAG TSAL
CHI NANG SANG SUM CHOD PAI SIN GYI PUNG
CHOD YON ZHAB SIL ME TOG DUG POE DRI
NANG SAL DRI CHAB ZHAL ZAE ROL MOI DRA
ZUG DRA DRI RO REG JA CHOE LA SOG
GYAL SID NA DUN TRA SHI DZAE GYE KYI**

*All of you, without exception, please come here and sit on these cushions. We make obeisance and offer great clouds of the outer, inner and secret offerings. Drinking water, water to bathe your feet, flowers, incense, lamps, perfumed water, food and music; forms, sound, smells, tastes, tangible objects, nature and so forth, the seven royal articles and the eight auspicious articles;*

THUG DAM KONG SHING NONG PA CHI CHI SHAG
KHO GUI LONG CHOD JUNG WAI SANG DUD KYI
MI TSANG NYE KYON SANG SHING KANG WAI DZAE
LHA LU MI YI PAL JOR DANG KYI KANG
MEN TOR RAKTA SER KYEM DI ZHE SHIG
MA HA PANTSA RAKTA BALINGTA
SARVA PUTSA KHA KHA KHA HI KHA HI

*By these offerings may your minds be satisfied and may you excuse whatever faults we have done. By the fragrant smoke from which the suitable articles arise the impure faults are purified from the satisfying articles. We satisfy you with all the shining wealth of gods, nagas and men. Please accept this amrita, torma, rakta and serkyim. Great five amritas, rakta, torma — all offerings, eat, eat, please eat, please eat.*

As GERMANY WAS, I'm sure, two thousand years ago, Tibet is a country where nature is very much alive. The mountains have gods, the rivers have gods, there are spirits in the sky, on the earth, under the earth. Every place, phenomenon, force, is under the power of some local group. When Padmasambhava went to Tibet, he encountered a lot of powerful, local gods and spirits who were worshipped and offered rituals according to many ancient traditions. By his meditation power he brought about, not so much their conversion, but the alignment of these energy forces with dharma, so that they become turned towards the dharma, and turned particularly towards protecting the dharma rather than attacking or undermining it.

For this reason alone, Padmasambhava should be a saint of the ecology movement. As far as I know, in all the other buddhist countries, when buddhism was introduced, you had a splitting between monastic buddhism and the local gods, and the local gods, although they weren't destroyed, were handed over to local shamans and local priests, who did particular kinds of trances and healings and so forth. The monks didn't do any of that, so you had a separation. Of course, in christian countries we killed off the shamans, so we had a very radical approach to dispatching local gods. Padmasambhava, however, managed to integrate a formal, sophisticated buddhist cosmology and meditation system with a very simple, village-level energy. That integration has been enormously important for sustaining a non-dual understanding. When Padmasambhava met these local gods, he forced them into a contract to support the dharma. He established certain rituals for worshipping them, or at least for making offerings to them, and certain mantras for controlling them. These practices continue today, as the contracts have to be maintained on a daily basis.

Generally speaking, we always visualise ourselves as Padmasambhava before we do protector practices. We have to remember that these are not just some kind of symbol or some kind of idea for Tibetans, these are energy forces and if you evoke them, you get some result, they actually do something. You have, on the one hand, very high dharma protectors who operate on the level of bodhisattvas like Mahakala, and on the other you get very wild and dangerous dharma protectors who are hardly buddhist at all, and who have to be managed with great care.

Buddhas, of course, have a lot of understanding. Therefore, if you say to a buddha, "I will pray to you every day", and then you don't do it, that buddha says, "Eh, people don't change very much!" They are not very surprised. But some of these dharma protectors, they're not like that at all. If you say, "I will make offerings to you every day," they come back and say, "Eh! Where are you?" They are like the Mafia, they don't forget to collect. Having made a connection, if you upset them they can cause all kind of illnesses, sickness, and trouble. So this is a kind of practice that one should do very carefully, whether one does it frequently or not.

We begin by purifying the offerings, and then we identify all the guests. These are the buddhas and the sangha, the three kayas, all the wishing gods, all the higher figures, including Padmasambhava and the great ones. Then there are the dharma protectors themselves. Tibetan culture was very, very hierarchical, a bit like Chinese culture, so if you go to a Tibetan house, traditionally you will sit on the floor in rows, and like in a monastery, you always get put into your place according to your rank. There is a great sensitivity to status and people take offence easily. The protectors and local gods are the same. There are eight main categories of spirits, and then there are many other kinds of groupings as well. They need to be dealt with in the proper way. If you put one ahead of the other, the gods get jealous and you can get trouble, so if you enter into this field, you have to be very careful. Very often it doesn't mean very much to western people, and you have to find your own way in this territory, because it's very, very foreign to our present culture.

For example, here you had a storm recently that knocked down many trees, so you can really get a sense of the power of something, the wind. Who blew the wind up the hill? In Tibet they would have a sense, somebody would think, "Oh we didn't make this offering on the hill." They then go and do a puja to placate the local god who has created the destruction. They believe that the puja will make a difference. This is a lot of the bread and butter of Tibetan lamas, because the villagers pay them to do pujas around these local things much more than the big things. so you have the life of the monastery for enlightenment, and you have the relationship with the villagers around the management of power, which means that rain falls on time and hailstones don't fall, so you have food. I mean, it's a very life-and-death struggle in many Tibetan valleys; having a sense of how to work these energies is very important.

So, we're holding the visualisation of ourselves as Padmasambhava, and we recite the text in a strong, clear way. You have to be strong, for these beings respect strength. The text lists the names of many deities. Then it says, 'Without exception, please come here. Sit on this seat. We offer salutation. We offer these outer and inner offerings, great piles of them, heaps of them. We offer you things to drink, to wash your feet, water, incense, so forth. General offerings we offer to you, and all the nice things of the world.' We want them to perform their function, which is to protect the dharma and to keep the world in harmony, and that's the purpose of making these offerings, so there is a harmony. In Tibetan monasteries the dharma protector practice was done for hours every day. There would be a special room for the protectors, and there would be two or three monks there doing practice many, many hours of the day.

## F. Dharma Protector Practice

We want our guests to be satisfied, peaceful. So we say 'Please be happy, be satisfied with this and forgive any faults or mistakes that we have made'. Very often people do a burned offering, offering *sang*, juniper leaves, or more generally any fragrant leaf. 'By this fragrant smoke all impurities are removed in the offerings, and therefore may you be satisfied with this and with all the shining wealth of gods, nagas and men'. It means all the wealth on the earth, above the earth, and beneath the earth. Then it says 'Please accept these usual offerings, the *amrita*, *torma*, *rakta*, and the *ser kyem*, the special offering cup for dharma protectors, usually filled with arak, sometimes with tea. Then we have the offering mantra which we recite three times.

དེ་ལྟར་སྐོང་ཤིང་ཕྲིན་ལས་བཅོལ་བ་ནི༔
མི་མཐུན་རྐྱེན་བཟློག་མཐུན་རྐྱེན་ཡིད་བཞིན་སྒྲུབས༔
རྗེས་སུ་འགྲོ་ན་བསུ་སྐྱེལ་ཁ་འཛིན་མཛོད༔
གཞི་ལ་འདུག་ན་སྟོང་གྲོགས་རྒྱབ་བརྟེན་གྱིས༔
བདག་གི་ལུས་སྲོག་ལོངས་སྤྱོད་མངའ་ཐང་རྣམས༔
ཁྱེད་ལ་བརྟེན་འཛུགས་མངའ་གསོལ་གཉེར་དུ་གཏད༔
ནམ་ཡང་འབྲལ་མེད་ལུས་དང་གྲིབ་བཞིན་འགྲོགས༔

**DE TAR KONG SHING THRIN LAE CHOL WA NI
MI THUN KYEN DOG THUN KYEN YID ZHIN DRUB
JE SU DRO NA SU KYEL KHA DZIN DZO
ZHI LA DUG NA DONG DROG GYAB TEN GYI
DAG GI LUE SOG LONG CHOD NGA THANG NAM
KHYE LA TEN DZUG NGA SOL NYER DU TAD
NAM YANG DRAL MED LUE DANG DRIB ZHIN DROG**

*Thus being satisfied, do your appointed tasks. Repel all difficult situations and establish helpful situations according to our wish. When we travel you must welcome us and ease the way, and when we stay at some place you must advance our interests and protect us. Therefore our bodies, wealth, positions and so on we offer to you and entrust ourselves to your friendly care. Never separating from us, you must be like a shadow accompanying the body.*

ཡིད་ལ་གང་བསམ་མ་ལུས་འགྲུབ་པ་དང༔

བསྟན་འཛིན་སྐྱེས་བུ་རིམ་བྱོན་དགེ་འདུན་སྡེ༔

དབྱར་མཚོ་ལྟར་འཕེལ་མི་ནུབ་རབ་བརྟན་ཞིང༔

སྙན་གྲགས་གདུལ་བྱ་མངའ་ཐང་ལོངས་སྤྱོད་རྒྱས༔

ས་དང་ལམ་གྱི་ཡོན་ཏན་གོང་འཕེལ་ཞིང༔

མཆོག་ཐུན་དངོས་གྲུབ་མ་ལུས་རྩལ་དུ་གསོལ༔

ཁྱེད་ལ་རྒྱུན་དུ་གསོལ་བ་བཏབ་པའི་མཐུས༔

ཚེ་འདིར་ཡིད་བཞིན་དབང་རྒྱལ་འགྲུབ་པ་དང༔

མཐར་ཐུག་ང་ཡབ་ཟངས་མདོག་དཔལ་གྱི་རིར༔

དག་པའི་ཞིང་དུ་འཁྲིད་པའི་གྲོགས་མཛོད་ཅིག༔

YID LA GANG SAM MA LUE DRUB PA DANG
TEN DZIN KYE BU RIM JON GE DUN DE
YAR TSO TAR PHEL MI NUB RAB TEN ZHING
NYAN DRAG DUL JA NGA THANG LONG CHOD GYAE
SA DANG LAM GYI YON TEN GONG PHEL ZHING
CHOG THUN NGOE DRUB MA LUE TSAL DU SOL
KHYE LA GYUN DU SOL WA TAB PAI THUE
TSE DIR YID ZHIN WANG GYAL DRUB PA DANG
THAR THUG NGA YAB ZANG DOG PAL GYI RIR
DAG PAI ZHING DU THRID PAI DROG DZOD CHIG

*All that our minds desire must be accomplished, and the doctrine-holders who come from time-to-time and the bhikshu sangha must increase steadily like the summer oceans, without decline. Their fame, disciples, position and wealth must spread. With the good qualities of the stages*

## F. Dharma Protector Practice

*and ways increasing please grant us all supreme and general siddhis without exception. By the power of always praying to you, whatever we wish for in this life must be fully accomplished, and when we die you must help and guide us to the pure realm of Ngayab Zangdopalri.*

OM AH HUNG SA MA YA AMRITA KHA KHA KHA HI KHA HI
HO NYING NYE DRAN PHO DRAN MOI TSOG
DAM LA MA DA SA MA YA
DAG GI SUNG MAR NGA SOL LO
SANG GYE TAN PA KHYOD KYI SUNG
KON CHOG WUE PHANG KHYOD KYI TOD
NAL JOR KU DRA KHYOD KYI DROL
CHOL WAI THRIN LAE DRUB PAR DZOD

*Body, speech and mind. Keep your vows. Eat this amrita, eat. You must eat! You must eat! Ho! You loving hosts of male and female servants do not go beyond your vows. Keep your vows! You are appointed as my guardians. You must protect the doctrine of the Buddha. You must praise the three jewels as high above your heads. You must kill the personal enemies of the yogis. You must carry out the activities I entrusted to you.*

གང་ཞིག་ཡིད་ལ་དྲན་པ་ཙམ་གྱིས་ཀྱང༈
འདོད་པའི་དངོས་གྲུབ་སྩོལ་བར་མཛད་པ་ཡི༈
ཆོས་སྐྱོང་ཡིད་བཞིན་ནོར་བུ་ཁྱེད་རྣམས་ཀྱིས༈
བདག་གིས་བསམ་དོན་མ་ལུས་འགྲུབ་པར་མཛོད༈

**GANG ZHIG YID LA DREN PA TSAM GYI KYANG
DOD PAI NGOE DRUB TSOL WAR DZAI PA YI
CHOE KYONG YID ZHIN NOR BU KYED NAM KYI
DAG GI SAM DON MA LUE DRUB PAR DZOD**

*If someone should merely remember you, just by that
you will grant them the real attainments they desire.
You dharma protectors who are like wish-fulfilling gems,
please satisfy all my desires and needs without exception.*

ཁྱེད་རྣམས་མཆོད་ཅིང་གསོལ་བ་བཏབ་པའི་མཐུས།
བདག་སོགས་གང་དུ་གནས་པའི་ས་ཕྱོགས་སུ།
ནད་དང་དབུལ་ཕོངས་འཐབ་རྩོད་ཞི་བ་དང་།
ཆོས་དང་བཀྲ་ཤིས་འཕེལ་བར་མཛད་དུ་གསོལ།

**KYE NAM CHOE CHING SOL WA TAB PAI THUE
DAG SOG GANG DU NAE PAI SA CHOG SU
NAD DANG UL PHONG THAB TSOD ZHI WA DANG
CHOE DANG TRA SHI PHEL WAR DZAD DU SOL**

*By the power of offering you praise and praying to you,
in whatever place we stay, may sickness, poverty and strife
be pacified, and may dharma and good fortune increase.*

Now, when they have been satisfied by these offerings we say to the protectors, "You must do your job." This job is not as general as, "Please give us enlightenment," or "Please give us this special kind of siddhi." Here we're talking about much more precise issues in terms of daily life. So the text says *mi thun kyen dog*, reverse situations or conditions which are unhelpful to us. *Dog pa* means to turn back. It's a function that is used in magic where if somebody has put a spell onto you, you can turn it back on them and they get burned up by it. The person is destroyed not by us but by their own bad intention. We also ask that the good things we like will happen.

Then the text requests that when we're travelling, to make life easy and make a good reception for us. In Tibet this was particularly important because, as you travel, you move across the realms of various protectors and local deities. Each one of these may say, "Oy, who are you, and what are you doing?" and give you some trouble. "Also, when we stay in a place, you should take care of us, make sure that our ideas go well, our desires go well, and also make sure that nobody causes trouble for us." Just because forms are empty it does not mean they have no existence, that would be the wrong view of nihilism. By maintaining the form of Padmasambhava throughout the protector practice we never forget that all the functions described are inseparable from emptiness, no matter how banal and dualistic they appear to be.

The text then says, 'My body and wealth, my social position, my whole existence, everything, I offer to you and I ask you to take care of me. I put myself in your care. Never separating from us, you must be like a shadow.' They will always be there. When we practise dharma and maintain an open state of awareness we drop our usual focus on self-protection. In that state we're potentially quite vulnerable since openness can integrate anything, but it doesn't blank dangerous energies out automatically. While you're doing your dharma practice and are going into non-ordinary states, shifted away from the ordinary resonances of the world, the dharma protectors, who are very much agents in the world, will keep you safe, so we can trust that the protection normally provided by the ego will occur without strengthening the ego. They will keep their eyes open for us, in this life and at the time of our death when we travel to Zangdopalri. It is a collaborative relationship in which their focused energy performs functions that allow us to relax, while our offerings, and reminders of their dharma contracts, keep them in check so they accumulate less bad karma, and remain close to Padmasambhava. Thus it is the energy of the mandala that acts for us, and as us, helping us to let go of the ego as the central site of security and activity.

Then the text describes setting out the offerings very nicely for a joyous festival. It's very important, especially if you're doing the practice on your own, to really have a good time when you do the offerings. You need to really build up the felt sense that these deities have actually come, and that the offerings are an interaction. In a sense you're creating a kind of mental drama here, and the more you bring your own feelings and hopes into this, the more alive it becomes. Always offer the best quality you can afford, fresh produce, and never left-overs from something else.

# G. Offerings

## a. Blessing the Offerings and Inviting the High Guests

### Blessing the Offering Articles (Tsog)

རཾ་ཡཾ་ཁཾ༔ ཨོཾ་ཨཱཿཧཱུྃ༔

**RAM YAM KHAM OM AH HUNG**

THE OFFERINGS ARE PURIFIED of all defects by the agency of fire, wind and water and the body, speech and mind of the buddhas. It is important to establish all offerings in emptiness so that that awareness helps us to deconstruct our grasping approach to the products of the world. Our body is a light body, so if we look at the *tsog*, at the food, and think, "Ooh, I want some of that," or "Mmm, I'll have more of that," we're abandoning our meditation for the sake of a little piece of chocolate, or a big strawberry or something. It's not very helpful. We eat and drink, but we shouldn't do it like pigs. We should always do it with an awareness.

ཧཱུྃ༔ ཨུ་རྒྱན་ཡུལ་གྱི་ནུབ་བྱང་མཚམས༔
པདྨ་གེ་སར་སྡོང་པོ་ལ༔
ཡ་མཚན་མཆོག་གི་དངོས་གྲུབ་བརྙེས༔
པདྨ་འབྱུང་གནས་ཞེས་སུ་གྲགས༔

HUNG UR GYEN YUL GYI NUB JANG TSHAM
PE MA GE SAR DONG PO LA
YAM TSEN CHOG GI NGOE DRUB NYE
PE MA JUNG NAE ZHE SU DRAG
KHOR DU KHAN DRO MANG POE KOR
KHYE KYI JE SU DAG DRUB KYI
JIN GYI LAB CHIR SHEG SU SOL
GU RU PE MA SID DHI HUNG

*Hung. In the north-west corner of the land of Urgyen, upon the stem and stamen of a lotus, are you who have the marvellous and supreme attainments, Padmasambhava of great renown, with a retinue of many dakinis around you. Following and relying on you, I do your practice; therefore, in order to grant your blessings, please come here! Guru Padmasambhava, give me the real attainment of buddhahood.*

**Invitation**

HUNG HRI RANG NANG DAG PA SANG CHEN NGA YAB ZHING
KU SUM DAG NYID RIG DZIN PAD MA JUNG

## G. Offerings

**DRUB NYE TSEN CHOG GYAD DANG DAK KI CHE
TSOG KYI KHOR LO DU WAR SHEG SU SOL**

*Hung. Hri. In my own mind's pure and very secret realm of Ngayab
is Padmasambhava, the vidyadhara with the nature of the three kayas,
together with the eight excellent forms and the dakinis.
Please come to this assembly of the offering circle.*

In this realm, the very secret, pure realm of Zangdopalri, which is one's own experience — *rang nang* here is *rigpai rang nang*, which means this is the manifestation arising out of emptiness — there arises the essence of the three kayas, Padmasambhava, together with the eight forms and the dakinis, and we say, 'Please come here to this gathering circle, please come here to this place where we are going to be together.' Ngayab, where Padmasambhava lives, is very secret because only those with initiation can go there. 'It is an aspect of my own mind, and I invoke the gods who inhabit it to come here to this feast'.

Within the state of meditation we imagine Padmasambhava and his entourage coming towards us through the clear blue sky of awareness. Rainbows are all around them and they exude happiness.

ཡེ་ཤེས་ལས་གྲུབ་བསྟན་སྲུང་དམ་ཅན་སྡེ༔
ཡང་དགོས་ཟབ་གཏེར་ཆོས་བཀའ་སྐྱོང་བ་ཡི༔
ཕོ་མོ་མ་ནིང་རྒྱུད་གསུམ་དྲེགས་ཚོགས་བཅས༔
འདོད་ཡོན་ཚོགས་ཀྱི་འཁོར་ལོ་འདུ་བར་གཤེགས༔

**YE SHE LAE DRUB TEN SUNG DAM CHEN CHI
YANG GOE ZAB TER CHOE KA KYONG WA YI
PHO MO MA NING GYUD SUM DREG TSOG CHE
DOD YON TSOG KYI KHOR LO DU WAR SHEG**

*Those having the nature of pristine cognition, the general doctrine* guardians, and vow-keepers, and in particular those who protect the words of the profound treasure dharma, the hosts of the fierce forms of the three groups, male, female and neuter — come to this assembly of the gathering circle where there is everything to please the senses.

དམ་རྫས་བཅུད་ཕོབ་སྐལ་ལྡན་དབང་བཞི་བསྐུར༔
བར་ཆད་ཀྱེན་ཞི་མཆོག་ཐུན་དངོས་གྲུབ་སྩོལ༔
བཛྲ་ས་མ་ཡ་ཛཿཛཿ

**DAM DZAE CHUD PHOB KAL DEN WANG ZHI KUR**
**BAR CHED KYEN ZHI CHOG THUN NGOE DRUB TSOL**
**BENDZA SA MA YA DZA DZA**

*Give substance to the offering articles and grant the four initiations to the fortunate ones. Pacify obstructing conditions and grant supreme and general real attainments. Keep your vajra vows! Come! Come!*

By their blessing, the honoured guests transform the offerings into liberating elixir. Through their presence at the feast, we want to receive the four initiations, have all our difficulties removed, and gain all attainments.

### Presenting the Offerings

ཧྲཱིཿ རྒྱལ་ཀུན་དབང་ཕྱུག་རིག་འཛིན་པདྨ་འབྱུང༔
མཚན་མཆོག་བརྒྱད་དང་རྗེ་འབངས་བཀྱེ་དི་ཚོགས༔
རྩ་གསུམ་ཀུན་འདུས་རྒྱལ་བའི་དཀྱིལ་འཁོར་དུ༔
འདོད་ཡོན་ལྷ་ལྷུན་ཟག་མེད་དྲིང་འཛིན་ཛམ༔
དམ་རྫས་ཚོགས་ཀྱི་མཆོད་པས་དགྱེས་པར་སྐྱོངས༔

## G. Offerings

**HRI GYAL KUN WANG CHUG RIG DZIN PAD MA JUNG**
**TSEN CHOG GYAD DANG JE BANG DAK KI TSOG**
**TSA SUM KUN DUE GYAL WAI KYIL KHOR DU**
**DOD YON NGA DEN ZAG MED TING DZIN ZAE**
**DAM DZAE TSOG KYI CHOD PAE GYE PA KONG**

*Hri. Vidyadhara Padmasambhava, who is mighty among all the jinas, and the eight excellent forms with the twenty-five disciples and the hosts of dakinis — in the Jina's mandala which encompasses the three roots we offer you all that is pleasing, with undefiled, absorbed contemplation. Be happily satisfied with the assembled offerings of the obligatory articles.*

We offer all the best things we have and that we can imagine, and we do this with one pointed meditation. So, if you can, stop for a moment and develop your visualisation of the offerings.

**HRI KA TER LA MA NAM KYI THUG DAM KANG**
**YI DAM LHA TSOG NAM KYI THUG DAM KANG**
**MA SING KHA DRO NAM KYI THUG DAM KANG**
**DAM CHEN NOR LHA NAM KYI THUG DAM KANG**

*Hri. The gurus of kama and terma must be fully satisfied and happy. The hosts of wishing gods must be fully satisfied and happy. The mother and sister dakinis must be fully satisfied and happy. The vow-keepers and wealth gods must be fully satisfied and happy.*

The *kama* lineage is the unbroken, open lineage from the time of Padmasambhava. It has been passed on from person to person, without being hidden, whereas the *terma* lineage includes a period when the teaching was hidden as treasure, entrusted to the dakinis. *Thug dam kang* means 'Don't be displeased with me, don't have any bile in your heart towards me. Don't be upset if I've hurt you in some way, or done something that made you unhappy. Don't hold that against me.' This is vital because we need to maintain a very clear line of connection with all of these gods, so when we say *thug dam kang* it means let's make our relationship good again. Be happy to be with me! This is necessary because we're trying to populate our experience with these deities. We need them to be alive in our lives.

**CHOD JIN OE PAI DRON KUN THAM CHE KYI**
**THUG DAM NYEN PO MA LUE DER KANG LA**
**NAD DON DIG DRIB ZHI DANG TSE SOD GYAE**
**MOE PA NAM ZHI WANG DUE LOG DREN DROL**
**CHOG DANG THUN MONG NGOE DRUB TSAL DU SOL**
**GU RU DE WA DAK KI NI SARVA PU TSA KHA HI**

*For all those guests who are worthy of offerings and gifts, all their sacred connections must be fully satisfied and restored. Then sickness, demons, sins and obscurations must be pacified, and life and merit must increase. The four kinds of satisfaction must come under our power, and the misleaders must be destroyed. Please grant us supreme and general real attainments. Guru, deva, dakini, please eat all these ceremonial offerings.*

By our offerings we wish all harmed vows and connections to be repaired. Then, with energy flowing easily between us and the three roots (guru, deva, dakini) and the dharma protectors, all the functions we require will be fulfilled. Negative phenomena, like sickness and difficulties, will be pacified, while positive phenomena, like wealth, merit, life span, will increase. We will gain the power of the four satisfactions, gaze, touch, embrace and intercourse, and all our troublesome demons will be destroyed. We shall gain enlightenment and all general attainments. Therefore, we are very keen indeed that they accept the offerings.

## b. Making Confession

ཧོ༔ བདག་ཅག་ཐོག་མེད་དུས་ནས་ད་ལྟའི་བར༔
རང་ངོ་མ་ཤེས་ལོག་ཏོག་འཁྲུལ་པས་བསྒྲིབ༔
སྡོམ་གསུམ་དམ་ཚིག་འདས་རལ་ཆག་ཉམས་ཀུན༔
ཚོགས་ཀྱི་འཁོར་ལོས་བསྐང་ཞིང་བཤགས་པར་བགྱི༔

**HO DAG CHAG THOG MED DUE NAE DA TAI BAR
RANG NGO MA SHE LOG TOG THRUL PAE DRIB
DOM SUM DAM TSIG DAE RAL CHAG NYAM KUN
TSOG KYI KHOR LOE KANG ZHING SHAG PAR GYI**

*Ho. All of us from beginningless time up until now,
due to the obscuration of the false understanding and confusion
of not knowing our own natures have broken, breached and
lapsed in our obligations of the three classes of vows.
Making restoration with this gathering circle, we offer our confession.*

The root cause of all our problems is ignorance. This is what we need to recognise and repair; repair by ceasing to ignore what is there, what has always been there, our own nature, pure from the very beginning. Because of not recognising it, we become confused, attached to wrong views, and become more lost even as we try to find our way. We confess these, and make up for any harm caused.

In particular, we have made breaches in our vows. In our vows of restraint and morality (vinaya), our commitment to control our behaviour and pacify our tendencies. In our bodhisattva vows, through being forgetful of the benefit of others. In our tantric vows, through forgetting that we are now inhabitants of the sacred mandala, with a specific view, meditation and activity. In particular, we forget the purity of our own nature, and identify with self-attacking thoughts, abandoning our buddha nature in favour of an attachment to ourselves as real, separate, self-existing and bad. All faults, errors, mistakes are contingent and impermanent! They do not have the power to contaminate and condition us without our participation, without our being willing to say, "I am bad," and feel that its true, right to our core. We fully confess these mistakes and meditate on Dorje Sempa in order to be reconnected with unchanging purity:

OM GURU PADMA SA MA YA MA NU PA LA YA
GURU PADMA TE NO PA TI SHTA DRI DHO ME BHA WA
SU TO KYIO ME BHAV WA SU PO KYIO ME BHA WA
A NU RAKTO ME BHA WA SAR VA SIDDHI MA ME PRA YA TSA
SAR VA KAR MA SU TSA ME TSI TAM SHRI YAM KU RU HUNG
HA HA HA HA HO
BHA GA WAN SARVA TA THA GATA GURU PADMA MA ME MUN TSA
GURU PADMA BHA WA MA HA SA MA YA SA TWA AA HUNG PHAT

## G. Offerings

*The five pristine cognitions. Guru Padma with the power of being strong in your vows, you must protect me and all who follow after you and rely on you! Guru Padma, you must hear me! You must keep me! You must think of me. Please purify all my sins. You must think strongly of me. You must stay with me and not separate from me. Grant me all real attainments. You must do all necessary deeds! All subtle karmic traces, living in the heart must become emptiness. Give me the dharmakaya, sambhogakaya, nirmanakaya and svabhavikakaya. Victorious one, you are like all the tathagatas. Guru Padma, please keep me strongly. Guru Padma, great vows. We must get attainments. We must get fulfilment of our vows.*

ཨོཾ་ས་མ་ཡ༔ ཨཱཿས་མ་ཡ༔ ཧཱུྃ་ས་མ་ཡ༔ བཛྲ་ས་མ་ཡ༔
བདག་གཞན་གྱི་ཚེ་རབས་འཁོར་བ་ཐོག་མ་མེད་པ་ནས་བསགས་པའི་
སྡིག་སྒྲིབ་ཉེས་ལྟུང་དྲི་མའི་ཚོགས་ཐམས་ཅད་རྩ་བ་ནས་
བྱང་ཞིང་དག་པར་བྱིན་གྱིས་བརླབས་ཏུ་གསོལ༔

**OM SA MA YA AA SAM MA YA HUNG SA MA YA BEN DZA SA MA YA
DAG ZHAN GYI TSE RAB KHOR WA THOG MA ME PA NAE SAG PAI
DIG DRIB NYE TUNG DRI MAI TSOG THAM CHE TSA WA NAE
JANG ZHING DAG PA JIN GYI LAB TU SOL**

*Body vows: forgive my lapses. Speech vows: forgive my lapses. Mind vows: forgive my lapses. Vajrayana vows: forgive my lapses. I and all beings in all our countless previous lives have collected sins, obscurations, faults, stains and causes for falling into states of sorrow. All these we beg you to cleanse from the root and so bless us with purity.*

Reading this we integrate fully with the state of Vajrasattva, the unchanging, indestructible purity, to which not the least imperfection can adhere.

## c. Sacrifice

### Preparing the Sacrifice

HUNG  OM AH HUNG  BENDZA GU RU PAD MA THOD THRENG TSAL
BENDZA SA MA YA DZA  SIDDHI PHA LA HUNG
EE RAM  PHAT RAM  DZVA LA RAM  NI YAM DZA  TRI YAM DZA
NA MO  KON CHOG SUM GYI DEN PA DANG
TSA WA SUM GYI JIN LAB DANG
KHAN DRO CHOE KYONG NUE THU YI
NOD JED DRA GEG GANG YIN PA
DA TA NYID DU DIR KHUG CHIG
DZA HUNG BAM HO

*Salutation. By the truth of the three jewels, the blessing of the three roots and the power of the dakinis and dharma protectors, may the trouble makers, enemies and obstacles (mainly one's own ego) immediately come here.*

Here we use the power of the truth of the three jewels, their lack of deception, and the power of the blessing of the three roots, their force for good, and the power of the force of the dakinis and protectors, all together, to create an irresistible pull on all the many kinds of troublemakers. We pull in all those who cause outer problems, like stealing yogis' food, and those who cause inner problems, like doubt, distraction, despair. The mantras catch and bind these demons so that they cannot escape. Although we may feel overwhelmed and persecuted by events in our lives, if we remember the dharma we will be able to face them from the infinity of the three kayas, and will always be more powerful than the demons, troublemakers and so forth. But you have to be clear what you are doing, for although these forms are empty of inherent self-nature, they do have an energetic presence that has an impact.

All of us, I'm sure, are frightened of something in our life. We're frightened of being tortured or raped or beaten to death. These kind of fears are important here. What you are dealing with are all the forces that can frighten you, forces outside yourself, forces inside yourself, so they have to be very clearly controlled. Otherwise, if your demons are not under your control, they are controlling you. So this is a life-and-death struggle. That's why it's put in very powerful language. We need to respond with energy, from the state of emptiness. This means not getting caught up in fearful retaliation but being relaxed, open, and focused, so that we can concentrate on re-merging this hostile, self-referential energy in its own ground, which is emptiness. It's not a game, and the intensity of cruel, contemptuous, dehumanising attitudes should never be underestimated. Shouting *phat* Is not enough, it won't drive them away. We need stability in emptiness and the fearlessness that comes with it.

## Making the Sacrifice

ཧཱུྃ༔ ཉོན་མོངས་ལོག་པའི་དགྲ་བགེགས་རུ་དྲའི་ཚོགས༔
མཚན་མའི་རྫས་ཀྱི་སྦུབ་ཁང་འབར་བའི་ནང༔
རྣོ་མྱུར་ཡེ་ཤེས་མཚོན་ཆའི་ཆར་ཆེན་པོས༔
དགྲ་བགེགས་ཕུང་ཁམས་མ་ལུས་དུལ་དུ་རློག༔
ཨ་མུ་ཀ་མ་ར་ཡ་བད༔

**HUNG NYON MONG LOG PAI DRA GEG RU DRAI TSOG
TSEN MAI DZAE KYI DRUB KHUNG BAR WAI NANG
NO NYUR YE SHE TSON CHAI CHAR CHEN POI
DRA GEG PHUNG KHAM MA LUE DUL DU LOG
A MU KA MA RA YA BAD**

*Hung. The hosts of demons, the enemies and obstructors and all the forms of the afflictions are put in the symbolic article of the blazing imprisoning pit. By the great rain of the sharp and penetrating weapons of wisdom, the substantial elements, of all the enemies and demons, without exception, are totally annihilated. The enemy must really be finished.*

Now that the demons have been captured and bound they have to be dispatched back into their source. The malignant consciousness will be shocked back into its original ground. We imagine that they are put into a blazing triangular pit, from which they can't escape. Then a storm of sharp weapons, the manifest forms of emptiness, comes raining down and chops them to pieces. The pieces are also chopped up finer and finer until the skandhas, the basic components of existence, and the sense organs and their consciousnesses are chopped to dust, to atoms, to nothingness. Not a trace remains, there is no basis for their return, they are gone. The basis for grasping, attachments, the five poisons, the stirrings of hateful and cruel intent are gone. All that's left is form inseparable from emptiness.

## G. Offerings

### Offering the Fruit of the Sacrifice

ཧྲཱིཿ རྩ་གསུམ་རིག་འཛིན་རྒྱལ་བའི་དཀྱིལ་འཁོར་དུཿ
དགྲ་བགེགས་བསྒྲལ་བའི་ཤ་རུས་བདུད་རྩིར་བསྒྱུརཿ
མཉམ་ཉིད་བདེ་བ་ཆེན་པོར་འབུལ་ལེགས་ནཿ
གཉིས་མེད་ཁྱབ་བདལ་ངང་དུ་བཞེས་སུ་གསོལཿ
སརྦ་པུ་ཛ་ཁ་ཧཱིཿ

**HRI TSA SUM RIG DZIN GYAL WAI KYIL KHOR DU
DRA GEG DRAL WAI SHA RUE DUD TSIR GYUR
NYAM NYID DE WA CHEN POR BUL LEG NA
NYI MED KHYAB DAL NGANG DU ZHE SU SOL
SAR VA PU TSA KHA HI**

*Hri. In the mandala of the vidyadhara Jina who contains the three roots, the flesh and bones of the enemies and obstructors killed becomes liberating elixir. When it is offered in the great happiness of perfect equality, please eat it in the state of all-pervasive non-duality. Eat all the ceremonial offerings!*

In the mandala, all is pure. Here, everything becomes elixir. The corpses, the remnants, are revealed for what they are and have always been: the manifestation of emptiness. Having the nature of emptiness, they become liberating for others. All the badness, that seemed to be so inherent in them, is gone. Now it's just form and emptiness. When accepted in the state of non-duality there is not the least trace of reification, attachment, selfishness. The corpse of the demon is just like everything else, no different. Seeing this, we experience the great happiness of perfect equality. The only true purity is in the nature of the mind, which from the very beginning has never been contaminated.

But activity arises into a field of great complexity. Whenever we meet people, they project things onto us, they have expectations of us, they want things from us. We can not possibly fulfil all the desires of the world. If you please one person, someone else will be pissed-off with you. If you try to please everyone, you go mad. So purity is not about being nice to everyone. That's impossible. Purity lies in the relationship one has with emptiness and then, out of that, behaviour arises due to causes and conditions.

We should recognise as a basic principle that everything is empty, but manifest action has many different forms. We have to learn how to manage these different forms. Some people are safe and easy, some people are dangerous. You have to know the difference. But of course this sweet person, the nice person, may actually be very, very dangerous for you. Because they are very sweet and they're very nice you think they're going to be nice to you. Even if they *are* very nice to you, they help you fall asleep, while the unkind person, the dangerous person, maybe frightens you and you waken up a little bit, so actually *they* have been kind to you. Life is not easy.

If demons came with tails and scales, smelling of sulphur, it would be easier. They are not marked in some special way, for demons are not entities, not beings that are always bad. We can't sort beings out: good ones to the right, bad beings to the left. Demons arise as aspects of our karma, they are a relationship. They get to us because we have something to do with them, we get what's coming to us. Trying to control the object, as object, does not work. We have to relax into the open ground nature that exists prior to all differentiation into subject and object, good and bad. Focusing on the object cannot bring a lasting solution. Ethnic cleansing doesn't work, and neither does demon cleansing. Integration and collaboration provide a sustainable future. In the Middle Ages, when people in Europe were very concerned about demons, and especially the devil, they were frightened about where he was. They had some basic identification, smell of sulphur, scales, maybe some horns, so if you see someone like that then this is the devil. It's the same in the Tibetan tradition. We look for these dangerous people but actually the demon is everywhere, everyone is a demon, and everyone is helpful. That is the issue.

## d. Offerings we Share

### The Consumable Offerings

**RAM YAM KHAM OM AH HUNG**

*The offerings are purified of all defects by the agency of fire, wind and water and the body, speech and mind of the buddhas. By this means there is not one speck of outer or inner defilement. All is pure, sunyata pure.*

**NGO WO TONG PAI TSOG ZHONG DU
RANG ZHIN SAL BAI TSO DZE SHAM
THUG JE KUN KHYAB JIN CHEN PHOB
CHOG SUM TZA SUM KU SUM LHA
KUN DUE LA MA DIR JON LA
DE WA CHEN POI TSOG CHOD ZHE**

*In the offering vessel with the essence of sunyata are placed the naturally radiant offering articles. The articles are blessed*

*by the all-pervading energy. May the three jewels, three roots,
three-kaya deities and the guru who encompasses them all,
please be present here and accept these assembled offerings of great bliss.*

ཉམས་ཆགས་ཉེས་ཚོགས་མཐོལ་ཞིང་བཤགས༔
འཁྲུལ་སྣང་རྟོག་ཚོགས་དབྱིངས་སུ་བསྒྲལ༔
ཀ་དག་རིག་པའི་ཀློང་དུ་བསྟབས༔
མགྲོན་བཞིའི་ཐུགས་དམ་བསྐང་གྱུར་ཅིག༔
ཚོགས་རྫོགས་དོན་གཉིས་ལྷུན་གྲུབ་ནས༔
སྐུ་བཞིའི་རྒྱལ་སྲིད་མྱུར་ཐོབ་ཤོག༔

**NYAM CHAG NYE TSOG THOL ZHING SHAG
TRUL NANG TOG TSOG YING SU DRAL
KA DAG RIG PAI LONG DU TAB
DRON ZHI THUG DAM KANG GUR CHIG
TSOG DZOG DON NYI LHUN DRUB NE
KU ZHI GYAL SID NYUR THOB SHOG**

*With my hands pressed together I confess all my many defects, shortcomings and broken vows! The host of confusing appearances and ideas are liberated in the dharmadhatu, and placed in the expanse of primordially pure awareness. The four classes of guests must be fully satisfied and happy. May our accumulations of merit and wisdom become complete and, having spontaneously accomplished the welfare of ourselves and others, may we quickly attain the four-kaya realm of the Buddha.*

We now make another offering to our guests, this time with the focus on the actual offerings we have assembled. We should, of course, imagine many more and much finer offerings than we have actually managed to assemble. The first three lines of the prayer establish the offering as being radiance displayed in the openness of the natural condition, which then manifests through the blessing of energy as being suitable for all the high-ranking enlightened guests.

We then again confess our errors and sacrifice/liberate confusion in the dharmadhatu. This removes all impediments to hospitality as there is nothing to interrupt or contaminate the proceedings. From this we gain the benefit of quickly and effortlessly gaining enlightenment. It is important to hold the confidence of this when we do the next part, of offering to ourselves.

### Offering to the Meditators

ཚོགས་རྫས་ཡེ་ཤེས་བདུད་རྩི་དགའ་སྟོན་རོལ༔
གཙང་མེ་གཉིས་འཛིན་རྟོག་བྲལ་ཨ་ལ་ལ་ཧོ༔

**TSOG DZAE YE SHE DUD TSII GA TON ROL**
**TSANG ME NYI DZIN TOG DRAL A LA LA HO**

*The assembled offerings are to be enjoyed as a festival of the liberating elixir of pristine cognition. Free of dualistic thoughts such as clean and dirty, it is wonderful.*

We eat the pure food in a state of non-distraction. Being aware of the food dissolving in our mouths, the arising of sensation and emptiness, relaxing, not busy, few thoughts. Clarity and emptiness. What is 'other' becomes 'self', there is no barrier, no difference. The food is pure, you are Padmasambhava, light flowing into light, just as in the dissolving practice. There is no hurry. Experience the integration, the co-emergence of subject and object. All attachment is gone, open.

Don't be busy passing things round, don't talk, don't select what you eat. Take the meat in the right hand and the alcohol in the left. Take them first, for they are the symbols of the sacrifice, the transformation of the demon. Experience your body moving and eating from within the state of stillness. Stillness welcomes activity, activity ornaments stillness. Collaboration, not conflict. Don't limit yourself, for your limits will limit others. No judgement.

## e. Remains

### Offering the Remainder

**PHEM HRING LHAG DRON DAM LA NAE PAI WANG CHUG DRAN
KING DANG LING KA BAR MA DAM CHEN TSOG
KHA THRU TAB PAI LHAG MAI ZAE ZHE LA
NYI MED RO CHIG DRUB PAI THRIN LAE DZOD
U TSU DA KHA HI**

*Phem! Hring! The guests for the left-overs, the vow-keeping dakinis, the Wongchuk Dran, and the hosts of messengers, workers, middle-workers and vow-keepers: eat this left-over food that has been sprinkled with nectar, then perform the activities of the attainment of the single flavour of non-duality. Eat the left-overs!*

It is important that everyone is included, that no one is left out. Yet here we have a hierarchical structure, and a hierarchy that indicates value, spiritual attainment, capacity to benefit others. Some of the guests are judged to be functionally inferior, though not different in their true nature. They are not entitled to enter the feast circle, but have to wait outside to get the left-overs, like beggars at a wedding in India. This is not a politically correct, equal opportunity system, Just because some being is alive, does it mean they have equal value in terms of function? The lower guests, the menial ones and the frightened, anxious ones get something, but at the end. Here, value is privileged over need. A very different view from that in modern European democracy. To forget value creates a homogenised, sibling society, where entitlement displaces respect, honour and gratitude. Dharma, having a phenomenological turn, is concerned to see situations and beings for what they are, and not to hide in idealistic fantasies.

**Reminder of Vows**

ཧཱུྃ་ཧྲཱིཿ སྔོན་ཚེ་འདས་དང་བར་བསྐལ་ད་ལྟ་རུཿ
བརྒྱུད་གསུམ་རིག་འཛིན་བླ་མའི་སྤྱན་སྔ་རུཿ
ཁས་བླངས་དམ་གནས་བཀའ་སྲུང་དྲེགས་ཚོགས་ཀྱིཿ
དམ་རྫས་གཏོར་མ་བཞེས་ལ་ཕྲིན་ལས་མཛོད༔

**HUNG HRI NGON TSE DAE DANG BAR KAL DA TA RU
GYUD SUM RIG DZIN LA MAI CHEN NGA RU
KHAE LANG DAM NAE KA SUNG DREG TSOG KYI
DAM DZAE TOR MA ZHE LA THRIN LAE DZOD**

*Hung. Hri. In former times in the past, in the middle period and up to the present, in front of the vidyadhara gurus of the three lineages you, the hosts of vow-keeping, order-guarding, strong forms made promises. Eat this torma, the article for your obligations, then perform your activities!*

Until enlightenment, we live in contracts: unconscious karmic contracts and explicit, formal contracts. Even after enlightenment we have obligations to benefit all beings. Here, we remind the protectors to do their duty. In accepting the torma, the sacrificial food, they agree to remain bound to the tasks given them by Padmasambhava.

## Offering to the Twelve Tenma

**HUNG JHO SANG NGAG TEN PA SUNG WAR KHAE LANG TE
DRUB PAI DROG DZAD TAN MA MA YAM TSOG
DIR JON SHAL CHUI DRU TOR DI ZHE LA
NAL JOR THRIN LAE DRUB PAR DZAD DU SOL
MA MA KHA KHA LA LA LI LI TA TA TE TE
MAMSA RAKTA AMRITA KHA HI**

*Hung. Jho. You promised to guard the vajrayana doctrines.
You, the host of mothers, the tenma, who act as friends to yogis,
come here and eat this torma of rice and plate washing water, then please
act to accomplish the activities of yogis. Ma, Ma, Kha, Kha, La, La,
Li, Li, Ta, Ta, Te, Te. Eat the meat, blood and liberating elixir!*

As before, the delegation of the tasks of protection from the ego to the guardians frees the yogi to focus on practice. The twelve *tenma* are a very useful group, and this offering helps to keep them working to support our dharma practice.

## G. Offerings

བདེ་སྟོང་དགྱེས་པའི་གླུ་ཆང་བྲོ་བརྡུང་དེ༔
རིག་རྩལ་དག་པའི་དབྱིངས་སུ་རྒྱས་གདབ་པོ༔
སརྦ་སྟྃ་བྷ་ཡ་ནན༔

**HUNG HRI TSA SUM RIG DZIN ROL PAI KYIL KHOR OG
NYI DZIN TSEN DZIN DAM SI JUNG PO NAN
DE TONG GYE PAI LU LANG DRO DUNG TE
RIG TSAL DAG PAI YING SU GYAE DAB PO
SAR VA STAM BHA YA NAN**

*Hung. Hri. Below this joyful mandala of the three roots vidyadhara,
we put pressure on the dualising, reifying spirits and vow-troublers.
Singing and dancing on them with the joy of happiness and emptiness
we are in the pure infinitude of the energy flow of natural awareness.
All demons are unable to move.*

Safe within the mandala, we look out and see that those who once troubled us are actually powerless. Before, when we were in samsara, these demons could penetrate us very easily. Somebody just had to shout at us, and we became angry or frightened. In that way we were easily invaded. Now our presence in non-duality, paradoxically, excludes them and they cannot come through. So life is peaceful, and we can sing and dance.

# H. Concluding Section

### The Seven-Line Prayer

ཧཱུྃཿ ཨུ་རྒྱན་ཡུལ་གྱི་ནུབ་བྱང་མཚམསཿ
པདྨ་གེ་སར་སྡོང་པོ་ལཿ
ཡ་མཚན་མཆོག་གི་དངོས་གྲུབ་བརྙེསཿ
པདྨ་འབྱུང་གནས་ཞེས་སུ་གྲགསཿ
འཁོར་དུ་མཁའ་འགྲོ་མང་པོས་བསྐོརཿ
ཁྱེད་ཀྱི་རྗེས་སུ་བདག་བསྒྲུབ་ཀྱིསཿ
བྱིན་གྱིས་བརླབ་ཕྱིར་གཤེགས་སུ་གསོལཿ
གུ་རུ་པདྨ་སིདྡྷི་ཧཱུྃཿ

**HUNG UR GYEN YUL GYI NUB JANG TSHAM**
**PE MA GE SAR DONG PO LA**
**YAM TSEN CHOG GI NGOE DRUB NYE**
**PE MA JUNG NAE ZHE SU DRAG**
**KHOR DU KHAN DRO MANG POE KOR**
**KHYE KYI JE SU DAG DRUB KYI**
**JIN GYI LAB CHIR SHEG SU SOL**
**GU RU PE MA SID DHI HUNG**

*Hung. In the north-west corner of the land of Urgyen,*
*upon the stem and stamen of a lotus, are you who have the marvellous*

*and supreme attainments, Padmasambhava of great renown, with a retinue of many dakinis around you. Following and relying on you I do your practice, therefore, in order to grant your blessings, please come here! Guru Padmasambhava, give me the real attainment of buddhahood.*

## a. Stabilising the Result

### The Flow of Blessing and Attainments

ཧཱུྂ་ཧྲཱིཿ ཆོས་དབྱིངས་བདེ་བ་ཆེན་པོའི་ཞིང་ཁམས་ནསཿ
རྒྱལ་ཀུན་འདུས་ཞལ་རིག་འཛིན་དཀྱིལ་འཁོར་ལྷཿ
གསང་གསུམ་མི་ཟད་ཕྲིན་ལས་རྒྱན་དུ་ཤརཿ
འབྲུ་གསུམ་འོད་ཟེར་དཀར་དམར་མཐིང་གསུམ་བཅསཿ
མོས་གདུང་དད་པས་བདག་གི་གནས་བཞིར་ཐིམཿ
དབང་ཐོབ་སྒྲིབ་དག་ཡེ་ཤེས་མངོན་དུ་གྱུརཿ
ཕྲིན་ལས་མཐར་ཕྱིན་ལས་བཞི་ལྷུན་གྱིས་གྲུབཿ
མཆོག་ཐུན་དངོས་གྲུབ་དམ་པ་དེང་འདིར་སྩོལཿ

ༀ་ཨཱཿཧཱུྂ་བཛྲ་གུ་རུ་པདྨ་སིདྡྷི་ཧཱུྂཿ
གུ་ཡ་བྷ་ག་ཙིཏྟ་སིདྡྷི་ཧཱུྂཿ

**HUNG HRI CHOE YING DE WA CHEN POI ZHING KHAM NAE**
**GYAL KUN DUE ZHAL RIG DZIN KYIL KHOR LHA**
**SANG SUM MI ZAD THRIN LAE GYEN DU SHAR**
**DRU SUM OD ZER KAR MAR THING SUM CHE**
**MOE DUNG DAD PAE DAG GI NAE ZHIR THIM**
**WANG THOB DRIB DAG YE SHE NGON DU GYUR**
**THRIN LAE THAR CHIN LAE ZHI LHUN GYI DRUB**
**CHOG THUN NGOE DRUB DAM PA DENG DIR TSOL**

## H. Concluding Section

**OM AH HUNG BENDZA GURU PEMA SIDDHI HUNG
KA YA WAKKA TSITTA SIDDHI HUNG**

*Hung. Hri. From the dharmadhatu realm of great happiness come the gods of the mandala of the vidyadhara whose nature encompasses all the jinas. The inexhaustible activity of the places of their body, speech and mind arise as ornaments, and from the three letters rays of white, red and blue light arise. Then, with intense faith and devotion they are absorbed into our four places. Thus the initiations are gained, the obscurations purified, and the pristine cognitions become manifest. With all activities complete may the four deeds arise effortlessly. Please grant us the excellent supreme and general real attainments here and now. Body, speech, mind — grant us their real attainments!*

THIS IS THE CONCLUDING PART of the practice, in which we receive a final blessing and initiation from the deities in order to establish us in the view, meditation, activity and result. The formal mandala will soon dissolve and our attention will once again be focused on the complex activities of our daily life. By visualising the flow of light from the deities to us, we stabilise ourselves in our inseparability from them. We are reconfirmed in the vajra, indestructible, empty nature of our body, voice and mind.

### Requesting Attainments

བླ་མ་རིག་འཛིན་ཡོངས་རྫོགས་འཁོར་བཅས་ལ༔
ཁྱད་པར་མཆོད་པ་པཉྩ་ཨ་མྲྀ་ཏ༔
མ་ཧཱ་བྷ་ལིང་རཀྟ་བཅས་ཏེ་འབུལ་ལ༔
བཞེས་ནས་བླ་མེད་དངོས་གྲུབ་རྩལ་དུ་གསོལ༔

**LA MA RIG DZIN YONG DZOG KHOR CHE LA
KHYAD PAR CHOD PA PANTSA AMRITA**

**MA HA BHA LING RAKTA CHE TE BUL**
**ZHE NAE LA MED NGOE DRUB TSAL DU SOL**

*To all gurus and vidyadharas and their circle we make the special offerings of the five liberating elixirs, the great torma and rakta, please enjoy, then grant us the unsurpassed real attainment.*

This text is recapitulating, again and again, the key point of the transformation. Why is it repeated? Because we don't get it! Even if we get it intellectually or experientially, it is a brief moment and then we let go of it again, more interested in the distractions of samsara than the ease of nirvana. This should alarm us, stop us in our tracks. No change will come if we are just going through the motions. Only a profound, heartfelt commitment and engagement brings change. So, investigate yourself. Sit down and explore why you don't really open to practice. Write an essay on why you prefer samsara to nirvana, for if that really is the case, why waste your life pretending to practice? But don't despair, the very fact that the text has all these repetitions indicates that we are not the only ones who find it difficult. Just take every chance you can to wake up.

### Praising the Guru

**HUNG MA CHOE TROE DRAL LA MA CHOE KYI KU**
**DE CHEN LONG CHOE LA MA CHOE KYI JE**
**PE DONG LE TRUNG LA MA TRUL PE KU**
**KU SUM DOR JE CHANG LA CHAK TSAL TOD**

## H. Concluding Section

*Hung. The guru without artifice, free of all relative positions is the dharmakaya. The guru of great happiness, the lord of dharma, is the sambhogakaya. The guru born from the lotus stem is the nirmanakaya. We salute and praise the three-kaya Vajradhara.*

Without the kindness of Padmasambhava, and all the lineage gurus, and in particular our own root guru, we would not have this rare chance of liberation. So we praise his kindness and his qualities.

### Making Confession

བླ་མ་རིག་འཛིན་ཡོངས་རྫོགས་འཁོར་བཅས་ཀྱི༔
བསྙེན་བསྒྲུབ་འཕྲིན་ལས་གཞུང་བཞིན་བགྱིས་པ་ལ༔
བདག་ཅག་མ་རིག་ལོག་རྟོག་དབང་སོང་བའི༔
འགལ་འཁྲུལ་ནོངས་པ་ཅི་མཆིས་བཟོད་པར་གསོལ༔

**LA MA RIG DZIN YONG DZOG KHOR CHE KYI
NYEN DRUB THRIN LAE ZHUNG ZHIN GYI PA LA
DAG CHAG MA RIG LOG TOG WANG SONG WAI
GAL THRUL NONG PA CHI CHI ZOD PAR SOL**

*When doing the practice of all the gurus and vidyadharas with their retinue according to the texts of the meditation services, having gone under the power of the false thoughts of ignorance, whatever confused errors and mistakes we made, we beg to be excused.*

We are so frequently under the power of the confusion that arises from ignorance that its not surprising that we've made some mistakes. Ah! We don't even know what mistakes we made, because we were distracted! So we say, 'Whatever confused errors and mistakes we made, we beg to be excused'. If you think of a ballerina like Sylvie Guillem, she has been practising for many, many years. She started to dance when she was four, and now she is this fantastic ballerina. Think how many thousands of hours she was practising on the bar, all the exercises she has done. How many hours have you practised the puja? It's not so many. So it's not surprising that you make mistakes. It is for this laziness, and all other errors, that we apologise. If you remember that we have invited these great beings as guests and then we have forgotten about them, such poor hospitality is shameful. We are men and women not little children playing. We have to take our lives seriously and, by respecting the practice, respect ourselves and our infinite potential.

**Purification**

OM GURU PADMA SA MA YA MA NU PA LA YA
GURU PADMA TE NO PA TI SHTA DRI DHO ME BHA WA
SU TO KYIO ME BHAV WA SU PO KYIO ME BHA WA
A NU RAKTO ME BHA WA SAR VA SIDDHI MA ME PRA YA TSA
SAR VA KAR MA SU TSA ME TSI TAM SHRI YAM KU RU HUNG
HA HA HA HA HO
BHA GA WAN SARVA TA THA GATA GURU PADMA MA ME MUN TSA
GURU PADMA BHA WA MA HA SA MA YA SA TWA AA HUNG PHAT

## H. Concluding Section

*The five pristine cognitions. Guru Padma with the power of being strong
in your vows: you must protect me and all who follow after you
and rely on you! Guru Padma, you must hear me! You must keep me!
You must think of me. Please purify all my sins. You must think strongly
of me. You must stay with me and not separate from me.
Grant me all real attainments. You must do all necessary deeds!
All subtle karmic traces, living in the heart must become emptiness.
Give me the dharmakaya, sambhogakaya, nirmanakaya and
svabhavikakaya. Victorious one, you are like all the tathagatas.
Guru Padma, please keep me strongly. Guru Padma. Great vows.
We must get attainments. We must get fulfilment of our vows.*

ཨོཾ་ས་མ་ཡ༔ ཨཱཿས་མ་ཡ༔ ཧཱུྃ་ས་མ་ཡ༔ བཛྲ་ས་མ་ཡ༔
བདག་གཞན་གྱི་ཚེ་རབས་འཁོར་བ་ཐོག་མ་མེད་པ་ནས་བསགས་པའི་
སྡིག་སྒྲིབ་ཉེས་ལྟུང་དྲི་མའི་ཚོགས་ཐམས་ཅད་རྩ་བ་ནས་
བྱང་ཞིང་དག་པར་བྱིན་གྱིས་བརླབས་ཏུ་གསོལ༔

**OM SA MA YA AA SAM MA YA HUNG SA MA YA BENDZA SA MA YA
DAG ZHAN GYI TSE RAB KHOR WA THOG MA ME PA NAE SAG PAI
DIG DRIB NYE TUNG DRI MAI TSOG THAM CHE TSA WA NAE
JANG ZHING DAG PAR JIN GYI LAB TU SOL**

*Body vows: forgive my lapses. Speech vows: forgive my lapses.
Mind vows: forgive my lapses. Vajrayana vows: forgive my lapses.
I, and all beings, in all our countless previous lives have collected sins,
obscurations, faults, stains and causes for falling into states of sorrow.
All these we beg you to cleanse from the root and so bless us with purity.*

## Prayers Requesting Forgiveness for Errors in the Practice

མ་འབྱོར་བ་དང་ཉམས་པ་དང་༔
གང་ཡང་བདག་རྨོངས་བློ་ཡིས་ནི༔
མ་རིག་འཁྲུལ་པ་ཅི་མཆིས་པ༔
དེ་ཡང་བཟོད་པར་མཛད་དུ་གསོལ༔

**MA JOR WA DANG NYAM PA DANG
GANG YANG DAG MONG LO YI NI
MA RIG THRUL PA CHI CHI PA
DE YANG ZOD PAR DZE DU SOL**

*Not having and not preparing the necessary articles, and not acting properly, and whatever I have done due to dull and stupid thinking, whatever I did in bewildered ignorance, for these things I also beg forgiveness.*

ལྷག་པ་དང་ནི་ཆད་པ་དང་༔
ཆོ་གའི་ཡན་ལག་ཉམས་པ་དང་༔
བདག་གིས་བརྗེད་ངེས་ཅི་མཆིས་པ༔
དེ་ཡང་བཟོད་པར་མཛད་དུ་གསོལ༔

**LHAG PA DANG NI CHAD PA DANG
CHO GAI YEN LAG NYAM PA DANG
DAG GI JED NGE CHI CHI PA
DE YANG ZOD PAR DZE DU SOL**

*Saying too much and missing out words, and not reading the extra parts of the ceremony's reading text, and whatever things I forgot to do, for these things I also beg forgiveness.*

## H. Concluding Section

བག་མེད་བརྗོད་བྱ་མ་དག་པ༔
རྒྱུད་ནས་གསུངས་པའི་ཆོ་ག་བཞིན༔
མ་ཕྱོགས་འཁྲུལ་པ་ཅི་མཆིས་པ༔
དེ་ཡང་བཟོད་པར་མཛད་དུ་གསོལ༔

**BAG MED JOD JA MA DAG PA
GYUD NAE SUNG PAI CHO GA ZHIN
MA CHOG THRUL PA CHI CHI PA
DE YANG ZOD PAR DZE DU SOL**

*Carelessly not reciting clearly and correctly, and not being able to practice according to the reading text which comes from the tantras. Whatever I did in confusion, for these things I also beg forgiveness.*

སེར་སྣའི་དབང་གྱུར་ཕུད་ཉམས་ཤིང༔
མཆོད་པ་ངན་ཞིང་བཤམས་ཉེས་པ༔
སྦྱོར་བ་གཙང་སྦྲ་མ་ཐོན་པ༔
དེ་ཡང་བཟོད་པར་མཛད་དུ་གསོལ༔

**SER NAI WANG GYUR PHUD NYAM SHING
CHOD PA NGEN ZHING SHAM NYE PA
JOR WA TSANG DRA MA THON PA
DE YANG ZOD PAR ZHE DU SOL**

*Going under the power of avarice and being stingy with offerings, making poor offerings and not arranging them correctly, not using pure and clean ingredients, for these things I also beg forgiveness.*

These prayers are self-explanatory. From ignorance come the five poisons. Due to the power of stupidity we become distracted during the practice, we lose attention, we read things in the wrong order, we forget the tunes, the mudras and so on. We are also distracted beforehand, we don't set things out properly with the correct ingredients. Sometimes we can't be bothered, or maybe we never learned properly. Branch faults occur easily, again and again. Cut the root!

### Final Requests to the Deities

ཁྱེད་ཐུགས་གསང་བ་གདམས་པའི་མཛོད༔
དགྱེས་པ་ཆེན་པོའི་སྒོ་ཕྱེས་ལ༔
དངོས་གྲུབ་འཕྲིན་ལས་བདུད་རྩི་ཡི༔
རྒྱུན་གྱིས་བདག་རྒྱུད་གཏམས་པར་མཛོད༔

**KHYED THUG SANG WA DAM PAI DZOD**
**GYE PA CHEN POI GO CHE LA**
**NGOE DRUB THRIN LAE DUD TSI YI**
**GYUN GYI DAG GYUD TAM PAR DZOD**

*Please open the door of the great happiness of the secret and holy treasure of your mind. Then, please fill my mind with the flow of the liberating elixir of the granting of real attainments.*

You shining ones, please open the door to great happiness. Please show us this secret and wonderful dimension of your mind which is our mind. Please fill my mind with the flow of the liberating elixir of your blessing, giving me attainment. It's a final request to them. Don't leave me here all alone in samsara. Before you go, give me integration with yourself, so that when you leave, when the mandala finally dissolves, I'm not standing in the station, crying, "Oh, baby please don't go. I'm lost without you!" Not like that! We translate *tam par dzod* as 'Please do' but actually it's more like 'Do', it's more like a function of things. "Hey, before you go, can you do the dishes?" "Before you go, can you make me enlightened? Come on, it's a simple request!"

## H. Concluding Section

### Requesting the Deity to Stay

ཨོཾ༔ འདིར་ནི་གཟུགས་དང་(རྟེན་དང་)ལྷན་ཅིག་ཏུ༔
འགྲོ་བའི་དོན་དུ་བཞུགས་ནས་ཀྱང་༔
ནད་མེད་ཚེ་དང་དབང་ཕྱུག་དང་༔
མཆོག་རྣམས་ལེགས་པར་རྩལ་དུ་གསོལ༔
ཨོཾ་སུ་པྲ་ཏི་ཥྛ་བཛྲ་ཡེ་སྭཱ་ཧཱ༔

**OM DIR NI ZUG DANG (TEN DANG) LHEN CHIG TU
DRO WAI DON DU ZHUG NAE KYANG
NAD MED TSE DANG WANG CHUG DANG
CHOG NAM LEG PAR TSAL DU SOL
OM SU PRA TI SHTA BENDZA YE SWA HA**

*Om. Please stay here, together with this form, for the benefit of beings.
Then also please grant life free of sickness, and wealth,
and all the best things well obtained. Om. Please sit down.
You must always stay very strongly and quietly.*

With this verse, we imagine the mandala being merged with our paintings and statues. The image of Padmasambhava functions as an icon. We believe that the image contains the living presence of the guru. This verse helps to potentiate your icons. They needn't be fancy, a photograph will do if it is all you have.

## Dissolving the Mandala

ཨོཾ༔ ཁྱེད་ཀྱིས་སེམས་ཅན་དོན་ཀུན་མཛོད༔
རྗེས་སུ་མཐུན་པའི་དངོས་གྲུབ་སྩོལ༔
སངས་རྒྱས་ཡུལ་དུ་གཤེགས་ནས་ཀྱང༔
སླར་ཡང་འབྱོན་པར་མཛད་དུ་གསོལ༔ བཛྲ་མུ༔

**OM KHYE KYI SEM CHEN DON KUN DZOD
JE SU THUN PAI NGOE DRUB TSOL
SANG GYAE YUL DU SHEG NAE KYANG
LAR YANG JON PAR DZAD DU SOL BEN DZA MU**

*Om. You who act for the benefit of all beings, please grant them real attainments according to their need. Go to the buddhas' realm, yet also please come again when we need you. Bendza Mu.*

At this point the mandala dissolves as Padmasambhava and all his retinue return to Zangdopalri. Yet we remain with the nature of Padmasambhava, maintaining the three kaya view under all circumstances. The sambhogakaya form of the guru departs, yet he remains fused in our being.

## Integration with the Deity

ཧཱུྃ༔ ད་ནི་དཀྱིལ་འཁོར་གསལ་བཏབ་ལ༔
ཕྱི་ནང་སྟོང་བཅུད་ཐམས་ཅད་ཀུན༔
ཨཱ་ག་འབྲུ་ཧྲཱིཿལ་ཧྲཱིཿལ་གྱིས་བསྡུ༔
ཧྲཱིཿཡང་མི་དམིགས་འཇའ་ལྟར་ཡལ༔

## H. Concluding Section

དེ་ནས་བདག་ཉིད་ལྷ་རུ་གསལ༔
རྟག་ཆད་གཉིས་ཀྱི་མཐའ་བསལ་ལོ༔

HUNG DA NI KYIL KHOR SAL TAB LA
CHI NANG NOD CHUD THAM CHE KUN
YIG DRU HRI LA HRIL GYI DU
HRI YANG MI MIG JA TAR YAL
DE NAE DAG NYID LHA RU SAL
TAG CHAD NYI KYI THA SAL LO

*Hung. Now make the mandala very clear: all appearances, outer and inner come together as the letter Hri. Then, without making an object of the letter Hri, it vanishes like a rainbow. Then I arise clearly as the god, free of the two extremes of permanence and nihilism.*

In the beginning Padmasambhava manifested out of a Hri in Amitabha's heart, and in this practice we manifest as Padmasambhava out of the letter Hri. The Hri is the energetic link between emptiness and manifestation. It is the symbol and the active function of potentiality. Because it is indestructible the mandala will reappear again according to need. Neither permanent nor nothing at all, the mandala is a relational gesture. It's not that when the mandala is there it should remain forever; it's not that when the mandala dissolves it is gone forever; it appears and then it vanishes. When you do the practice again, the mandala comes back again. It's not a new mandala, but once again a revelation of the sambhogakaya dimension.

## b. Prayers of Aspiration

**HUNG LA MA YI DAM KHA DRO CHOD LA SOG
CHAD DANG KUL DANG YI RANG LAE JUNG WAI
SO NAM GE TSOG PAG ME DI DAG GI
TSE DIR LA ME JANG CHUB DRAE THOB NAE
KU SUM DE CHEN ZHING DU CHOD JED CHING
ZUG KUE DRO DON LAB CHEN CHOD PAR SHOG**

*Hung. To the gurus, wishing gods and dakinis I made offerings,
and I encouraged others to make offerings, and rejoiced when they did so.
By all the limitless accumulations of merit and virtue coming from these,
in this life may we gain the result of the unsurpassed enlightenment.
Then, enjoying the realm of the great happiness of the three kayas,
by manifesting form bodies we will make great waves of benefit
for those who move in samsara.*

## H. Concluding Section

**HUNG CHI YI LA MA NA TSOG THRUL PAI KU
NANG GI LA MA KUN ZANG HE RU KA
SANG WAI LA MA RANG RIG NYUG MAI SHI
TSE DIR NGON DU JAL WAR JIN GYI LOB**

*Hung. The outer guru of the many different nirmanakayas, the inner guru of Kunzang heruka, the secret guru of the unchanging nature of one's own natural awareness: may we have the blessing of clearly seeing them in this life.*

རིག་པའི་ངོ་བོ་གསལ་སྟོང་འཛིན་པ་མེད༈
རྗེན་པར་མཐོང་བ་ཡེ་སྟོང་ཀ་ནས་དག༈
སྒྲོན་དྲུག་ལམ་ལ་བརྟེན་ནས་ཟག་བཅས་ཀྱི༈
ཕུང་པོ་འཇའ་ལུས་རྡོ་རྗེར་འགྲུབ་པར་ཤོག༈

**RIG PAI NGO WO SAL TONG DZIN PA MED
JEN PAR THONG WA YE TONG KA NAE DAG
DRON DRUG LAM LA TEN NAE ZAG CHAE KYI
PHUNG PO JA LUE DOR JER DRUB PAR SHOG**

*The real nature of natural awareness is clear and empty, free of grasping. Clearly seen it is primordially empty, pure from the very beginning. By following the path of the six lamps, with the sinful flesh body becoming a rainbow body, may we get the indestructible attainment.*

སྐལ་བ་དམན་ནས་བར་དོའི་གནས་སྐབས་སུ༈
སྐྱེ་བའི་སྒྱིད་པ་འཛིན་ཚེ་པདྨ་འབྱུང་༈
བོན་ནས་མངོན་པར་མཐོ་དང་ངེས་ལེགས་ཀྱི༈
ཡང་དག་ལམ་དུ་ཁྲིད་པར་བྱིན་གྱིས་རློབས༈

KAL WA MEN NAE BAR DOI NAE KAB DU
KYE WAI SRID PA DZIN TSE PAD MA JUNG
JON NAE NGON PAR THO DANG NGE LEG KYI
YANG DAG LAM DU THRID PAR JIN GYI LOB

*If we are not fortunate enough to gain that, then may we be blessed that in the bardo at death and when starting on a new birth, Padmasambhava will come and lead us on the very good way to heaven and the high heavens.*

PHEN DEI TSA LAG GYAL WAI TEN PA DANG
THA LAE KYE GUI DE KYID MA LUE PA
YAR NGOI DA WA TA BUR RAB GYAE SHING
MI THUN NYE PAI TSOG KUN ZHI GYUR CHIG

*The root of help and happiness, the Jina's doctrines, and every happiness for all the numberless beings —
with these spreading large like the waxing moon, all the hosts of unhelpful situations and sins must be pacified.*

## H. Concluding Section

KHYAD PAR SANG CHEN DOR JE THEG PA DANG
YANG GOE PAD MAI JE JUG GAR NAE SAR
NAD RIM MU GE SAD SER THEN PA DANG
THRUG TSOD THA MAG NOD PA ZHI WAR SHOG

*Especially for the followers of the very secret vajrayana, and most especially for the followers of Padmasambhava, in the places where they stay — sickness, flu, famine, frost, hail, drought, and fighting, arguing, border war and all troubles must be pacified.*

THUG JE DRO KUN YOL MED JE DZIN KYANG
NYIG MAI DRO WA KYOB PAI ZHAL ZHE KA
THRI SONG GYAL POR TSOL WAI NYING POI DON
RE WA JI ZHIN KONG WAI DUE LA BAB

*I will hold all beings unceasingly with compassion, and I will protect the beings of the present degenerate times — thus Padmasambhava gave his promise. To King Trisong Deutsan he gave this essential teaching, and now at this time all our hopes can be fulfilled.*

DE CHIR DE ZHII PAG SAM YONG DUI JON
TSO KYE JIN LAB CHID KYI MA MA YI
NYE WAR KYANG LAE DRUB PAI DON NYI DRAE
LONG SU CHOD PAI GA TON GYAE GYUR CHIG

*Therefore he is like a wishfulfilling tree for the four aims in life.*
*By the blessing of Padmasambhava which is like the spring time cuckoo,*
*may we all see him and then gain the result of benefit for ourselves*
*and for all others. Then by using that result*
*the festival of happiness for all must expand and grow!*

Prayers of aspiration are very important in Tibetan buddhism. They are seen not just as a hope or a wish, but as an intention, as an act which brings about definite effects. We get what we pray for, not because some big powerful person gives it to us, but by the power of aspiration itself. Our intention is brought into the world, we set out out values, our agenda, and this helps to modify the impact of negative karma, the force of our habitual assumptions, impulses, tendencies. Positive thinking, especially when it involves linking out to other beings and to the shining, compassionate deities, is very helpful in lifting our mood, in re-contextualising the daily problems that arise. Wishing the best helps to populate our mind with kindliness, warmth, friendliness. May all beings be happy! The Tibetan word we translate as 'aspiration' is *monlam*. *Mon* means wish, hope, and *lam* means path. The wish is a road we can travel, it sets out a track for us to follow so that we avoid the swamp of samsara. It is a useful practice to memorise these verses and sing them from time to time in your daily activities.

## c. Auspicious Verses

རྒྱལ་མཚན་རྩེ་མོར་དབང་གི་རྒྱལ་པོ་ལྟར།
ལྷག་པ་ལྷ་ཡི་གཙུག་གི་རྒྱན་གྱུར་པའི།
སྒྲུབ་པ་པོ་ལ་དངོས་གྲུབ་མཆོག་སྩོལ་བའི།
དཔལ་ལྡན་བླ་མ་རྣམས་ཀྱིས་བཀྲ་ཤིས་ཤོག།

**GYAL TSEN TSE MOR WANG GI GYAL PO TAR
LHAG PA LHA YI TSUG GYI GYEN GYUR PAI
DRUB PA PO LA NGOE DRUB CHOG TSOL WAI
PAL DEN LA MA NAM KYI TRA SHI SHOG**

*Like the jewel on the top point of the victory banner, you are the crest jewel of the wishing god, the ones who grant supreme real attainments to practitioners. May the glorious gurus grant good luck!*

ཀུན་བཟང་རྡོར་སེམས་དགའ་རབ་ཤྲཱི་སིང་།
ཨུ་རྒྱན་པདྨ་རྗེ་འབངས་ཉི་ཤུ་ལྔ།
བཀའ་གཏེར་བརྒྱུད་ལྡན་རྩ་བའི་བླ་མ་སོགས།
འདྲེན་མཆོག་ཡབ་སྲས་ཡོངས་ཀྱིས་བཀྲ་ཤིས་ཤོག།

**KUN ZANG DOR SEM GA RAB SHI RI SING
UR GYEN PAD MA JE BANG NYI SHU NGA
KA TER GYUD DEN TSA WAI LA MA SOG
DREN CHOG YAB SRAE YONG KYI TRA SHI SHOG**

*Kunto Zangpo, Dorje Sempa, Garab Dorje, and Shri Singha,
Padmasambhava and his twenty five disciples,
my root guru who possesses the lineages of kama and terma,
may the supreme guides, both gurus and disciples, grant good luck!*

རྒྱལ་བ་ཉིད་ལས་ལྷག་པའི་ལུང་མངའ་ཞིང་།
འཕྲིན་ལས་མཛད་པ་བསམ་གྱིས་མི་ཁྱབ་པ།
བསྟན་དང་འགྲོ་བའི་རྩ་ལག་མཆོག་གྱུར་པའི།
ཨུ་རྒྱན་རིན་པོ་ཆེ་ཡིས་བཀྲ་ཤིས་ཤོག

**GYAL WA NYID LAE LAG PAI LUNG NGA ZHING
THRIN LAE DZAD PA SAM GYI MI KHYAB PA
TEN DANG DRO WAI TSA LAG CHOG GYUR PAI
UR GYEN RIN PO CHE YI TRA SHI SHOG**

*You whose teachings are more excellent than those of the Jina himself,
who perform activities beyond the reach of thought, most excellent cause
for the growth of both the doctrine and sentient beings,
may Guru Rinpoche grant good luck!*

བལྟས་པ་ཙམ་གྱིས་འགྲོ་རྣམས་དབང་དུ་སྡུད།
བསྒྲགས་པ་ཙམ་གྱིས་སྡེ་བརྒྱད་བྲན་དུ་ཁོལ།
བསམས་པ་ཙམ་གྱིས་དགོས་འདོད་ཆར་ལྟར་འབེབས།
ཨུ་རྒྱན་བརྒྱུད་པར་བཅས་པས་བཀྲ་ཤིས་ཤོག

**TAE PA TSAM GYI DRO NAM WANG DU DUD
DIG PA TSAM GYI DE GYAD DREN DU KHOL
SAM PA TSAM GYI GOE DOD CHAR TAR BEB
UR GYEN GYUD PAR CHAE PAE TRA SHI SHOG**

*By your mere glance all beings are gathered under your power,
by your mere command the eight classes of spirits attend you as servants,
by your mere thought all we need and desire falls like rain.
May Padmasambhava with his lineage grant good luck!*

## H. Concluding Section

སྟོན་པ་སངས་རྒྱས་རྣམས་ཀྱིས་བཀྲ་ཤིས་ཤོག
སྐྱོབ་པ་དམ་ཆོས་རྣམས་ཀྱིས་བཀྲ་ཤིས་ཤོག
འདྲེན་པ་དགེ་འདུན་རྣམས་ཀྱིས་བཀྲ་ཤིས་ཤོག
སྐྱབས་གནས་དཀོན་མཆོག་གསུམ་གྱིས་བཀྲ་ཤིས་ཤོག

TON PA SANG GYE NAM KYI TRA SHI SHOG
KYOB PA DAM CHOE NAM KYI TRA SHI SHOG
DREN PA GEN DUN NAM KYI TRA SHI SHOG
KYAB NAE KON CHOG SUM GYI TRA SHI SHOG

*May the teachers, the buddhas, grant good luck! May the protectors, the holy dharmas, grant good luck! May the guides, the sanghas, grant good luck! May the refuge places, the three jewels, grant good luck!*

ཆོས་སྐུ་ནམ་མཁའ་བཞིན་དུ་དབྱེར་མེད་ཅིང་།
གཟུགས་སྐུ་འཇའ་ཚོན་བཞིན་དུ་སོ་སོར་གསལ།
ཐབས་དང་ཤེས་རབ་མཆོག་ལ་མངའ་བརྙེས་པའི།
རིགས་ལྔ་བདེ་བར་གཤེགས་པས་བཀྲ་ཤིས་ཤོག

CHOE KU NAM KHA ZHIN DU YER MED CHING
ZUG KU JA TSON ZHIN DU SO SOR SAL
THAB DANG SHE RAB CHOG LA NGA NYE PAI
RIG NGA DE WAR SHEG PAE TRA SHI SHOG

*Although you are not different from the dharmakaya which is like space, you show form kayas like rainbows, each clear and distinct. You have the power of supreme method and superior knowledge. May the sugatas of the five kulas grant good luck!*

ཧྲཱིཿ རིག་འཛིན་བླ་མ་སྒྲུབ་པའི་མཐུ་བྱིན་གྱིས༔
འགྲོ་ཀུན་ཡང་དག་དོད་མའི་ས་ཐོབ་ཅིང༔
ཟབ་གསང་བསྟན་པ་རྒྱས་ཤིང་ཚེ་བསོད་འཕེལ༔
བར་ཆད་ཀྱེན་ཞི་དགེ་བའི་བཀྲ་ཤིས་ཤོག༔

HRI RIG DZIN LA MA DRUB PAI THU JIN GYI
DRO KUN YANG DAG DOD MAI SA THOB CHING
ZAB SANG TEN PA GYAE SHING TSE SOD PHEL
BAR CHAD KYEN ZHI GE WAI TRA SHI SHOG

*Hri. By the blessing of the effective power of the practice of the vidyadhara guru, with all beings gaining the very pure original stage, the profound secret doctrines must spread, and life and merit increase, and the obstructing causal situations must be pacified. May there be this virtuous good fortune!*

བདག་སོགས་རྣམས་ཀྱི་ཆོས་དང་མཐུན་པའི་དོན།
ཇི་ལྟར་བསམ་པ་ཡིད་བཞིན་འགྲུབ་པ་དང་།
ནད་གདོན་བགེགས་སོགས་བར་དུ་གཅོད་པའི་ཚོགས།
ཉེ་བར་ཞི་བའི་བཀྲ་ཤིས་བདེ་ལེགས་ཤོག།

DAG SOG NAM KYI CHOE DANG THUN PAI DON
JI TAR SAM PA YID ZHIN DRUB PA DANG
NAD DON GEG SOG BAR DU CHOD PAI TSOG
NYE WAR ZHI WAI TRA SHI DE LEG SHOG

*Being in harmony with the dharma, and whatever we think being accomplished according to our wish, and the complete pacification of the hosts of sickness causing demons, obstructors and interrupters, may there be the good luck, happiness and well-being of these things!*

## H. Concluding Section

དཀྱིལ་འཁོར་གཞལ་ཡས་འདིར་ཡང་བཀྲ་ཤིས་ཤིང་།
ཉིན་ཡང་བཀྲ་ཤིས་དཔལ་འབར་ད་ལ་ལ།
མཚན་ཡང་བཀྲ་ཤིས་དཔལ་འབར་འཁྱིལ་ལི་ལི།
ཉིན་མཚན་རྟག་ཏུ་བཀྲ་ཤིས་བདེ་ལེགས་ཤོག

**KYIL KHOR ZHAL YAE DIR YANG TRA SHI SHING**
**NYIN YANG TRA SHI PAL BAR DA LA LA**
**TSEN YANG TRA SHI PAL BAR KHYIL LI LI**
**NYIN TSEN TAG TU TRA SHI DE LEG SHOG**

*This religious assembly here having good luck, in the daytime also good luck blazing out, da-la-la, in the night time also good luck blazing, swirling khyi-li-li, always in both day and night, there must be good luck, happiness and well being!*

རྒྱལ་བསྟན་སྤྱི་དང་རྡོ་རྗེ་ཐེག་པ་ཡི།
བསྟན་པ་འཛིན་སྐྱོང་སྤེལ་ལ་བླ་མེད་པ།
གུ་རུ་པདྨའི་རང་ལུགས་སྟ་འགྱུར་གྱི།
བསྟན་པ་ཡུན་རིང་གནས་པའི་བཀྲ་ཤིས་ཤོག

**GYAL TEN CHI DANG DOR JE THEG PA YI**
**TEN PA DZIN KYONG PEL LA LA MED PA**
**GU RU PAD MAI RANG LU NGA GYUR GYI**
**TEN PA YUN RING NAE PAI TRA SHI SHOG**

*Guru Padmasambhava, the unsurpassed one who upholds, preserves and spreads the Vajrayana teachings and the general doctrines of the Buddha — may there be the good fortune of the doctrines of the Early Translation School (Nyingmapa) remaining for a long time.*

གནས་འདིར་ཉིན་མོ་བདེ་ལེགས་མཚན་བདེ་ལེགས། 
ཉི་མའི་གུང་ཡང་བདེ་ལེགས་ཤིང་། 
ཉིན་མཚན་རྟག་ཏུ་བདེ་ལེགས་པ། 
དཀོན་མཆོག་གསུམ་གྱིས་དེང་འདིར་བདེ་ལེགས་ཤོག 

**NAE DIR NYIN MO DE LEG TSEN DE LEG  
NYI MAI GUNG YANG DE LEG SHING  
NYIN TSEN TAG TU DE LEG PA  
KON CHOG SUM GYI DENG DIR DE LEG SHOG**

*In this place, happiness in the daytime and happiness at night, and happiness and well-being in both day and night. By the three jewels, there must be happiness and well-being here and now!*

At a time when so many peoples' minds are full of hatred, confident that they know the truth, that they are good and right and that the other is wrong and bad, we need some sweet, hopeful good wishes. Wishing good for ourselves and bad for our enemies is easy and popular, but conflict simply increases delusion and the five poisons. So we say these simple, naïve, hopeful verses with love in our hearts and a wish for happiness for all. All of us have the same mother, the Great Mother, Prajnaparamita. Remembering that, may we avoid prejudice, partiality, and practice open hospitality to all!

## H. Concluding Section

## Empowerment of the Aspirations and Good wishes

དེ་ལྟར་དུ་གྱུར་བཞང་དགོན་མཆོག་གསུམ་གྱི་བདེན་པ་དང་
སངས་རྒྱས་དང་བྱང་ཆུབ་སེམས་དཔའ་ཐམས་ཅད་ཀྱིས་བྱིན་གྱིས་བརླབས་པ་
དང་ཚོགས་གཉིས་ཡོངས་སུ་རྫོགས་པའི་མངའ་ཐང་
ཆེན་པོ་དང་ཆོས་ཀྱི་དབྱིངས་རྣམ་པར་དག་ཅིང་བསམ་
གྱིས་མི་ཁྱབ་པའི་སྟོབས་ཀྱིས་དེ་དེ་བཞིན་དུ་འགྲུབ་པར་གྱུར་ཅིག།

**DE TAR DU GYUR WANG KON CHOG SUM KYI DEN PA DANG
SANG GYE DANG JANG CHUB SEM PA THAM CHE KYI JIN GYI LAB PA
DANG TSOG NYI YONG SU DZOG PAI NGA THANG
CHEN PO DANG CHOE KYI YING NAM PAR DAG CHING SAM
GYI MI KHYAB PAI TOB KYI DE DE ZHIN DU
DRUB PAR GYUR CHIG**

*All that has been mentioned, coming as is wished, and also
the truth of the three jewels, and blessings by all the buddhas and
bodhisattvas, and the great splendour of the full completion of the
two accumulations, and the inconceivable, very pure dharmadhatu:
by their power, all the dharma we have done today must be accomplished.*

As we recite this we should throw flowers in the air. Beauty, truth, love, all come together. The true nature, how things are, is good, open, available, welcoming. The buddhas are on our side. We are not alone, and so we rejoice in the spreading of love, light and happiness in the world.

## Prayer to Spread the Dharma

NYER TSE MA LU ZHI WA DANG
THUN KYEN NAM KHAI DZOD ZHIN DU
GYAL WANG PE MA JUNG NAE KYI
TAN PA YUN RING BAR GYUR CHIG
OM AA HUNG BENDZA GURU PAD MA SID DHI HUNG

*All difficulties without exception being pacified, and with harmonious situations like the treasure of the sky, Padmasambhava lord of the jinas, your doctrines must live long and shine brightly. Indestructible guru Padmasambhava, having the three kayas, grant real attainments.*

## From the Bodhicaryavatara

PHAN PAR SAM PA TSAM GYI KYANG
SANG GYAE CHOD LAE KHYAD PHAG NA

## H. Concluding Section

**SEM CHAN MA LUE THAM CHAD KYI
DE DON TSON PA MOE CHI GOE**

*When merely the thought of helping others is more excellent than the worship of the buddhas, it is unnecessary even to mention the greatness of striving for the happiness and welfare of all beings without exception.*

### Prayer for the Swift Rebirth of H.H. Khordong Terchen Tulku Chhimed Rigdzin Rinpoche[13]

**OM SOTI
LA ME TSO KYE GYAL WAI RING LUG CHOG
KA TER MIN DROL MEN NGAG SAM MI KYAB
PEL DZE CHI WA MED PAI RIG DZIN JE
YANG TRUL NYUR JON DZAE TRIN LHUN DRUB SHOG**

*Wonderful! Chhimed Rigdzin, you who spread the inconceivable instructions of initiation and teachings of the Buddha's oral lineage and the hidden treasures belonging to the ancient tradition of the unsurpassed lake-born Buddha. May your tulku incarnation come quickly and may all activities be spontaneously accomplished.*

---

[13] Written by H.H. Dilgo Khyentse Rinpoche as a long-life prayer, and altered by Chhimed Rigdzin Rinpoche shortly before his death.

By the power of this prayer we evoke the guru to return. Our desire and his intention come together, to create the auspicious situation of his return.

*May any virtue arising from this brief commentary*
*and the good intentions of all involved*
*lead to the rapid rebirth of*
*Chhimed Rigdzin Rinpoche.*

# Appendices

## Authorisation to Practice

This book contains the complete practice text of the Vidyadhara Guru Sadhana. Many such texts from different lineages have been translated and are available in the west. According to tradition, little benefit will arise from practising any sadhana without transmission i.e. permission (*lung*), empowerment (*wang*) and instruction (*tri*) from someone who is authorised to do so within the lineage. The contact details below can give details of when and where this might be available for this practice.

## Contact Details and Further Reading

The Khordong main website gives details of regional groups and of activities at the main centres in India and Poland: http://www.khordong.net

The Diamond Heart Foundation near Manchester in UK: http://www.diamondheartfoundation.org.uk

James Low: http://www.simplybeing.co.uk (under construction)

Other related books by James Low include

- *Being Right Here: The Mirror of Clear Meaning* (Snow Lion Publications, 2004). Also available in German and Polish.
- *Simply Being: Texts in the Dzogchen Tradition* (Wisdom Books, 1998). Also available in German and French.
- *The Yogins of Ladakh: A Pilgrimage Among the Hermits of the Buddhist Himalayas*. With John Crook. (Motilal Banarsidass, 1997)

The painting on the front cover was done by Katharina Winkelmann, Hamburg: katharinaw@khordong.net. The photograph on the back cover was taken by Hans-Maria Darnov, Munich.

Cover design by Lisi Poller-Frischengruber. http://poller.frischengruber.net. Book layout and typesetting by Andreas Ruft, Berlin: andreas@khordong.net

## Table of Pictures

| | |
|---|---|
| Guru Rinpoche, painted by Katharina Winkelman | Cover |
| Guru Rinpoche (Padmasambhava) | 30 |
| Dorje Sempa (Vajrasattva) | 53 |
| Lineage | 86 |
| Guru Rinpoche with his Consorts | 120 |
| Tsogye Dorje | 121 |
| Padmasambhava | 122 |
| Loden Chogsae | 123 |
| Padma Gyalpo | 124 |
| Nyingma Odzer | 125 |
| Shakya Senge | 126 |
| Senge Dradog | 127 |
| Dorje Drolo | 128 |

## Available Titles of Khordong Commentaries

MARTIN J. BOORD, *A Bolt Of Lightning From The Blue. The vast commentary on Vajrakila that clearly defines the essential points,* edition khordong, Berlin, 2002

JAMES LOW, *Being Right Here. Commentary on The Mirror of Clear Meaning by Nuden Dorje,* Snow Lion, 2004

ISBN 141208407-5

Printed in Great Britain
by Amazon